THE GARDEN OF LEADERS

THE GARDEN OF LEADERS

Revolutionizing Higher Education

Paul Woodruff

OXFORD
UNIVERSITY PRESS

OXFORD
UNIVERSITY PRESS

Oxford University Press is a department of the University of Oxford. It furthers
the University's objective of excellence in research, scholarship, and education
by publishing worldwide. Oxford is a registered trade mark of Oxford University
Press in the UK and certain other countries.

Published in the United States of America by Oxford University Press
198 Madison Avenue, New York, NY 10016, United States of America.

© Oxford University Press 2019

Library of Congress Cataloging-in-Publication Data
Names: Woodruff, Paul, 1943– author.
Title: The Garden of leaders : revolutionizing higher education / Paul Woodruff.
Description: New York, NY : Oxford University Press, [2018]
Identifiers: LCCN 2018013260 | ISBN 978-0-19-088364-5 (hardcover) |
ISBN 978-0-19-088365-2 (updf)
Subjects: LCSH: Leadership—Philosophy. | Leadership—Study and teaching (Higher)
Classification: LCC HM1261.W66 2018 | DDC 303.3/4—dc23 LC record available at
https://lccn.loc.gov/2018013260

*Dedicated to Ernesto Cortes
and the many community leaders who have been enlarged
by his teaching*

CONTENTS

PART II

WHAT FUTURE LEADERS SHOULD LEARN

APPENDICES

PREFACE

What should colleges and universities do to back up their claims to educate students who are prepared for leadership?

Leaders are not born. Leaders are not made, either. Leaders grow in conditions that are conducive to leadership. Higher education ought to provide those conditions. In other words, a campus ought to be a garden of leaders.

Colleges and universities often claim that their graduates are prepared to be leaders. Their plans of study, however, show little evidence to support the claim. What is leadership? And what sort of education would prepare young people to be leaders? This book explores those two questions. The education should be broad, because we need leaders for all seasons and in every profession—not only in the military or in business, but in teaching, in coaching, in the arts, and, of course, in politics. In all of these areas, leaders must communicate well, and they must understand the human situation, which is often ugly. Leadership is inherently ethical, but leaders must learn to navigate moral dilemmas that may leave them with moral injury.

Should all students prepare to be leaders? If they do, you might ask, who will prepare to follow them all? Readers of this book will find out (if they do not already know) why leaders and followers need to develop the same qualities, such as trustworthiness, and why the best way to learn to lead is to take turns leading and following. A bad follower will not be a good leader.

A college or university ought to be a good place to learn these things. But is it? Do professors understand how to teach their subjects in ways that prepare students for leadership? Are students ready to practice leadership in the classroom? This book argues that we must all change. For centuries, universities have been fertile ground for leaders. But we could make the ground better, and we should. Students should learn more than they do now that would help them grow into leadership, and they should learn in better ways. At the same time, professors should be planning their classes in better ways, fostering more independence and more critical thinking. In giving team assignments they should pay attention to leadership in the teams.

Moreover, we must all recognize that our classrooms provide only part of a student's education. Students can learn on their own through joining and leading groups of all kinds—clubs, teams, prayer groups, theater troupes, political action groups, and so forth. A very young student can launch a project and see success in short order. A successful entrepreneur told me that he came to appreciate his own ability to change his world through starting a student newsletter in his second year. His was a small project, but it was new, and he made it work.

In and out of the classroom, a campus can be a garden of leaders. The image of gardening for education is an ancient one, with roots especially deep in the Chinese tradition. But the image is not quite right, because people are not plants. Followers of Confucius offered aids to *self-cultivation*, but no plant cultivates itself.

The garden of leaders must be a collaborative project between students and professors. Professors may prepare the ground, but students are responsible for cultivating themselves. In the garden of leaders, both professors and students should practice leadership. Leadership works best within groups of people who have goals in common. And leadership does not work at all unless all parties have their goals at least in alignment.

What should the goals be in the garden of leaders? Whatever the answer, these goals should be ones that students and professors can share. This book is about those goals. That is why it is aimed at both professors and students. If we all work seriously at these goals, we will change the way we teach and learn.

READERSHIP

The book is aimed at a wide audience:

- Anyone interested in the concept of leadership
- The general public, who have every reason to want to know the value of higher education, and who may wish to lobby for reforms of the kind this book advocates
- All who teach at the college level: This book will encourage them to teach whatever they teach intentionally—with intentions for leadership. Any class can be designed to give students practice in leadership.
- Those who wish to defend the liberal arts: The book shows how liberal arts are especially important to the growth of leadership. In teaching literature, history, or philosophy, professors can—and should—intentionally relate these subjects to leadership.
- Those who design college curriculum or course reform: They need to ask how their reforms will support student growth toward leadership.
- Students: This book may be used as a textbook for a course on the conceptual basis of leadership; it is written at a level that is open to student readers.

HOW TO USE THIS BOOK

Since Parts I and II can be used as the basis for a course in leadership studies, I have provided supplementary material to support such a course. Appendix A is a defense of the use of the humanities in leadership studies, while Appendix B is a set of study guides with suggestions for further reading relating to each chapter. Part III calls for major changes in the way professors work in the classroom. In Appendix C, I develop one practical suggestion, which can be used in almost any course on any subject: using teams for leadership.

ACKNOWLEDGMENTS

Thanks first of all to Ernesto Cortes, who started me on this book by correcting me about Billy Budd. I had used Billy as a positive example in my *Ajax Dilemma*, but Ernesto rightly said that Billy would be a terrible leader. Then to my dearest friend Reuben McDaniel (ob. 2016), whose wisdom has buoyed me in all my writing over the last twenty years; no one knew better than he the importance of community to the virtues. Veteran and friend William Gibson has challenged me on many points, especially my military examples; he helped me see the value of understanding virtue as commitment. Jess Miner asked the right questions at the start of the project. Betty Sue Flowers read the entire manuscript more than once and gave wonderful advice. Baker Duncan, who has educated young leaders, helped me out on several points. Jake Galgon guided me through the tangle of moral dilemmas. Patrick Haley dug up references and made useful editorial comments on every chapter, giving the text better clarity and consistency; he also helped by supplying an undergraduate perspective on the university. James Collins helped me see how performance leads to learning. Bjorn Bilhardt gave me the perspective of an entrepreneur with a liberal education. Andrew Ingram introduced me to Karl Jaspers' book about guilt and self-knowledge. John Deigh has helped me in many ways to understand modern ethical thought. Art Markman has shown me the way to valuable research in psychology. I owe thanks to him as well for founding the MA program in the Human Dimensions of Organizations at the University of Texas at Austin. Through that program I have been able to test my ideas about leadership on students who are in mid-career as managers, using many of the texts I discuss in this book. Their positive response has given me confidence in the approach.

And endless gratitude to Lucia Norton Woodruff for many conversations about these topics, and for everything.

THE GARDEN OF LEADERS

PART I

UNDERSTANDING LEADERSHIP

Leaders give shape to freedom. Leadership is what it takes to bring a free community to pursue a goal, its members willingly sharing that goal. Leadership sets an example, inspires, communicates, and pulls people together. Leadership is the only form of power that is compatible with total freedom and equality. From this understanding of leadership we can derive an account of what leaders need to know.

Chapter 1

Alexander the Great Had Aristotle

Alexander the Great had Aristotle. Abraham Lincoln read "all the books he could lay his hands on" and memorized much that he read.[1] George Washington did not read widely, but what he read he read well and took to heart.[2] These commanders changed the world with their armies. Perhaps you too could change your world with an army, if you had one. And if you were given an obedient army at the outset, you would not need to show much leadership. But none of these three commanders would have had an army if they had not been leaders first and commanders second.

Not all great leaders had armies behind them, but all of them had the education they needed to change the world. Leaders without armies give us the best illustrations of leadership, because they have no source of influence other than the qualities and abilities that make up leadership. Harriet Beecher Stowe came from an intellectual family and was extremely well read; she knew how to give voice to a cause that would inspire an army to victory.[3] Rosa Parks had a husband who insisted she finish her high-school education, and she evidently learned much from her experience of life with segregation—in her hometown—and outside it—on a military base. She had no position of power, but she took an action that changed a nation.[4] Marie Stopes had scholars for parents and a PhD in paleobotany from the University of Munich; she wrote books, plays, and poetry popularizing birth control in the English-speaking world and ultimately winning this battle of ideas over women's rights. She went on to found the first birth-control clinics in Britain.[5]

None of these leaders—not even Alexander—was born into leadership, although all were born with capacities that could grow into leadership under the right conditions. The right conditions include education, but teachers and books were not enough: They were lucky to have experiences thrust on them, and these experiences helped them take shape as leaders. And besides experience, they had opportunities. As the son of a king, Alexander was born with a golden opportunity, but many young people have had similar opportunities and done nothing of note. Rosa Parks had few opportunities, but she rose to the opportunities she had.

FREEDOM

The most important opportunity granted to these future leaders was freedom—primarily the freedom of others not to follow their lead. Washington would have had no need to grow into a leader if he had won his heart's desire: an officer's commission in the army of His Majesty King George. No freedom there. In the King's army, an officer would have soldiers killed for disobedience, so officers had no need to lead their troops toward willing obedience. Command was enough in the King's army. But members of the army Washington actually came to lead, the Continental Army, simply went home when they were unhappy; to prevent this, he had to learn to command as a leader.[6] Because his power did not come from a king, it had to come from somewhere else—and that somewhere is the heart of leadership. Alexander's army came from a confederation of Macedonians who were under no obligation to follow him after his father died; when they felt he had led them too far into India, they were free to stop. They would not have followed him so far had he not been more than a king. The freedoms enjoyed by the Macedonians show how much their king was also a leader. Stopes had no power but the power of her writing, and she had little freedom to bring her ideas to the public. But she was determined to bring her message past the censors, and she succeeded.

Freedom demands leadership. Leadership is what it takes to bring a free community to pursue a goal, its members willingly sharing that goal. Leadership sets an example, inspires, communicates, pulls people together. It is the opposite of tyranny. Tyranny terrifies people into working toward the tyrant's goals; leadership inspires people to form a community around goals that they make their own. Leadership picks up precisely where freedom begins. Leadership is at work whenever you influence people to go beyond what you require them to do. If you have authority—if you are a boss or a commander or a director or a coach or even a teacher—you will not show leadership all the time. Your authority will limit the freedom of your followers. Only when you invite them past that limit—and they follow—are you a leader.

Leadership is an ideal, just as freedom is an ideal. History offers no examples of ideal leaders, but plenty of examples of leadership. So don't think you will learn leadership merely by studying an individual such as George Washington. We know he was human, like us, riddled with imperfections. Don't look at the man; look at the things he did that showed leadership. His decision to step down from the presidency—that was leadership. Even the most loathsome dictator—remember, don't look at the individual—may show leadership from time to time.

NATURE

All the leaders I mentioned had natural advantages. Lincoln and Washington were tall, and their height gave them a commanding presence.[7] Alexander had captivating good looks.[8] Parks had a natural grace that made her an ideal champion for her cause, Stopes had a brilliant mind, and Stowe had an extraordinary capacity for human sympathy. Washington's stature would not have made Parks a better leader, and her grace would not have done much for Washington. You will find a type of leadership to suit every sort of personality, every set of natural gifts. Natural charisma won't make you a leader: Not every charismatic person is a leader, and not every leader is charismatic. Do you think you fail at charisma? So what? That is no excuse for setting out to fail at leadership.

No doubt all the leaders we could list will have had natural talents too numerous to list. Nature's gifts may be necessary, but the gifts that leaders are born with do not suffice for leadership. Leaders-to-be need at least three additional gifts that only society can give them: education, experience, and opportunity. What kind of education? What kind of experience? What kind of opportunity? We need answers to these questions. If any of these three gifts is missing, or is of the wrong sort, leadership cannot grow.

SOCIETY

Leaders emerge in a healthy community, but leaders also bring health to their communities. A healthy community gives its members the breathing room to become leaders, along with education and opportunities. Which comes first, the health or the leadership? The answer must be that they come at the same time. We cannot have one without the other.

Think of a healthy classroom—a community that builds itself around learning. The teacher is the authority—at least the teacher knows more. But the teacher in a healthy classroom is also a leader, inspiring the students to learn by example. This the teacher could not do if the community did not allow it, if the culture of the school were utterly resistant to learning. The most gifted teacher will not have the opportunity to be a leader in a classroom that is seriously unhealthy.

In a really healthy classroom, the teacher is not the only leader. In the perfect case, all the students will be exercising leadership in one way or another. But in my classrooms, which have been far from perfect, some students have been passive and others disengaged. No teacher can force active engagement on students.

Society cannot force its children to become leaders, but it can present them with the gifts they need. None of these gifts is simply a matter of luck. Society can choose to provide for a liberating education, offer the kind of experiences that shape leaders, and open up opportunities for young people to lead from early age. On the other hand, society can deny young people opportunities for leadership, and, in place of education, foist on them training for low-level jobs, leaving them most fit for obeying orders. Effective leaders need education more than they need job training; they can usually delegate tasks that require training to those who have it.[9]

This book is about the education, experience, and opportunities that young people need if they are to grow into leadership. Specifically, it is about what higher education, as we have it today, can contribute. What can we do in a modern university that would help our students emerge as leaders, on campus or later in life? What could we do better? And are we doing anything now that stands in the way of leadership?

My thesis is simple. A college or university ought to be a garden of leaders. It may be many other things besides that, but it should at least be ground on which leaders can grow. In this light, look at what we do—all of us who teach or study or manage things in a modern university—and ask these questions as we tend the garden: Which, of the things we are doing, should we keep doing? Which should we do differently? And is there anything we should stop doing?

WHERE DO LEADERS COME FROM?

Leaders emerge when the conditions are right. The most important condition for leaders to emerge is freedom. Freedom is like sunlight in the garden of leaders. Block sunlight, and the plants die. If you agree with this, then you will see that a lot of what people say about leaders is wrong.

Leaders are not born. A plant is not born with everything it needs for good health; in order to be healthy, a plant needs sunlight and water and good soil and safety from weeds. In the same way, no one is born to be a leader. Of course, a plant could germinate with defects so bad that it could never be healthy; but no plant germinates with advantages so great that it will be healthy no matter what.

Leadership is not the same as inborn charisma. Gifts of nature such as height, physical beauty, or a powerful voice can get people's attention. But after you get people's attention, what then? It is what you do with your gifts that could make you a leader. Many successful leaders have none of those gifts. Leaders can be short, ugly, and weak-voiced. Whatever gifts nature has given you, you can probably use as a leader—if you know how to lead and have an opportunity to do so.

Leaders are not made. A gardener cannot force a plant to grow; in the same way, teachers cannot transform you into a leader through their teaching. Leadership ability is not learned in leadership courses. Such courses may help, but in general they fail to teach what leaders really need to know. Military academies give cadets experience in leadership roles. Experience like that is more valuable than courses on leadership. Taking my course or reading this book will not make you a leader. If we knew how to make leaders, and used that knowledge wisely, we would live in a far better world. But we do not.

Leadership is not earned. If it were possible to earn leadership, you would have to do so by exercising leadership. But this you cannot do unless you were already leading. If you had to earn leadership, you would never get started.

Leadership is not management.[10] Leaders do not come from management schools. Management, unlike leadership, can be taught and learned. It is a set of techniques for achieving goals that belong to management— usually targets that management sets. With leadership, a team can achieve goals that belong to every member of the team. Is this an arbitrary distinction? Many people use "management" and "leadership" as synonyms, and some use "management" for what I am calling "leadership" or for a combination of the two. The dictionary allows that—but dictionaries allow a lot of fuzzy thinking. If we want to understand leadership, we have to be clear about whose goals matter. If it's your goals, then you are a manager; if it's goals you share with your team, then you are acting as a leader. Remember also that management can thrive without freedom, but leadership cannot.

If management and leadership are two different things, but both have influence, then there are two ways a university can prepare people to have influence in real life. Many universities offer training for managers, but a university can also offer the sort of education that will help people grow into leadership. If a university takes on the second role, then it may become a garden of leaders.

Knowledge, experience, and opportunity are all necessary for leaders to grow. You will not emerge as a leader unless you have found all three of these. Leadership emerges in a community that welcomes leadership— and that is just the sort of community that a college or university should be.

CAN WE HAVE TOO MANY LEADERS?

You might ask this: "If every student becomes a leader, where will we find the people to follow them?" Can't we grow too many leaders? Not really. We could promote too many generals, of course, and we want only one CEO to a company. But leadership is not the same as command or management. As the military knows well, we need to cultivate the same qualities in leaders and followers. A good example is trust: Both leaders and followers need to be trustworthy. So in educating people to be leaders we are also preparing them to be followers. We are not teaching them all to be generals or CEOs. Keep in mind also that you can exercise leadership at any level, and at any rank. The lowest-ranking member of a team can be a leader, by speaking up at the right time and reminding the team of its values.

WHY A UNIVERSITY?

Alexander the Great did not go to Harvard. Plainly, you can be a great leader without attending a university. But universities as we know them today are especially well designed to be gardens of leaders.

A residential university or college of the kind we enjoy today is capable of presenting all three of society's gifts to young leaders as they emerge—education, experience, and opportunity. Education may seem obvious, but not everything we do by way of education counts toward leadership. (This book will touch on the main topics a future leader should study.) A residential campus also offers unique experiences and opportunities for leaders to grow. Where else can a student start a vibrant new organization in a few weeks? Where else can a young person rise through the ranks in a few short years to lead a student government?

Online universities and communities can offer virtual equivalents of a physical campus, so we will want to ask to what extent a nonresidential virtual campus can be a garden of leaders. We are not ready to be sure of an answer.[11]

THE RANGE OF LEADERSHIP STUDIES

Some leaders command armies, some run businesses, others create new kinds of organizations for new purposes. And some leaders work outside organizations altogether. The genius of Harriet Beecher Stowe was in writing, the genius of Dr. Martin Luther King, Jr., was in speaking. Military leaders need to know how to deploy firepower to best effect, while leaders in commerce need to master fundamentals of marketing and accounting. Business leaders should be acquainted with organizational psychology, information science, and management studies. Teachers should know something of pedagogy and learning science. And in these days, most leaders should know the uses of technology and social media—but not all. Many leaders need to know how to manage a complex organization. But not all: Joan of Arc had the gift to inspire an army and a natural grasp of tactics, but she didn't have to manage anything. Different leaders need to know different things. One sort of education would not be enough for all leaders.

Certain things, however, all leaders should know. All need to be able to communicate, all need to inspire trust, and all need the wisdom to understand what motivates their fellow humans. This book is about that sort of knowledge—the sort that should be helpful to leaders of every kind. This is the core of leadership education. The other subjects I have mentioned are complementary to this core. They are not strictly necessary. Great leaders can hire people with expert knowledge in complementary areas such as technology or accounting, but they cannot hire people to inspire trust for them. They may hire people to help them with communication, but in the end they must know how to listen well and to speak for themselves. And they must have the human wisdom to choose staff well and guide them appropriately. There is no substitute for the core—the education every leader should have.

THE PLAN OF THIS BOOK

I begin by exploring the concept of leadership (Chapter 2), and then proceed to look at two kinds of leadership that do not tolerate education. Messianic leaders and natural leaders depend on gifts from God and nature, respectively. Both sorts of gifts do not equal the kind of education I discuss in this book; both sorts of gifts fall short of what a leader needs. In two brief chapters (3 and 4), I discuss the shortfalls in such cases and then ask what we must add to divine or natural gifts in order to help a young person grow into leadership (Chapter 5).

Our messianic and natural leaders are stumped by evil and totally innocent of the sort of political arrangements that must be made for a community to survive. That is why both of our examples—Joan of Arc and Billy Budd—die very young. A priority in education, then, is learning to recognize and deal with evil. We will have to look into guile and cunning for dealing with evil in others (Chapter 6). But we will also find evil in ourselves, and that calls for compassion and justice, to be treated next (Chapter 7).

The moral world into which we will put our leaders is tangled up; our leaders will have to cope with complexity, and they will have to find their ways through dilemmas, such as the leadership dilemma—choosing between the interests of the home team and those of the world (Chapter 8).

Leadership is courageous. Why do leaders, more than anyone else, need courage? How do we cultivate courage in ourselves and others? We will first consider the effects of courageous leaders on a team (Chapter 9). Then, as we analyze courage, we will see that courage involves both habits and skills, as well as commitment (Chapter 10).

A leader must aim for qualities of character such as justice and wisdom and compassion, in addition to courage. I call all of these "beauties of soul"; traditionally they have been called "virtues," but that word makes them sound unattractive, and these qualities must be attractive. Leaders cannot be perfect, not in courage or any of the other virtues, but they must at least exhibit attractive qualities. When it is appropriate for leaders to seem more courageous than they are? Chapter 11 looks at the need of leaders to put on the appearance of good qualities they are only striving to have.

Leadership knows how to communicate, in order to bring people into a community around shared goals. What kind of communication? I will discuss that in Chapter 12, "Good Ears, Strong Voices."

In the end, the most important quality of leaders is their personal attractiveness—not their physical beauty (though that might help), but the beauty of their souls. Beauty is goodness made evident. Good character in a leader must be evident to the whole team; hidden goodness is no use. So our leaders must not only cultivate good characters but also learn to let that goodness shine. They must try, in my words, to have beautiful souls (Chapter 13).

The humanities can help with both voice and soul, if they are taught well, though they may do more harm than good if taught poorly. Indeed, teaching in any field of study presents models of authority—examples that may or may not express leadership. Not all teaching styles are conducive to the growth of leaders. Some teachers are little better than tyrants (Chapter 14). Others undermine leadership by thoughtlessly teaching ethical failure (Chapter 15).

Leaders are independent. How can a campus promote independence in and out of class? Both are important (Chapter 16). Better teaching promotes independence in students. Time for extracurricular activities does too. Learning without experience will not make a student a leader. Residential universities and colleges can provide extraordinary leadership experiences for every student. Perhaps a virtual campus can provide such experiences as well, but living away from one's parents and home is helpful to developing independence. At present, however, higher education is not doing what it should: All colleges and universities need to consider a revolution that would make them more fertile grounds for leadership. We will outline the goals of such a revolution in the final chapter.

That looks like a lot of chapters, but don't worry: They are all short, some of them very short indeed. None of them exhausts its subject. All of them point to questions and further reading. I am writing for the general reader who is interested in education or leadership or both. I am also writing for students, who could follow these chapters to give themselves a course on leadership. For teachers and students, I have included recommendations on how this material could be studied further (Appendix B).

WHY I WRITE THIS BOOK

Where in modern life is there more freedom than on a university or college campus? Students make their own decisions regarding what to study, how much to study, and with whom to study. They choose their friends and companions. They are free to start, overnight, a new organization that can change the campus on which they live. They make time for whatever they decide they want to do.

All of this is under threat as I write this book. Politicians from left and right are attacking the humanities as useless. Efficiency experts want students to take more course work and graduate sooner, leaving less time for experiences outside the classroom. Rising costs are driving efforts to change the university in such a way that it spends fewer resources on education and more on job training. Pundits want the university to become more efficient in generating graduates with credentials. They want the university to limit the time students may spend outside the classroom, and they want to clamp severe constraints on the freedom of students to choose their destinies as their minds expand through higher education. "Choose a lucrative profession at age eighteen," say the pundits, "and study only those matters that pertain to that profession. Graduate as soon as you can and start earning your living. Don't waste time in clubs or sports; especially don't waste time in exploration, trying to find the subjects in which you will flourish best." These pundits do not mean to be cruel to young people, but they are. They are enemies to the freedom of the young.

Universities have long been fertile gardens of leaders; and they could, if well managed, become even more fertile. Such gardens are threatened in a day of industrial agriculture. There are those who would lock young minds away like hens in an industrial henhouse, with productivity the only goal and efficiency the only measure of success. Perhaps the university can be saved from these threats, but only if enough of us understand what the real value of a university is.

A false economic model for education has become popular, and this threatens the garden of leaders. Pundits speak of developing "human capital," as if a human being were an investment like factory equipment. And we speak of "investing" in higher education, insisting that the cost of education can only be justified in terms of financial return. This may be true of training people to be cogs in an industrial machine, and it would be useful if we still had industrial machines. But our economy no longer looks like a machine: Human cogs are rapidly being replaced by robots. The connectivity on which the new economy depends calls for creative and flexible minds, and there is no training regimen for either flexibility or creativity. Training is not education.

The economic model of education is nonsense for the new economy, and it is dangerous nonsense for education. The best way to see this is to consider leadership. The value of leadership is not to be measured in dollars earned, but in freedom gained, maintained, or restored.

That is why I am writing this book. A free society needs leaders, and leaders need freedom. For this, leaders of the future need the gifts that, in our day, can be offered nowhere better than in a university. They need to be nurtured in a garden of leaders.

NOTES

1. On Lincoln's self-education, see Kaplan (2008), especially the first three chapters, and Wilson (1998), Chapter 2. The "all the books" quotation comes from Lincoln's cousins and friends (Wilson 55 and 330, n. 15). As a teenager Lincoln memorized speeches by the great senator Henry Clay (Kaplan 24). Lincoln's reading habits earned him a reputation for laziness (Wilson 57).
2. Washington produced a hand-copied list of all 110 precepts from *The Rules of Civility and Decent Behaviour in Company and Conversation* (Ellis 2004, 9). See also Brookhiser's account of Washington's self-cultivation (1996).
3. Harriet's father, Lyman Beecher, was a well-known Presbyterian minister, who married Harriet's mother, Roxana Foote Beecher, for her intelligence (Hedrick 1994, 3–5). Harriet spent three years of her adolescence (1824–1827) at the Hartford Female Seminary, considered "a republican experiment in women's education," where Stowe received an education equivalent to that of a contemporary man, began writing letters on religion, and was editor of the student newspaper (31–43).
4. Brinkley 2000, 41–43.
5. Hall 1977, 15ff.
6. During the winter in Valley Forge, desertions grew so bad that Washington wrote to Congress that soon "we shall be obliged to detach one-half of the army to bring back the other" (Chidsey 1959, 26).
7. According to Joseph Ellis, "Washington was at least two inches taller than six feet and disproportionately made, with very broad shoulders and huge hips" (45). Lincoln was six foot four, and contemporaries commented on his enlivened appearance when humored (Wilson 1998, 150).
8. Keegan 1987, 22.
9. An entrepreneur I knew in his student days reports that he makes little use of what he learned at a famous business school, as he delegates that kind of work. But the skills and habits of thought he gained with his liberal arts degree he uses every day. I do not wish to disparage job training. Leaders in most fields (but not all) need appropriate training: A sea captain must know how to sail and navigate, a CFO must understand accounting, and so on. But there is no particular training that a political leader needs, and training is no substitute for the education discussed in this book.

10. Keohane (2012, 36–37) has a useful discussion of the relation between leaders and managers. A recent study of differences and similarities between the two concepts is by a former student of mine, O'Leary (2016). Kotter argues for the value of both management and leadership while insisting that change in organizations requires the latter (2014, Chapter 4).
11. Can there be virtual gardens of leaders? Time will tell. We have no a priori reasons for us to rule this out, because we have no a priori way of predicting the limits of technology. But experience so far is not encouraging. All barriers will be down when (if possible) we are as happy to attend our children's weddings by digital means as we are in person. On issues about digital presence, see Woodruff (2011).

WORKS CITED

Brinkley, Douglas (2000). *Rosa Parks*. New York: Penguin Books.

Brookhiser, Richard (1996). *Founding Father: Rediscovering George Washington*. New York: Simon & Schuster.

Chernow, Ron (2010). *Washington: A Life*. New York: Penguin Books.

Chidsey, Donald Barr (1959). *Valley Forge*. New York: Crown Publishers, Inc.

Ellis, Joseph J. (2004). *His Excellency: George Washington*. New York: Alfred A. Knopf.

Fischer, David Hackett (2004). *Washington's Crossing*. New York: Oxford University Press.

Hall, Ruth (1977). *Marie Stopes: A Biography*. London: André Deutsch Limited.

Hedrick, Joan D. (1994). *Harriet Beecher Stowe: A Life*. Oxford: Oxford University Press.

Kaplan, Freed (2008). *Lincoln: The Biography of a Writer*. New York: Harper Perennial.

Keegan, John (1987). *The Mask of Command*. New York: Penguin Books.

Keohane, Nannerl O. (2012. *Thinking about Leadership*. Princeton, NJ: Princeton University Press.

Kotter, John P. (2014). *XLR8: Accelerate: Building Strategic Agility for a Faster-Moving World*. Boston: Harvard Business Review Press.

O'Leary, John (2016, June 20). "Do Managers and Leaders Really Do Different Things?" *Harvard Business Review*. https://hbr.org/2016/06/do-managers-and-leaders-really-do-different-things

Wilson, Douglas L. (1998). *Honor's Voice: The Transformation of Abraham Lincoln*. New York: Vintage Books.

Woodruff, Paul (2011). "Lighting up the Lizard Brain: The New Necessity of Theater." *Topoi* 30.2, 151–155. http://www.springerlink.com/openurl.asp?genre=article&id=doi:10.1007/s11245-011-9101-z

Chapter 2

Leading from Freedom

THE UN-TYRANT

Freedom is the key to leadership. We follow a true leader freely, without thought of rebellion. No one serves a slave-master or a tyrant willingly. We recognize tyrannical behavior in authority figures whenever they do things that make us want to rebel. From that recognition we can start thinking about leadership: First list the qualities that make a tyrant a tyrant, then list the opposites, the ones that would make an un-tyrant. My students all say that they have been under the thumb of a tyrannical personality—of someone who made them want to rebel—at least once in their lives. It may be a coach, a band director, a teacher, a stepparent, or even a parent.

Perhaps the band director is acting with the best of intentions but has not explained those intentions clearly, instead forcing his students to comply. He is not a tyrant through and through, but he has fallen into a tyrannical pattern, which the students recognize. I ask them what the terrible band director was doing wrong. Common answers include:

He wouldn't listen to me.
She wasn't fair.
He didn't follow his own rules.
She tried to frighten me into doing what she wanted.
He put his goals ahead of ours.

A profile of the tyrant emerges quickly. He is disrespectful, selfish, and unfair. He is a bully, and probably a coward as well. Tyrants, like all bullies, are often given to fear. Afraid of being supplanted, or simply afraid of failure, the tyrant drives fear into others. The ancient Greeks developed this concept of the tyrant at precisely the time they were inventing democracy. Their playwrights frequently put tyrannical figures on stage in the tragic theater to illustrate how bad life could be under the sway of a tyrant. Sometimes their stage showed a tyrant who was all bad, but the great plays give us mixed figures, like Oedipus, called *Tyrannos*, who truly cared for the welfare of his people but was so terrified of being overthrown that he could not listen to good advice. He is so frightened he even threatens his wife's brother with death.[1]

The band director that my students complain about may be a good person on the whole. He may care about his students, and he may succeed in driving them to the victory they all covet. But he does have tyrant qualities. The students resent these, and hold back from giving him their best. Most of them feel that they would have performed better under the leadership of someone who treated them better.

We can draw a profile of a leader by contrast. Let's start with courage. The band director who is a leader is not afraid. Her confidence allows her to treat the students better. She is (at least) respectful, fair-minded, and unselfish. Of course the students want more from their band director than courage, respect, and justice: They also want the director to have musical knowledge, speaking ability, conducting experience, and much more.

Our students have experienced plenty of tyranny in their short lives, but very little freedom. We adults on the whole have considered them too young for freedom. So we have given them few opportunities to follow a leader freely. We bear down on our teachers, threatening them with dismissal if they do not get good test results from their students. The teachers' fear rubs off on the students, who are made to be afraid of doing badly. And, as a result, they do worse. Fear is one of the enemies of learning.

Think about this: If we care about freedom, why do we give so little of it to our children? If we want our children to grow into leadership, are we doing right by them in their education if we restrict their freedom? We will have to change the way we teach before we can honestly claim to be preparing our students for leadership roles. Later chapters in this book address the changes we must make in college teaching.

GIVING SHAPE TO FREEDOM: THE LIFEBOAT

Leadership is the only form of power that is compatible with total freedom and equality. To imagine pure leadership, we have to create an extreme situation, like a lifeboat at sea. Suppose you find yourself in a lifeboat with other passengers who have escaped a sinking vessel. No one is a sailor. No one has been given a position of authority. If you are lucky, one of you (at least) will emerge as a leader; if no one shows leadership, you will probably not survive. If a leader does emerge, she will have no rank, no carrots to give out, and no sticks to beat you with (apart from what the rest of you willingly provide). You in the lifeboat are free; you will follow a leader only if . . . only if what? What must a leader be like to give shape to the huddled mass of humanity in your lifeboat?

Your leader, if you are lucky enough to have one, will inspire trust. You will believe that, on the whole, she is fair and that she aims to save everyone—not only herself. She knows the limits of her knowledge, and asks for advice when she needs it. She is willing to listen to unsolicited advice, when time allows. She speaks clearly and pays attention to what others say. She is not afraid; her confidence rubs off on the rest of you. When she asks you to bail the boat, you will feel like doing so, if you can. If you can't, and you tell her why, she will find an alternative.

Quickly, she organizes the huddle of people into a crew. Those strong enough to row or bail will take turns at those tasks. Others are given charge of signaling equipment. Two are asked to take an inventory of food, water, and medical supplies. Still others look after the children on board. Everyone is willing to take on the assigned tasks. A ship's officer with pistol or cutlass might have forced such an arrangement on the survivors. In that case they would have shape but not freedom. But the leader in our lifeboat case has given shape to freedom.

To be a leader, she would have to do more than give shape to this group. She would not try to take charge in the first place without some confidence that she could work out how to keep the boat afloat and its people safe. She would find out how to steer the boat and where to steer it, for the benefit of all. She doesn't have to know everything, but she has to be prepared to use the best knowledge in the boat. As a leader, she would

not capitalize on her charisma to make the others steer the boat to a desti-
nation that was in her interest but not that of the others; if she did that, she
would be a tyrant disguised as a leader. Such disguises are all too common
in real life.

Once she satisfies herself that she has something to offer as leader, she
must work out how to influence the others in the boat, with no recourse
to rank, resources, or even expert knowledge. All she has to offer is leadership. But that will save lives.

LEADING WITHOUT AUTHORITY: BEYOND CARROTS AND STICKS

Of course, in real life, leadership usually emerges in people who do have
rank or resources or knowledge. That makes leadership hard to distinguish
from other ways of getting people to do things, such as using commands,
incentives, or threats—or striking awe into people by superior knowledge
or strength or charisma.

Suppose the crown makes you captain of a ship and gives you permission to punish without limit anyone who disobeys you. Or suppose a ven-
ture capitalist gives you unlimited means to reward members of your team
as they develop new software. You may accomplish great things by waving
sticks or holding out carrots; a good course in management may teach you
how to use carrots and sticks most effectively to secure your goals. But
would you be quite satisfied by the result? Your well-flogged sailors may
be too frightened to warn you of impending danger, and your rich software
designers may not care to go beyond the goals you have set for them. They
garner all the rewards you are willing to give them simply by doing what
you say. Why should they do more? Leadership gives reasons to go beyond
the carrot and the stick.

In the age of sail, Horatio Nelson was given command of a ship that
was simmering on the edge of mutiny. He was chosen not because he was
a fierce disciplinarian (he was not) but because of his leadership ability.
Melville tells us: "An officer like Nelson was the one, not indeed to ter-
rorize the crew into base subjection, but to win them by force of his mere

presence and heroic personality, back to an allegiance not perhaps as enthusiastic as his own, yet as true." [2]

The same goes for teaching. Imagine yourself teaching in a classroom, with the ability to punish laggards and reward the quick learners. Testing your students may show that by these means you are meeting the goals laid down by the school authorities. But would this satisfy your goals as a teacher? Would the tests convince you that your students really understand what you taught? That they now love learning enough to continue discovering things on their own? Great teachers inspire in their students a desire to learn, and to learn in a certain way.

Carrots and sticks are not enough, no matter how delicious the carrots or how fearful the sticks. Going beyond carrots and sticks is what I mean by leadership. There is a science for the effective use of carrots or sticks, and we can train students in that science. But can we train students in going beyond the carrot and the stick? I doubt it. I believe that leadership can be learned, but I do not believe it can be taught. We learn leadership through the experience of trying to lead people. But most importantly, we learn leadership by example.

Effective teachers are leaders because they go beyond carrot and stick. In doing this they provide models of leadership for their students. Teachers, coaches, and music directors have opportunities to model leadership for students. Are those of us who teach making the best use of our opportunities? Or should we change the way we teach?

DESCRIBING LEADERS?

I could begin by describing famous figures that have been studied—say, Jack Welch or Steve Jobs in the business world, General Patton in the military, or Franklin Roosevelt in politics. Social science can have a field day studying the traits or behaviors of people who are thought to be great leaders because they have achieved great things. But there will be none of that in this book. Instead, we will look selectively and critically at behaviors that appear to belong to leadership. Would we follow such people? Do we wish to emulate them? These choices ride on values; they cannot be determined by descriptions. To clarify such choices, fiction is as useful as history.

I have three objections to the descriptive approach. First, the people to be studied were mostly men, so they were not role models for half the world. Second, they all did some appalling things. Third, such men are often manipulative and sometimes violent; they did not leave their followers entirely free not to follow them.

So it's no use describing famous figures until we know how to pry apart their leadership from their manhood, from their misbehaviors, and from their use of force and manipulation. We need prying tools for this exercise, and these must come from the mind. We need conceptual tools, and these must be normative, not descriptive.

Anyone who holds what we call a leadership position will at one time or another look like a bully or a tyrant. And sometimes a bully or tyrant wins where a leader would fail.

I have a fourth reason for not building on descriptions of people regarded as leaders. Choosing a leader to study is in itself a choice of values. We should ask whether we really count as successes the things that Patton or Welch or Jobs or Roosevelt accomplished. Is a tyrant's victory really something to celebrate? Leadership breathes the language of values. What is worth fighting for? What sort of person is worth following at risk of my life? What sort of person must I be, if I want to be worth following? How do I induce others to agree with me about what is worth fighting for?

Think of this book, then, as a series of questions about your values. The stories I tell here are designed to make you think about the values you would pursue as a leader—or those values which, as a follower, would make you willingly follow a leader.

Warning: Responding to questions like these may change your life.

CHARISMA AND THE DICTATOR

History gives us examples of people who have had nature's gifts[3] but have not used them in a context of freedom. Such people may accomplish great things, and they may exercise leadership along the way, but they are not leaders. They have no stake in freedom. Stalin, for example, led his nation to victory in the great patriotic war; part of this he achieved through leadership, but much of it through terror. Indeed, he killed, enslaved, imprisoned, and terrified his people as only a badly frightened tyrant would do. He was a prisoner of his own fears, and he locked his own people away in a prison of fear.

What is missing in such a case? Most people who accomplish great things show some ability as leaders, but whenever they violate freedom, forcing their own goals on the community, they are using tools that do not belong to leadership. Stalin showed leadership, but was not a leader in the full sense. That is why I speak of *leadership* in this book, rather than of *leaders*: Freedom is rarely complete; where freedom is limited, leadership too is constrained. Therefore most high achievers in real life are leaders only in part, and in this book I will examine examples of leadership, not examples of leaders. In other words, I will try to isolate the leadership from the person who exercises it. Human beings are never perfect; a supposed leader will never be a good example altogether. But we will find actions—even the actions of a tyrant like Stalin—that are good examples of leadership.

I have said that leadership picks up where freedom begins. Stalin's subjects went beyond what he forced them to do; otherwise Russia would not have won its great patriotic war. So it appears that Stalin showed leadership—or at least put on a convincing show of leadership. A charismatic dictator such as Stalin communicates brilliantly, as do all brilliant leaders. He takes control of information and the media, and uses them to manipulate public opinion in his favor. No doubt some of what he says is honest and heartfelt, but some is dishonest and manipulative. The same goes for a demagogue in a democracy, who pretends to take on the values of the people. How can we distinguish a leader's honest speeches from the lies of the charismatic dictator or the clever crowd-pleasing politician? Both kinds of speakers seem honest and sincere enough.

Two problems: First, some demagogues make no attempt to hide. They present themselves as the violent, freedom-hating, dangerous people that they are. Why, then, do others follow them? Erich Fromm wrote a famous book about this, partly inspired by the need to explain the popularity of Hitler—*Escape from Freedom*. Other writers have taken up the theme recently.[4] Authority is comforting to some people, even when it is cruel, and especially comforting when contrasted with chaotic freedom.

Second is what I will call "the cosmetic problem"—demagogues who present themselves as far better than they are. Machiavelli urges the prince to appear good even when he is not—in effect, to wear moral cosmetics.[5] I will have a lot to say about this when I discuss good character. Cosmetics work for a while, and in certain circumstances, but the true face of the dictator will be hard to hide in the long run. The "dear leaders" of North Korea appear to have carried off a massive deception of their people, up to a point. But the deception is not sufficient, or these "dear leaders" would not have to supplement it with fear. No regime has more terrible prison camps.[6] If they trusted their own cosmetics, they would not resort to fear. But obviously they understand the limit of moral cosmetics.

What do people like about a charismatic dictator? He is decisive, and he demands absolute obedience. In a crisis, those qualities can save us all. Of course, we are not always in a crisis (though many dictators would like us to think so). Absolute obedience is hard to maintain, and it is limiting. If all you do is obey, you will do only what the dictator thinks should be done—and one mind will not compass all the possibilities. A successful community must go beyond obedience. It must learn the art of following.

THE ART OF FOLLOWING

To follow is not the same as to obey. To be a leader, you need to be around people who know how to follow. To be a leader you also need to know how to be a good follower when it is time to be a follower. The charismatic dictator does not know how to follow. Leaders are willing to take their turns and then cede leadership to others, whom they follow. Military training in leadership requires you to take turns leading and following.

Obedience is, simply, doing what you're told. All you need to know, in order to obey, is what you have been told to do and how to do it; you do not need to know why you are doing it, and you need not believe that doing it is a good thing. You simply do it. Following is not the same as obeying orders. To follow well, you need to understand what you are doing and why you are doing it; you need to agree to the goals you have been asked to promote.

Good followers are free not to follow, not to obey, and they know how to use their freedom wisely. They will question orders that don't seem to make sense, if time allows. They will not be afraid to disobey an order if their mission requires them to do so. In following orders, they will try to carry out the full spirit of the orders. Good followers are not afraid to offer criticism to their leaders, but they will do so as quietly as possible, so as not to make their leaders lose face with others.

There are times to obey without question or delay: The lifeboat will sink if we don't act quickly when a squall threatens to capsize us. The skipper gives orders and we obey instantly. This is no time for consultative leading or wise following; this is a time for captain's orders and crew's obedience. We need to have a clear sense of when to be the obedient crew, and when to be the wise followers. Similarly, our leader needs to know when to be captain and when not—when to bark orders, and to punish those who dally or disobey—and when to explain what we are doing, where we are headed, and why.

Good followers have all the skills and graces of good leaders. They are trustworthy, courageous, and wise. They are just and compassionate. They have the good judgment necessary to negotiate tough moral problems. The education that's needed is the same for both leaders and followers. If we aim to help our students grow into leadership, we must also help them grow into followership.

LEARNING FROM WOMEN

When asked to name great leaders, most of us start listing men who have achieved great things. But men typically have had advantages that clutter the picture of leadership. George Washington had a commanding presence and many other traits of masculine power, along with advantages offered only to men in his time—military training and the experience of managing a plantation. Lacking such advantages, women who have achieved great things typically illustrate leadership more clearly. In contemplating them, we are less likely to be distracted by factors other than leadership.

Who are the women leaders who achieved great things, and how did they do it? History generally has failed to notice people who achieved great things outside of the traditionally male worlds of conquest, statecraft, or business. Still we all know of people who have done great things in families or communities, but will never make the history books. Many of these are women. We should take them into account—asking older relatives for their memories, or looking into the local histories of communities.

As for women who have been recognized by history as leaders, some of the most famous of them drew their power from men—from fathers or husbands.[7] Cleopatra was daughter of a king, wife of a king, and consort of a great commander. Elizabeth I was daughter of Henry VIII. Eleanor Roosevelt was married to a great president. Joan the Maid dressed as a man and drew her authority from God (who of course was visualized as male). These women were nevertheless great leaders in their own right. But let's look beyond these examples of male-dependent leadership to women leaders whose success is untouched by male influence. For this we need to stretch our minds to models of leadership less familiar from the male world.

Pure leadership in women has generally been distinct from organization and management. Joan of Arc did not organize or manage the French army, but she gave it heart and led it to victory. Harriet Beecher Stowe gave the army of the Union the motivation that was essential to its success, but that is all she did. She was a brilliant communicator, not an organizer or activist. Marie Stopes, by contrast, was more than a communicator. She organized a long-lasting network of clinics. In the business world, Mary Kay was both a communicator and an organizer; she depended very much on character, or at least the language and appearance of character, to build her direct marketing empire—which, after all, was about cosmetics.

In the next chapter we will turn to Joan of Arc, who called herself Joan the Maid. She is the most astonishingly successful woman leader in history. What explains her success? And her ultimate failure? But first, a question:

ARE LEADERS AN ENDANGERED SPECIES?

"Don't turn the next page!" I hear a critic say. "The way Woodruff defines leadership there is no place for leaders in our world, because Woodruff says leadership requires freedom. There is precious little place for leaders in the business world because there's no freedom in business. Business is all about carrots and sticks: big juicy carrots for the top crust, and sticks for the losers who do the real work. Let's talk about success and the kind of people who succeed in business."

The critic is part right. History is full of people who cheated or bullied their way to great wealth or power.[8] Even if you do not want to be a shark, as long as you want to be a leader of fish, you had better learn how to survive in an ocean that belongs to sharks. You owe it to your followers not to lead them into a shark's belly. That's why this book must owe a lot to Machiavelli. The Big M will show up in several chapters.

The critic is wrong about freedom, however. Freedom abounds in the business world, and so does leadership. When no one is looking, a waiter is free to spit in the soup. Even when people are looking, an employee is free to invent plausible reasons for slowing down. Disgruntled airline pilots are free to delay flights over trivial errors in a log. And anyone at any rank can start looking for other jobs. Maintaining a loyal, well-trained staff does require the sort of leadership that speaks to freedom. And look outside business. Soldiers are free in battle to run away, as mercenaries so often do. No commander has the power to make soldiers feel willing to die for a cause. Or consider the classroom. No teacher has the power to make students curious, or attentive; no teacher can force young people to believe that they can succeed. No power on earth can prevent students from giving their minds over to delicious fantasies of sex during a long and boring lecture. In all these areas of freedom, only leadership can succeed.

Only leadership spikes morale, raises curiosity, evokes dedication. We can find elements of leadership in the career of anyone who rises to great heights—yes, even Stalin and Hitler and Mao. They all had willing followers, along with the unwilling ones. How did they manage that?

Yes, pure leaders are rare as hen's teeth. They are an endangered species. If I ask students for examples of leaders, they think quickly of Dr. Martin Luther King Jr., or Malala, or Rosa Parks. These leaders had extraordinary gifts and extraordinary opportunities. We can try to emulate their qualities, but not their careers. Few of us will have their strength, their selflessness—or their opportunities. In the shark's world of business, self-less *leaders* are endangered and may even be dangerous to their followers. But that does not mean that selfless *leadership* is scarce or dangerous in itself. That is why this book is not about leaders, but about leadership.

Yes, pure leaders are an endangered species. But leadership abounds.[9]

Now we will turn to the brief and dangerous career of a leader who made purity her trademark—Joan, who called herself, and was, "The Maid."

NOTES

1. Sophocles' *Oedipus Tyrannus*, line 622.
2. On charisma and leadership, see Cain (2013).
3. Melville 5.72/59.
4. E.g., Reese (2012) and Pfeffer on what he calls "toxic leadership" (2015, 180ff).
5. Machiavelli 1994, Chapter 18, p. 55.
6. Hassig and Oh 2009, 204–211.
7. On women leaders and their connections with men, see Flowers (2011).
8. This is the main theme of Pfeffer (2015).
9. On the general concept of leadership, see Keohane (2012).

WORKS CITED

Cain, Susan (2013). "The Myth of Charismatic Leadership." In *Quiet: The Power of Introverts in a World that Can't Stop Talking.* New York: Broadway Books, 34–70.

Flowers, Betty Sue (2011). "The Shield of Athena: Archetypal Images and Women as Political Leaders." In *Ancient Myth, Modern Psyche: Archetypes in the Making.* Ed. Virginia Beane Rutter and Thomas Singer. New Orleans: Spring Journal Books, 205–217.

Fromm, Erich (1941). *Escape from Freedom.* New York: Farrar & Rinehart.

Hassig, Ralph, and Oh, Kongdan (2009). *The Hidden People of North Korea: Everyday Life in the Hermit Kingdom.* Lanham, MD: Rowman & Littlefield Publishers, Inc.

Keohane, Nannerl O. (2012). *Thinking About Leadership.* Princeton, NJ: Princeton University Press.

Machiavelli, Niccolò (1994). *Selected Political Writings.* Ed. David Wootton. Indianapolis: Hackett Publishing Company, Inc.

Melville, Herman (1962). *Billy Budd, Sailor; The Definitive Text*. Ed. by Harrison Hayford and Merton M. Sealts, Jr. Chicago: University of Chicago Press.

Pfeffer, Jeffrey (2015). *Leadership BS: Fixing Workplaces and Careers One Truth at a Time*. New York: Harper Business.

Reese, Laurence (2012). *Hitler's Charisma: Leading Millions into the Abyss*. New York: Vintage Books (Vintage edition 2014).

Chapter 3

Messianic Leadership

Joan the Maid

The French army has been demoralized by one defeat after another. Every major city in France is now in the possession of the enemy, except for Orléans, which is under siege. France has no leader, and no French king wears a crown. There is an heir, Charles, but he has a rival, and in any case the French do not control the cathedral where they might crown him. It is 1429, and the English and Burgundian allies have every reason to believe that they have virtually won the war that will later be known as the Hundred Years War—that France will be a footnote in European history.[1] The English have besieged the French at Orléans, and the French have been unable to reinforce the city. Now a teenage peasant girl appears and makes a proclamation. None of the English believe what she says:

> You men of England, who have no right to this kingdom of France, the king of heaven orders and commands you through me, Joan the Maid, to abandon your strongholds and go back to your own country. If not, I will make a war-cry that will be remembered forever.[2]

The English did not believe it, but enough of the French did to drive the English from Orléans and eventually from all of France. How did Joan have the power to be believed?

COMMANDER WITHOUT RANK

Joan says that she has been receiving visions from saints, telling her that only she can save France, and that it is God's will that she do so. Enough people believe her that she is given a chance. Dressed like a man, she rides into battle with her banner as the French army liberates Orléans from the siege. One victory leads to another. The emboldened French army goes on a winning spree and crowns their king two months later. The tide has changed in favor of France, and the leader who made the difference is Joan.

Joan must be a brilliant leader, to turn the tide of battle against the enemies of France. She can make an army believe they can win under her guidance. Her advice to the generals is right, time after time, so she must be telling the truth when she says the advice is coming from her visions and the visions come from God by way of the saints. So the French believe.

Everything about Joan's story seems wrong. She is a woman, a peasant, a teenager, uneducated, and totally inexperienced in war. She has no authority and no power beyond what her mere presence conveys. She has no rewards to give to good soldiers—except for victory—and no penalties to give to the bad ones—except to be left out of the action. Her victory astonishes both her friends and her enemies. She has nothing going for her but whatever it is that makes soldiers of all ranks want to follow her. That "whatever it is" is leadership.

Her leadership is brief, however. The gift that makes her a leader is her capacity to hear the voices of saints, but these voices are limited. They don't see the point of diplomacy in war, and they don't know how to advise Joan in her hour of need. The English and Burgundians recognize Joan's power and move to eliminate it. At the same time, the French want to have her out of the way. Her simple devotion to the French cause runs up against diplomatic and political considerations.

The Burgundians capture her in a skirmish, and the English put her on trial for heresy in front of churchmen who are under English control. The French abandon her with a sense of relief. She is only nineteen. She will never understand why the French do not wish to save her. Her voices fail to tell her how to answer her accusers successfully; she does not know how to defend herself in a politicized environment. She says and does what her enemies need in order for them to convict her as a relapsed heretic. She recants, then courageously reasserts the truth of her voices. The English lay a trap for her, and she steps into it, to the joy of her accusers: Threatened with abuse by her male guards, she resumes male clothing for safety and comfort—evidence to her accusers that she is a relapsed heretic. Only a heretic woman would wear a man's garments.

On May 30, 1431, they burn her at the stake. Twenty years later, with the Maid safely dead, the French will arrange for the church to rehabilitate her memory for political reasons, and the trial will be nullified on procedural grounds. Then, in 1920, the church will declare her a saint.

To us in the twenty-first century she is an enigma. Joan's visions make up for her ignorance, but can such visions really come from God? We have more reasons now than ever to shudder when a warrior claims a God-given mission. Could a warrior like Joan really be a saint? Could God really take a side in this dynastic war? Did His saints really give Joan sound advice on tactics and gunnery? And if Joan really was His agent, why did He let a group of churchmen kill her? Surely God had the power to give true visions to her accusers as readily as to Joan.

SHAW'S *SAINT JOAN*

Joan is a figure of history, myth, and literature. We will look at her here through the lens of the play by George Bernard Shaw, who set out to resolve the enigma in a play he wrote shortly after Joan was canonized as a saint. Shaw accepts Joan's visions and voices: She really has them, they really tell her what to do, and she really is a saint—a person who is simply too good for this world. Shaw's subject is not her sainthood, but the effects of her saintliness on her interactions with others. As a saint, she is a holy innocent, totally unprepared for the ways of human beings; and as human beings, the men on both sides (and they are all men) are totally unprepared to deal with a saint.

She arrives at an army that has been demoralized by defeat. In Shaw's version, she knows exactly why the army has been defeated:

> Our soldiers are always beaten because they are fighting only to save their skins; and the shortest way to save your skin is to run away. Our knights are thinking only of the money they will make in ransoms: it is not kill or be killed with them, but pay or be paid. But I will teach them all to fight that the will of God may be done in France; and then they will drive the poor goddams [the English] before them like sheep. (70)[3]

She believes she brings a message from God, that God wishes France to be an independent nation. "I tell thee it's God's business we are here to do: not our own" (86). Shaw puts to one side the question whether God really did support nationalist warfare in France in the 1400s. Instead, he shows how Joan makes herself believed. She infuses the army with a new spirit by giving it, for the first time, shared ideals and a shared goal. Under her influence, the soldiers forget their private concerns, put behind them their individual fears of defeat, and fight together for France. Soldiers see her as an angel dressed as a soldier (73). In her vicinity they stop swearing (65), and under her influence, even the cowardly dauphin grows toward courage (84, 87). Joan is an inspiration.

This is the soul of leadership—to unite a team behind an ideal and a goal. Management has the power to offer incentives for good work, as well as to threaten penalties for failure. In doing so it touches people only through their individual interests. In good times, that works fine. But in defeat, a team of soldiers will come apart, if each of them is out mainly for number one. Defeated armies tend to come apart, especially if they are mercenaries. George Washington achieved something almost miraculous when he kept sufficient force of his army together at Valley Forge after a series of defeats that left the British in control of the Delaware Valley. Washington had little to offer his troops aside from his leadership. Commanders who have rank and other traditional powers still need to show leadership, especially if they hope to rally troops in defeat. Defeat is the ultimate test of leadership, and the French army is as miserably defeated as any in history. Joan has naked leadership, uncluttered by rank. Yet she puts heart into a demoralized army. She passes this leadership test with flying colors. She will fail others.

JOAN'S HOLY IGNORANCE

Joan is an innocent, totally unprepared for the politics of the situation in which she thrusts herself. Shaw says of her, "Her want of academic education disabled her" (23). She was unable to understand any nuances of speech; she would not be able to recognize a joke if it hit her between the eyes (92). And during her trial she was at a loss. She could not grasp the fact that she had made enemies who would destroy her (110, 138, 139, 145). The same goodness that drew people to her blinded her to the snares of evil among which she moved. Simply, she was too ignorant of the world to survive in it. And if she could not survive in it, she could not lead others to survive. Luckily, she did not lead others over a cliff, but she might well have done so.

In fact, the war would not be won by military means alone. Shaw does not bring this out, but history does: The chief turning point in the war would come after Joan's death, when French diplomacy brought Burgundy over to the French side.[4] Joan's unwavering devotion to fighting against Burgundy and England was not in French interests; that was one reason the French did not ransom her or otherwise attempt to rescue her. She was, simply, in the way. Her voices apparently knew only one sort of thing, and that was military.

In Shaw's Epilogue, she comes to see that she has no place in the world of selfish, conniving human beings. "You are not fit that I should live among you" (144), she declares, and wonders when, if ever, the world will be safe for saints. As Shaw sees Joan, she does not know how to rub shoulders with evil. Every leader needs to know that.

Her ignorance is more serious than that, however. She casts herself as a messiah in a war between powerful interests, not realizing that one side's messiah is another side's devil. As we read about Joan, we are tempted to demonize her English accusers, but from a Christian point of view the facts are with the English: It *is* blasphemous to claim that Jesus chose a side in a war for temporal power. Her claim is irreverent as well as blasphemous; it is never reverent to suppose that a human being knows precisely what God wants in political matters. In our time we know well the horrors of warfare that has been inspired by people who claim to speak for God.

Hubris is the vice of those who think that their voices and the Voice of God are the same, and reverence is the antidote—a reverent acceptance of human limitations.[5] Joan's claim was on the right side of history, and her extraordinary persona lent it charm. But whether or not she was a heretic, she certainly lacked reverence.

Reverence has no place in messianic leadership, and Joan is a messianic leader— a leader whose influence stems mainly from the belief that she has been sent by God to lead in a cause that God favors. Joan had to believe that about herself, before she could make others believe it. But this is not a reverent belief to have about oneself.

EDUCATING JOAN?

Education would have ruined Joan. As a messianic leader, she needs only to believe that God has sent her to lead the army that will drive the English from France. She does not need to *know* anything. Of course, Joan knows what a peasant girl of nineteen would know, but this is mostly irrelevant to her mission. She is observant and quick-witted. She has a way with words, or she would not convince people that she comes from God.

She has her visions and her voices, and these tell her what she seems to need to conduct her successful campaigns. Shaw thinks she is lucky to have escaped an academic education.[6] But he recognizes that she is crippled by her ignorance of politics in feudal France.

Now suppose Joan had been identified as a prodigy (which she surely was) by a benefactor and sent to the court, where she would learn the ways of palace intrigue. Or suppose she had been able to study (in disguise as a man) at the university in Paris, where she could sharpen her skills at critical thinking and ponder the monarchy's claim to have God behind it. Or suppose she had studied the background of the various claimants to the throne of France, and found that both Charles of France and Henry of England have reasonable claims, though both are subject to dispute. Could she, educated in any of these ways, have been the leader she was? I doubt it.

Education is not for messianic leaders. But messianic leaders are severely limited. They are also dangerous to all around them. They do not live long. Joan's early death is no accident. In our time, messianic warrior leaders are prime targets for death by drone attack or special operations. No established government wants to keep them around. There are far better ways to be a leader, but these call for education.

Joan did have the talent to be a leader, given education and opportunity. But she was a woman. A boy with her talent would have been sponsored by the church and would have risen rapidly in the church hierarchy. But that path was denied to Joan. Perhaps the only kind of leader she could have been was messianic. What paths have been open to women who were destined for leadership? And what difference does education make for women on the way to being leaders?

NOTES

1. For the life of Joan, see especially the sources in Taylor (2006). For further discussion, readers may choose among the works by Castor (2015), Harrison (2014), Perroy (1965), Warner (1981), and Wilson-Smith (2006). All are valuable; they are discussed in Appendix B (223).
2. Joan to the English at Orléans, May 5, 1429. Quoted in Castor 2015, 108. For its provenance, see Castor's note (270).
3. The full play can be found in Shaw 2005.
4. Perroy 1965, 290–296.
5. Woodruff 2014, 1–2.
6. Shaw 2005 (first published 1951), "The Modern Education Which Joan Escaped," a section of his Preface, pp. 20–22.

WORKS CITED

Castor, Helen (2015). *Joan of Arc: A History.* New York: Harper (first published in London, 2014, by Faber and Faber Ltd.).

Harrison, Kathryn (2014). *Joan of Arc; A Life Transfigured.* New York: Doubleday.

Perroy, Edouard (1965). *The Hundred Years War.* Ed. David C. Douglas. New York: Capricorn Books.

Shaw, George Bernard (2005). *Saint Joan.* London: Penguin Books.

Taylor, Craig (2006). *Joan of Arc, La Pucelle; Selected Sources Translated and Annotated.* Manchester and New York: Manchester University Press.

Warner, Marina (1981). *Joan of Arc: The Image of Female Heroism*. New York: Alfred A. Knopf.

Wilson-Smith, Timothy (2006). *Joan of Arc, Maid, Myth and History*. Stroud, UK: Sutton Publishing.

Woodruff, Paul (2014). *Reverence: Renewing a Forgotten Virtue*. 2d ed. Oxford: Oxford University Press.

Chapter 4

Natural Leadership

Billy Budd

NATURE'S BEST CHILD

A natural leader—if we could find one—would have no leadership gifts but those that nature gave to her. No education, no experience of living in human society, no opportunities to practice leadership. She would be, simply, a born leader. Of course, there is no such thing. Wherever there are human beings, nature is not pure. Since emerging as a species, we humans have always had a taming effect on our landscape. The same goes for our human landscape: Humans have always had languages, customs, and living arrangements, none of which are given by nature. If language were given by nature, we would all speak the same one; and the same goes for customs and living arrangements. Human languages and customs vary a great deal across the human landscape, though they all supply basic human needs. Our survival depends on learning a language and living in a community. But we don't all need to have the same language. Each of us needs to learn the particular skills of at least one community—how to speak, how to listen, how to behave—in order to get along in that particular group.

Still, we can try to imagine what it would be like to be a wild child, to grow up knowing none of these things. History records a few sad examples of children who have grown up deprived, to some extent, of human society,[1] but fiction serves my purpose better. Imagine a child who has every gift that nature could give a leader—beauty, strength, a sweet and unselfish character, a nature that inspires trust—in a word, the child has charisma. And then imagine that the child has not received any of society's gifts—no education, no experience of human interaction. Imagine him now a young adult.

Let's give him a name—Adam, Adam before his encounters with Eve and the serpent. He has a perfect body and a perfect soul. Pluck him out of Eden and drop him into the Bronx or Wall Street or onto an aircraft carrier. How will he handle himself in our world of sin and striving? Herman Melville played this thought experiment as he wrote the final versions of *Billy Budd*. Billy is an innocent young Adam, stolen from Eden and given to the tender mercies of a British warship. He is not ready for this, and his shipmates are not ready for him. He dazzles them with his beauty and goodness; some of them would follow him anywhere. But he has no idea how to navigate this world. Nature's best child—Adam before the Fall—is not fit to live among us fallen human beings.

Now ask what is missing in Adam before the Fall. Leaders do not emerge from an Eden or from a wilderness; they grow in what I am calling a garden—a place where human life is cultivated. In such a garden, what must society add to natural-born leaders to give them what they would need if they are to function as leaders in real life?

That is the main question of this book. History offers us no examples of purely natural leadership, so we have to conduct a thought experiment. Luckily, most of the work developing this experiment has already been done, by Herman Melville.

MELVILLE'S *BILLY BUDD*

Not that he preached to them or said anything in particular; but a virtue went out of him, sugaring the sour ones.[2]

Melville's fable helps us visualize the answer. Billy Budd has many of the attributes of a leader. He has every gift that nature could give a leader. But these gifts are all he has. People follow him because of those gifts, but because those gifts are all he has, he will never lead his followers anywhere new or change any situation for the better.

At age twenty-one, Billy Budd looks like the Adam in an Italian Old Masters painting and he has all the innocence and simple goodness that the human race lost when Adam and Eve left the garden. The other sailors view him with an amazed and amused reverence. But he cannot survive or help them survive in such a moral atmosphere—in a warship at a time of war. He will have to lose his innocence or his life. And in this fable, it is his life he loses. This Adam has not been prepared in Eden to learn from the serpents on board his ship.[3]

Beauty is goodness made visible, according to the Platonic tradition from which Melville worked. Billy's startling beauty, in this fable, is a sign of his natural goodness. The goodness shines out, like beauty, and radiates through his first ship, *The Rights of Man*. This was a merchant ship, a ship where peace should be the norm. The *Bellipotent* ("Powerful-for-War") intercepts Billy's peaceful ship and sends a party to impress sailors (i.e., force them to change ships). They choose to take only Billy. Captain Graveling of *The Rights of Man* is devastated:

> Before I shipped that young fellow, my forecastle was a rat-pit of quarrels. It was black times, I tell you, aboard the *Rights* here. I was worried to that degree my pipe had no comfort for me. But Billy came; and it was like a Catholic priest striking peace in an Irish shindy. Not that he preached to them or said anything in particular; but a virtue went out of him, sugaring the sour ones. (1.19.46–47)

He goes on to say, "Anybody will do anything for Billy Budd" and calls him his "peacemaker" (1.23/47). We would expect that the peacemaker on a ship would be a disciplinarian, one who had the authority to stop fights and either punish those who start them or reward those who keep their hands clean. Billy is the lowest-ranking sailor on the boat, the newest foretopman, but—with no authority whatever, and without consciously doing so—he exercises an uncanny power over his peers.

What is the source of Billy's power? He holds out no carrots and wields no sticks. Moreover, he has no education and very little experience. Billy does not know much about sailing, he is dangerously ignorant of human character, and he cannot utter a word if he has something important to say. So his power cannot come from what he knows or what he says. It comes from his character, just as his old captain says, his simple goodness.

In his new, more warlike, environment, Billy is puzzled to find himself the victim of a series of subtle attacks that bring down on him minor but annoying discipline. He has been unquestioningly obedient, obedient to a fault (1.12/45). But someone is making a mess of his few possessions, and he is being punished for the mess. These attacks puzzle him, because he has totally acquiesced to the rules of the ship. Who is putting his things in disarray, and why is he being punished for this? A man named Claggart, Master-at-Arms, disciplinarian of the crew, has orchestrated all this through his toadies. Claggart smiles at Billy but hates him for his beauty and goodness.

To Captain Vere, the noble commander of the *Bellipotent*, Claggart accuses Billy of fomenting mutiny. When asked to defend himself, Billy is speechless, owing to his one natural defect—the stutter that stops his tongue when he falls under any heartfelt emotion. Asked a second time, he lashes out at Claggart and kills him with a single blow. Captain Vere is experienced enough to recognize the perjury in Claggart and the outraged innocence in Billy. "Struck dead by an angel of God!" he exclaims. "Yet the angel must hang" (19.232/101). A drumhead court convicts Billy of the crime and he is hanged at dawn. He faces death with the same courage as that with which he has been facing the danger of hauling in a billowing sail on the highest yardarm in a gale. His last words are "God bless Captain Vere!" (25.317/123). The words echo through the ship's crew, and the signal is given to hoist Billy by his neck to the main yardarm.

> At the same moment it chanced that the vapory fleece hanging low over the East was shot through with the a soft glory as of the fleece of the Lamb of God seen in a mystical vision, and simultaneously therewith, watched by the wedged mass of upturned faces, Billy ascended; and, ascending, took the full rose of the dawn. (25.319–320/124)

Years later, sailors will still revere the yardarm as a sacred object. No dissension, no mutiny interrupts the order on the *Bellipotent*. Captain Vere will die with Billy's name on his lips. Billy has been a peacemaker to the end; he has found the words to forestall any anger the crew might feel over his death.

What did Melville mean by this story? In the years he was writing and rewriting *Billy Budd* he changed many fundamentals of the tale. Most notably, he replaced an older guilty Billy with the young innocent one we have today and developed the characters of Claggart and Vere. He may have contemplated further changes. But we can make of the story what we will. For my purposes, it is a thought experiment: What happens when a young Adam, untouched by sin or knowledge, finds himself among the war-plagued human race? What would he need to learn in order to survive? More to my purpose, what would he need to learn in order to be a successful leader? For leader he is, by nature's gifts, but a severely defective one.

At the moment the silent order is given for Billy's execution, the first rays of sun shoot over the horizon and set the fleecy clouds aglow. As Billy's lifeless body—miraculously still before the noose cuts into his tender neck—ascends to the main yardarm, it "takes the full rose of the dawn." The sailors, seeing in his death a crucifixion, treasure the yardarm afterwards, venerating pieces of wood as if they came from the Holy Cross. Billy has somehow become a holy sacrifice.

But to what end? Nothing has changed. Billy has done no good in the world.[4] The British Navy will continue to recruit Claggarts to keep their men in line. Intimidation, flogging, and hanging will not cease. This brutality is done for the sake of war, as Melville sees clearly. War follows war marching down the annals of history into our own lives, brutalizing those who are made to fight as well as all those who are affected by its violence. Thrust out of Eden into a world at war, what can an innocent would-be leader do but make a graceful exit? Not knowing where to go, he cannot lead.

THE BILLYS AMONG US

Melville's Billy Budd belongs to the world of fable. No one among us is as innocent as he; no one has been transported into our colleges direct from the Garden of Eden. But we can easily imagine young people who are almost as tongue-tied as Billy or share Billy's ignorance of evil in self and others. But, having grown up this side of paradise, they will know a number of things.

Our Billys might have been immersed in the writing of code at an early age. Or perhaps they have had an ideal education in one of the so-called STEM disciplines, or a superb technical training. But can you imagine young people who have never learned how to write a coherent paragraph or prepare a compelling short speech explaining the virtues of their ideas? Who, when asked what they love to do, speak in halting phrases, almost inaudibly? Can you imagine young people who have read few books of history or fiction and lived in protected suburbs, so their knowledge of the human potential is sketchy at best? Can you imagine young people who have never had to think their way around a moral dilemma? Who have not considered what sort of person they would want for a leader or a follower?

These young people know more than Billy Budd, but not much. Steeping young people in science or math or engineering can leave them almost as helpless as Billy. Great leaders came on the human scene long before there was education in science, but they had skills speaking or writing, and they knew something of the human condition. They had the education that befits leaders, whether from Aristotle or from books, from a university or from the school of life.

WHY EDUCATE FOR LEADERSHIP?

There is much to do. Faced with the evil of slavery, many Americans took the false ethics of slavery into their hearts, and most of the rest believed that nothing could be done about it. But leaders did emerge against this evil, starting with Benjamin Franklin, who was not afraid to speak against it.[5] William Lloyd Garrison knew how to give voice to the leaders of the cause against slavery.[6] And Frederick Douglass stole an education from his masters and used it to raise his own voice for freedom.[7] Thanks to such leadership, slavery in the United States and in most of the rest of the world has been outlawed. Of course it continues in lawless places, and in our own cities it festers underground. But legally, it has been abolished.

Billy Budd accomplished nothing; he was not prepared to do anything but hang from a yardarm. Perhaps—but not in my lifetime—some day we will find leaders who will help us to abolish war. In any case, we have leaders today with the courage and the voices to push back the lesser evils of our world. And we ought to have more such leaders.

We who teach should be asking what we can do to provide young people with an environment in which they can grow into leadership. Long service on a warship might help, but for the young and innocent a few good books can make up for the experience they have not had. Our students may not be as visionary as Joan or as sweet as Billy, but they are almost as innocent when they arrive on our campus. They have a lot to learn.

NOTES

1. Susan Curtiss's 1977 book *Genie* details such a case. See also Kitchen 2001.
2. Citations for *Billy Budd* are from the Hayford and Sealts edition (1962), in this format: chapter.print page/ms. page. This passage is from 1.23/47; that is, Chapter 1, p. 23 in Hayford and Sealts, p. 47 in the ms.
3. Rollo May (1972) calls Budd's condition "pseudoinnocence," and diagnoses it as "a childhood that is never outgrown, a kind of fixation on the past (p. 49, cf. pp. 206–211). May misunderstands the fable-like quality of Melville's story, however. Billy is not fixated on the past; he does not seem to have a past at all.
4. Thanks to Ernesto Cortes for making me see how badly Billy would perform in a real-life leadership position.
5. Brands 2000, 701–704.
6. For a remarkable biography of Garrison written by his children, see Garrison and Garrison (1885).
7. Douglass 1982, 78–87.

WORKS CITED

Brands, H. W. (2000). *The First American: The Life and Times of Benjamin Franklin.* New York: Doubleday.

Curtiss, Susan (1977). *Genie: A Psycholinguistic Study of a Modern-day "Wild Child."* New York: Academic Press, Inc.

Douglass, Frederick (1982). *Narrative of the Life of Frederick Douglass, An American Slave.* New York: Penguin.

Garrison, Wendell Phillips, and Garrison, Francis Jackson (1885). *William Lloyd Garrison: The Story of His Life Told by His Children.* New York: The Century Co.

Kitchen, Martin (2001). *Kaspar Hauser: Europe's Child*. London: Palgrave Macmillan.

May, Rollo (1972). *Power and Innocence; a Search for the Sources of Violence*. New York: W. W. Norton & Company, Inc.

Melville, Herman (1962). *Billy Budd, Sailor; The Definitive Text*. Ed. by Harrison Hayford and Merton M. Sealts, Jr. Chicago: University of Chicago Press.

PART II

WHAT FUTURE LEADERS SHOULD LEARN

All students, regardless of major, should have a general education that gives them an understanding of the human condition and makes up for their lack of experience. History, literature, and philosophy are central to this, as are the social sciences. At the same time they should be thinking through the values they wish to express as leaders and followers—such as courage and trustworthiness. Reading philosophy helps with that. In addition, all students should practice communication—writing, speaking, and listening— throughout their studies. Technical degree programs should make room for these subjects in their curricula, and liberal arts departments should make sure that they are teaching these subjects in ways that will be most useful to students in their lives after college.

Chapter 5

Educating Billy

THE GARDEN OF NOT EDEN

The garden of leaders is not the Garden of Eden. Sin grows even in the finest garden of leaders, and opportunities for sin are abundant. Leaders-to-be will have ground to sow their wild oats in our garden. They will emerge with regrets, if they know themselves well enough. Under the weight of regret they should not be self-righteous. A sense of how easy it is to go astray will grow in them, leading to compassion for others. But there is more. In the garden of not Eden, young people watch older people, some coping well with the tangles and temptations of the garden, others going down in disgrace or disaster. The young people experiment with their own lives. Friends will find good or bad qualities in them; the better friends will call them on their faults and recognize their virtues. A fertile garden of leaders will be teeming with friends of that sort. Although it will give space for wild oats, this garden will be a community that cultivates the best in its members—courage, compassion, justice, wisdom, and reverence.

Perhaps some folks are born like Billy Budd, innocent and good. But more likely not. Billy grew up in Eden. A young man growing up in our warship could not develop a character as simple as Billy's at all, and he could not even approach that state unless he knew something of our world. A course in ethics taught by my colleagues or by me will probably not do much good for anyone's ethical character.

Good character does not grow by itself. Philosophers who hold that goodness is based in nature still insist that it must be cultivated. Mencius, a founder of ethical theory in the Confucian tradition, taught that the virtues begin as delicate seedlings.[1] Goodness requires nurture. We cannot force goodness to take shape, the way we might force wood into the form of a chair. But neither can we expect goodness to grow by itself. It is not a weed. Virtue needs a garden.

But let's allow Melville his fable: Imagine that goodness has grown in Billy Budd without any cultivation at all. Billy is "One to whom had not yet been proffered the questionable apple of knowledge (2.42/52) . . . such perhaps as Adam presumably might have been before the urbane serpent wriggled into his company (2.44/52)." Parents may well feel that when they send their innocent children to a university they are exposing them to the serpent's knowledge. But of course these children are not as innocent as the parents want to believe. Besides, the devil is no more active on a campus than anywhere else. We cannot make our Billy relive Adam's Fall; he is already fallen. But our Billy still needs to learn many things, some of which we offer on our campus—experience living outside family and classroom, of course, but also education.

Our Billy could find what he needs outside our campus (as Lincoln did), but much of what he needs is available here. If he does not go to college, today's Billy would have a poor range of choices—join the military, seek a low-paying job, hang out with shiftless friends. Higher education will do more for him than any of these. The low-paying job may not give him time to read, and may not expose him to a wide range of human possibilities. The military will expose him to much that is human, and may give him opportunities to lead. But military training will probably not help him overcome the obedience that is one of Billy's defects. Hanging out will give him time to grow older and possibly also provide him with some useful experience, but that is his riskiest option.

So now let's imagine Billy as a first-year student at our university, our garden of leaders. And let's suppose that along with his beauty and goodness he has the capacity to learn: He has a good, curious mind; he is willing to change his views as new information arrives; he is willing to learn on his own; and he has the courage to challenge his teachers and fellow students when he thinks they go wrong. He also has the energy and drive to engage with other students outside the classroom. Let's start there: What can be gained outside the classroom?

LEARNING FROM THE OUTSIDE WORLD

Training

Melville's Billy is a novice sailor. He is strong, enthusiastic, and brave, but he does not know enough to be in charge of others. He does not have the kind of technical knowledge that commands obedience from those assigned to follow him. Give Billy a gang of older sailors to command and—although they might love him—they would see no reason to carry out any of his instructions. Billy needs on-the-job training. This he would not find in the classroom. Had he lived longer, he would have learned all the technical knowledge he needed on the *Bellipotent*. Of course a maritime academy might have taught him some useful skills in a classroom, but only experience on a square-rigger would prepare him for furling the foretopsail in a gale.[2]

Understanding Oneself

Billy is not yet conscious of being a leader; he does not know who he is or how he affects people. Melville writes, "Of self-consciousness he seemed to have little or none, or about as much as we may reasonably impute to a dog of Saint Bernard's breed" (2.42/52). I might say the same of many first-year students I have known. I do not believe that self-knowledge grows well in the classroom. It grows in people who are active and reflect on the actions they have taken. At most, schooling might prompt people to reflect on what they have done, how their actions affect others, and how their actions reflect on themselves.

A real-life Billy would have some potential for evil that he would not recognize until he had found himself going wrong ethically—as we all do, and as we can all recognize if we pay attention. Leaders need to know all of their human vulnerabilities, including their vulnerability to evil. Self-knowledge of this kind would have helped Melville's Billy—if he had had the capacity for evil—to understand evil in others. Obviously, you need to understand evil in order to protect against it. Less obviously, you need to understand evil in yourself in order to develop the compassion that a leader must have. But Billy has no experience of sin, no experience of having gone wrong. Adam before the Fall cannot look into himself and see anything that might mirror, even to the smallest extent, the evil in others. After all, the fruit that leads to the Fall yields knowledge of good and evil. Billy needs to sow wild oats.

Understanding People: Experience

Book learning can be a substitute for experience only up to a point. Melville shows us that Captain Vere knows things about people that he could only have learned by experience. He has served in a court at which a witness testified falsely, and he remembers the look of the man who perjured himself. Claggart has a similar look about him, and so Vere senses that his testimony may be false (18.205/94). Moreover, Vere has acquired over the years an ability to judge people wisely, and although he has had little contact with Claggart, he has seen enough of him to be suspicious of his character. As for Billy, the captain cannot possibly have met his like before, but he had a schoolmate with a speech defect like Billy's. He recognizes this in Billy and understands the situation. A less experienced commander might have heard Billy's silence as a confession of guilt, but Vere knows otherwise (19.224–225/99).

This is the sort of knowledge Billy would need in order to be a mature leader. Book learning can be at best a partial substitute. Billy has grown in intelligence as he advanced to the age of twenty-one, but, Melville tells us, "in Billy Budd intelligence, such as it was, had advanced while yet his simple-mindedness remained for the most part unaffected" (16.171/86). Book learning might have the same effect, advancing students' intelligence while leaving them innocent about the ways of their fellow human beings. That is why book learning has to be tempered by experience.

Authority

Billy has never had a position of authority. On a campus, outside the classroom, he could find a group in which he could exercise the kind of leadership that has authority. In a few short years he could be in charge of an important campus organization. Such a rapid rise would be unlikely off campus.

Independence

Melville's Billy has never really left the Garden of Eden. The Billys in our classroom are usually away from their parents for the first time, with a grand opportunity to develop independence—so long as their parents do not intrude too much, and so long as their professors use teaching methods that foster independence.

LEARNING IN THE CLASSROOM

Communication

Billy does not know how to read or write (2.42/52). This defect cuts him off from many treasures of human knowledge. He might thrive in an oral culture, but only if he filled his memory with the wisdom of his people, packaged in the form of verse that is easy to memorize. We no longer have such a culture. Billy needs to learn to read and write.

Billy cannot speak under emotional pressure: "Under sudden provocation of strong heart-feeling . . . [he suffers] a stutter or even worse" (2.47–48/53). As his beauty is an outward sign of his goodness, his paralyzing stutter is a sign of his inability to communicate, and he is left, like an Adam before the invention of words, with only his body as a means of expression. At his trial for killing Claggart, he is able to say, with difficulty:

> I am sorry that he is dead. I did not mean to kill him. Could I have used my tongue I would not have struck him. But he lied foully to my face and in presence of my captain, and I had to say something, and I could say it only with a blow, God help me! (21.251–252/106)

To make matters worse, he does not know what other people really mean when they speak to him. He is deaf to the irony in Claggart's kind-sounding but contemptuous remarks (1.30/49). Billy needs to learn to listen wisely as well as to talk fluently. Billy will never be an effective leader until he masters both sides of communication—listening and speaking. These skills Billy could develop in a healthy classroom.

Understanding People: Books

"Experience is a teacher indeed; yet did Billy's years make his experience small" (16.171/86). This is as true of our students as it is of Billy; they are too young to have had much experience of the world. If Billy lived to be an old sailor, and if he paid attention, he would acquire the experience he needs. Melville draws a portrait of a cynical older sailor whose experience suffices to make him apprehensive about Billy. The crew call him the Dansker, because of his Danish origin. The Dansker wonders

> what might eventually befall a nature like that [i.e., Billy's], dropped into a world not without some mantraps and against whose subtleties simple courage lacking experience and address, and without any touch of defensive ugliness, is of little avail; and where such innocence as man is capable of does yet in a moral emergency not always sharpen the faculties or enlighten the will. (9.111/70)

The Dansker's words are as convoluted as his thoughts. He is thinking that Billy's courage won't save him from the traps a man like Claggart might lay for him. For that he would need both experience and what the Dansker calls "defensive ugliness"—the capacity to be nasty when necessary in his own defense. But Billy will not live long enough to acquire what the Dansker knows by experience. In his short life, he would need a surrogate for experience. So does the Billy in our classroom, and, fortunately, surrogates for experience may be found in books.

Literature, history, and (within recent history) case studies may supply the want of experience in our young Billy, if they are well taught. What you have not seen yourself you may see through other's eyes.

Evil

Melville insists that even experience is not enough. The Dansker's experience has left him cynical and passive—hardly with the qualities of a leader. Without falling into that trap, Billy needs to know something about evil that no experience could teach him. Melville tells us "he had none of that intuitive knowledge of the bad which in natures not so good or incompletely so foreruns experience" (16.171/86). In other words, Billy, like Adam before the Fall, is too good. He cannot imagine the possibility of evil in himself, and so he fails to recognize evil in others. "Innocence was his blinder" (17.182/88).

Claggart's evil is especially hard to recognize because of his guile. He does his dirty work through toadies (8.103/67) and presents a friendly face to those he hates. He speaks double meanings. The Dansker sees through this and tells Billy what is going on: "Why *Jemmy Legs* is *down* on you" (15.168/86)—"Jemmy Legs" being the slang name for any master-at-arms. Billy hears but cannot understand. He does not believe the man *could* be down on him; after all, Billy knows he has done no wrong, and the man has been nice to him.

Claggart was moved against Billy Budd by his beauty and goodness (12.137/77). He "could even have loved Billy but for fate and ban" (17.178/88). Hate is close to love. Claggart's sexuality might be twisted against itself; he might hate Billy for arousing in him a desire he abominates in himself. But this cannot be the whole story. What Claggart hates most about Billy is not his beauty but his goodness, a quality he cannot share (12.141–142/78). And so he envies Billy. Envy turns to hatred, and hatred kills them both.

How could Billy possibly understand such hatred? Could our Billy in the classroom understand it in a professor who takes against him for similarly perverse reasons? Such things do happen in the university. The Billy in our classroom would not be so good as Melville's Billy, but he too would not know enough about evil to protect himself from a Claggart. For that, Melville says, knowledge of the world is not enough. Citing Plato, he hints that we might have to turn to philosophy or theology to understand the natural depravity of a Claggart (11.127/74). History, I think, does better than philosophy or theology. Fiction is even better, because it can sharpen the issues. In my classroom, I would ask Billy to read and try to understand *Confidence Man*, the last novel written by Herman Melville.[3] It may be the best introduction to evil ever written.

Guile

Billy has no guile and hears no guile in others. "To deal in double meanings and insinuations of any sort was quite foreign to his nature" (1.30/49). If Billy had guile himself he could use it to manipulate evil, even to turn it against itself. The study of literature alerts students to double meanings and might help Billy meet Claggart on Claggart's own ground. Of course he could learn this from experience as well, if he spent time with people who joke and tease.

There is more to guile than double meanings. Outside Paradise, as we are, we are often tempted to meet evil with evil. Leaders face ethical dilemmas. On the one hand they have an obligation to their followers, to people who may trust them with their lives. On the other hand, they are expected, like anyone else, to tell the truth, keep their promises, and so on. Machiavelli understood the problem as a prince might face it and offered a solution that has horrified many.

Ethical complexity can be horrifying. It would certainly horrify Melville's Billy, who is single-mindedly devoted to simple goodness and cannot imagine a world in which evil calls to be met by evil. Here philosophy in the classroom may be of some use.

Independence

Billy is too obedient for his own good, or for anyone else's. He does not know how to say "no" (14.154/81). The highest goal for our Billy's education is independence. This he can develop in or out of the classroom. Classroom education can be designed to foster his independence or to clip his wings. Quite young students can engage in research, and research calls for independent thinking. Nothing matters more than fostering independent thinking in our classrooms, and yet we teachers do not pay much attention to independence.

Diversity

Even a ship of Billy's time had a diverse crew. A leader's education should deal with the many differences that will crop up in a team—differences in ethnic background, gender, sexual identity, language, and so forth. So should the leader's experience outside the classroom. That is why I urge administrators to insist that campus organizations not be segregated by sex or race.

USING DATA

We now have ready access to a flood of data based on research on organizations, much of it tagged to the word "leadership." Our Billy needs to know how to use data in decision-making; for this he will need at least a smattering of statistics. But he must be cautious in using information if he takes it from the Internet. He will have to learn the difference between research and opinion. He will have to learn the use of academic databases, as opposed to general search engines, and he will have to know what numbers mean.

Billy will encounter research on what team members regard as leadership, but he should not be too impressed by this. Data may show him what succeeds for certain purposes, or what specific followers say they want in a boss, a manager, a commander, or a leader. But no data will show what Billy ought to count as success, or how he should define the sort of leader he wants to be, or the type of leader he would want to follow. Social science research on organizations tends to shy away from values (as it should) and to be short on definitions of leadership (as it probably should not).[4]

If Billy chose his values on the basis of data from research into organizational success, he would be adapting his values to suit his environment, as many people feel they have to do. That may be a successful strategy for a time. It belongs to what I call "moral cosmetics"—the art of making people think you have values that you don't have. Machiavelli recommends moral cosmetics, but Billy needs to realize that cosmetics wear off, and even when they do not, people often see through them. Billy also needs to ask whether he would want to follow a leader who used moral cosmetics heavily. If he would not willingly follow such a hypocrite, why would he want to ask others to follow him if he is a hypocrite?

It ought not to matter to Billy what other people think about leadership. Billy should focus on what *he* thinks about the subject after deep reflection. He will find that there are many ways to be a leader, and many different kinds of situations calling for leadership. Most of the scholars who have gathered data on leadership have not thought of Rosa Parks or Harriet Beecher Stowe as leaders. But if Billy learns to think of these people as leaders too, then he will start asking questions that the data won't address.

Of course the data will show him that a Rosa Parks would never rise to the top of General Electric. And if he expects his captain or his boss to be a Rosa Parks he will be sadly disappointed. In a cutthroat corporation he is likely to have bosses who care most about their own advancement and are happy to climb over the bodies of defeated colleagues.[5]

Social science research into organizations is valuable in many ways: You can't succeed in an environment unless you know something about it. Our students should know how to evaluate the results of quantitative and qualitative studies. To do that they should learn at least the rudiments of conducting surveys and gathering data. They need to know what people think. If they don't, how will they communicate? How will they adjust their expectations to social reality? The essence of communication is listening, and listening today entails knowing how to make use of data.

Data will not give you your values, however, or determine your commitments. Leadership in the context of freedom—the subject of this book—entails a sharing of values between the leaders and the led. Billy would not freely follow a captain who was committed to values antithetical to his own. That is why leadership is ethical.[6] It is found in people who are committed to certain values. What does that mean? To be committed to justice, for example, is to put the quest for justice at the core of your life—to try to understand what justice calls for, and to try to work out how to put active justice into whatever you do, wherever you are.

That kind of commitment does not allow for what Kant calls heteronomy—for letting outside factors determine what you take justice to be.[7] If you are committed to justice, you must take responsibility for what you think justice requires. You must, in other words, try to be autonomous in thought and action.

Your commitment to justice will serve you in any context. Your principles of justice may not deliver justice in every situation or in every culture, but your commitment can be stable nevertheless.[8] Social science can tell you about different cultures, and it can even tell you useful facts about situations—how moral failure becomes more common under certain stresses.[9] But what counts as moral failure—that is for you to work out.

That is why I base this book mainly on the humanities—on history, fiction, and philosophy.[10] Through the humanities I ask you as a reader to choose for yourself, using examples to focus your attention on crucial questions: What values do you want to see in the actions of a leader? Do you want to exhibit those values in your own actions? These questions are too vague and general as they stand, but I try to make them specific through examples from history or fiction.

The fictional examples are thought experiments. Billy Budd is a good example of a thought experiment: Drop a young Adam from Eden into a world of violence and competition. What then? If we could delay the drop until he had an education, what would you want his education to be? That is a thought experiment. It forces you to reflect on your values and organize them, to make sense of who you are and what you care about.

READINGS FOR FUTURE LEADERS

Our students would do well to read *Saint Joan* and *Billy Budd*. After that they should start facing moral complexity. They could do this by reading selections from Thucydides and Machiavelli. They should have plenty of time to think about these books, write about them, and discuss them. This will begin to overcome their innocence, and give them practice wrestling with the dilemmas of leadership. The good thing about these books is that they do not give definitive answers. In a good classroom such books will liberate our heroes to think for themselves.

Later in their education, to help cope with complexity, I would ask them to read at least the opening of Plato's *Republic*. And to understand the pull of moral imperatives, I would send them to read at least the first two sections of Kant's *Groundwork*. To put this in context, they should be aware of Kant's reasoning about the sorts of cases to be met with in the real world.[11]

Then our students need to face cultural complexity as well. In any workplace they will encounter colleagues from backgrounds different from their own, and many of them will work in international organizations. The essentials of ethics and leadership do not differ widely across cultures— courage and trustworthiness, for example, count for a lot anywhere. So does respect, but respect is expressed quite differently in different cultures. The more our students know of cultures other than their own, the better. They can learn a lot from books and also from travel abroad if they keep their eyes and ears open. In my courses on leadership I pay special attention to Chinese classics, as these are wise about quiet leadership and have been influential for over two millennia. Whatever our students read, they need to learn that the customs they have been taught to live by are not the only ones in the world.

Billy and Joan do not have to read whole books, but they should make the acquaintance of the best books we have. These books should be presented not as monuments to past history, but as living documents. We need not try to make scholars of Billy and Joan; they are too much engaged in the present to respond to an invitation to spend their lives in research. Instead, we should challenge Joan and Billy to think their way around the issues such books present.

Why assign old books, classics? Three reasons. First, old books have stood the test of time, which is as good a test as we have for the value of a book. Second, they have been widely read for a long time and have shaped the culture in which Billy and Joan must operate. In reading old books, our future leaders form bonds with leaders from many countries and many times. Third, each of these books is a trailhead to other valuable destinations. From Thucydides a trail leads by way of Hobbes to much of modern political theory, which our students will understand better if they start from the original trailhead. Machiavelli has been the source for enormous fertile debates about the tension between ethics and authority. From Kant a trail leads to John Rawls and much of the most recent political theory.

I admit that many newer books would serve the same purposes as these classics or as supplements to them, introducing students to guile and complexity. Recent history is especially valuable, because it helps explain the context in which our students will be leaders. From whatever source, our heroes need to learn that this world is no Paradise, and that coping with its complexity is no simple matter. They must grow beyond visions and simple goodness.

Education alone will not make Billy and Joan leaders. They will also need training in their line of work, experience in following and leading, and—yes—a good dose of luck. These things they may have while in college, in addition to general education; we will deal with these topics in later chapters.

NOTES

1. Mencius 1970, bk. 6, pt. A, par. 7. Confucius (Kong Zi) (551–479) left an oral tradition of his teachings which were compiled in various forms, principally the *Analects*. These have been subject to a number of interpretations, but Mencius (Meng Zi), who wrote during the fourth century BCE, produced an interpretation that has prevailed on the whole over others. For the history of Confucianism, see Ivanhoe 2000.
2. Lawyers, doctors, engineers, and businesspeople all assure me that on-the-job training has been essential for their success.
3. Melville 2007.
4. Pfeffer (2015) advocates the use of hard data but does not define "leadership," simply assuming that a person who rises to the top in a corporation has succeeded as a leader. The book is, nevertheless, very useful.
5. Pfeffer (2015) rightly argues that business schools that teach idealistic models of leadership are doing their students a disservice.
6. On the leadership shown for evil causes, see p. 21–23 on charismatic dictators. Such leadership does show a limited commitment to virtues such as justice; the boss of an evil team will not hold its members together unless they have some agreement as to what counts as justice.
7. Kant 1785/2002, 58–59 and 68–69.
8. On relativism, see Woodruff 2011, 157. Justice resolves quarrels, but not every culture or situation allows for the same sorts of resolution. The idea that fairness is the same as justice is a fantasy: Fairness does not resolve quarrels.
9. The historian Thucydides, writing in the late fifth century BCE, was the first to take this line in European thought. He shows how civil war and plague brought out the worst in people (1993, 89–95, and 46–50, iii.81–85 and ii.47–51). Citations of Thucydides are by page number to the 1993 edition, followed by book and chapter numbers. John Doris (2002) and his followers have written

influentially on the effect of situations on ethical behavior, basing their work on recent studies in psychology.

10.   See also Appendix A on the humanities.

11.   Plato sees nothing wrong with a noble lie that represents a Platonic truth in the form of a myth for common people (*Republic* 3.414b), though he says that philosophers abhor what is false (6.490b). Writing in the fourth century BCE, Plato develops his concept of an ideal state in his *Republic*. I use the 1992 translation by Grube, revised by Reeve. Citations of Plato are by book number, followed by the number and letter in the margins (Stephanus pages).

Kant appears to forbid lying absolutely (1785/2002, 58–59), but his theory does not require him to do so, and he is prepared to think through difficult situations (1797/1996, 184). On this see Wood 2005, 130–132 and 187n2.

WORKS CITED

Ciulla, Joanne, Price, Terry L., and Murphy, Susan E., eds. (2005). *The Quest for Moral Leaders: Essays on Leadership Ethics*. Cheltenham: Edward Elgar.

Doris, John H. (2002). *Lack of Character: Personality and Moral Behavior*. Cambridge, UK: Cambridge University Press.

Ivanhoe, Philip J. (2000). *Confucian Moral Self-Cultivation*. 2nd ed. Indianapolis: Hackett Publishing Company.

Kant, Immanuel (1785/2002). *Groundwork for the Metaphysics of Morals*. Trans. and ed. Allen W. Wood. New Haven and London: Yale University Press.

Kant, Immanuel (1797/1996). *The Metaphysics of Morals*. Ed. Mary Gregor. Cambridge: Cambridge University Press.

Melville, Herman (2007). *The Confidence-Man: His Masquerade*. Ed. H. Bruce Franklin. Champaign, IL: Dalkey Archive Press.

Mencius (1970). *Mencius*. Trans. D. C. Lau. London: Penguin Books.

Pfeffer, Jeffrey (2015). *Leadership BS: Fixing Workplaces and Careers One Truth at a Time*. New York: Harper Business.

Plato (1992). *Republic*. Trans. G. M. A. Grube, Rev. C. D. C. Reeve. Indianapolis: Hackett Publishing Company, Inc.

Thucydides (1993). *On Justice, Power, and Human Nature: Selections from The History of the Peloponnesian War*. Ed. and trans. Paul Woodruff. Indianapolis: Hackett Publishing Company, Inc.

Wood, Allen J. (2005). *Kant*. Oxford: Blackwell Publishing.

Woodruff, Paul (2011). *The Ajax Dilemma: Justice, Fairness, and Rewards*. New York: Oxford University Press.

Wren, Thomas J., Riggio, Ronald E., and Genovese, Michael A., eds. (2009). *Leadership and the Liberal Arts: Achieving the Promise of a Liberal Education*. New York: Palgrave Macmillan.

Chapter 6

Facing Evil, Learning Guile

Well this side of Paradise! . . .
There's little comfort in the wise.

—Rupert Brooke[1]

We need to show the Othellos of this world how to spot an Iago.

—Ernesto Cortes[2]

THIS SIDE OF PARADISE

I began with simple, innocent goodness, which we saw can be powerful. Followers are drawn to anyone they see with a beautiful character. Billy's goodness might have been hidden, but it was plainly visible to all, even to Claggart. Goodness visible is what I will call beauty of soul. Leaders with beautiful souls can draw people after them the way gorgeous flowers draw butterflies and honeybees. But where will they lead their followers? In his simple goodness, a Billy Budd would not know where to lead or how to lead the people who are drawn to him. Beauty of soul might be enough in the Paradise from which Billy is an uncanny visitor. But it is not enough in a warship—or in life on this Earth.

If you choose the way of simple goodness, you may well wind up hanging from a yardarm like Billy. I will feel a pang of sorrow for you if you do, but I will shake my head and think, "I told them so." If you lead others to the yardarm, I will be furious with them and with you. No one should follow an angel this side of Paradise, and angels should know better than to set themselves up as leaders here. In our messy, mixed-up world—which Melville represents as a warship—we might do better to follow a demon than an angel. But only if the demon understands that a leader bears a heavy load of responsibility for those who follow.

In our classroom there are two books our Billy must read from if he is to understand the difference between Paradise and the world into which he has been dropped: Thucydides' *History of the Peloponnesian Wars* and Machiavelli's *The Prince*. Thucydides wrote his history as a record of a great war, of course, but his main purpose was to develop a theory about how human beings behave under extreme conditions such as war, civil strife, and plague: very badly. Such conditions are all too common, and Thucydides believed that his readers should have his book "as a treasure for all time" so that they would know what to expect. Our Billy needs to know what to expect in our world of sin.

Machiavelli knew what to expect from his own experience of observing rulers and from suffering the cruelest torture for suspicion of mutiny.[3] He understood that a leader may have to be cruel and deceitful in order to do right by his followers. He realizes, however, that what he says here would be out of place in a paradise: "Of course, if all men were good, this advice would be bad; but since men are wicked and will not keep faith with you, you need not keep faith with them."[4] But could you be a Machiavelli and still have a leader's beautiful soul? Or is it enough to have merely an appearance of goodness, like an ugly face disguised by makeup? That is the dilemma of leadership. Machiavelli has been admired and abhorred; his detractors see him as a demon of immorality ("Old Nick").[5] His fans admire his grasp of the moral complexity of leadership in an imperfect world. Both sides should agree that he is master of guile. Like simple goodness, guile can be powerful, but only within limits.

FAILURES OF LEADERSHIP AT MELOS (THUCYDIDES)

A catastrophe still famous after more than two thousand years: The men of Melos will all be killed and the women enslaved, along with their children.[6] The Athenian army will do this in 415 BCE. A false promise would have saved the people of Melos, but false promising is a clear violation of moral law. Much later, Kant will use false promising as his star example to illustrate the force of the categorical imperative. But even at the height of the Athenian Empire, everyone knew that a false promise was wrong, *anosion* as they would say in Greek, "unholy," "irreverent."

An Athenian army lands on the little island of Melos and puts siege to the city there. The people of Melos believe they have done nothing to deserve this. True, they have so far refused to join the Athenian empire, but they have done nothing to hinder the Athenians in their war with Sparta, and they have not aided the Spartans in any way. The Athenians say that if they allow Melos to remain independent, that will make their empire seem weak, and apparent weakness would be an invitation for the subject states to revolt. The army of Athens orders the people of Melos to surrender; if Melos does not surrender, Athens promises to kill the men of Melos, enslave their women, and plant a new colony on the ruins of their city. That is precisely what will happen. The leaders of Melos attempt to negotiate with the Athenian commanders but fail to save their people. These are the leaders from hell, the ones who lead you to destruction.

The rulers of Melos, rich oligarchs, meet with the generals of Athens to negotiate. The Athenians make their position clear from the start: Surrender or die. Don't waste time over morality.

> *Athenians*: For our part, we will not make a long speech no one would believe, full of fine moral arguments—that our empire is justified because we defeated the Persians, or that we are coming against you for an injustice you have done to us. And we don't want you to think you can persuade us by saying that you did not fight on the side of the Spartans in the war, though you were their colony, or that you have done us no injustice. Instead, let's work out what we can do on the basis of what both sides truly accept: We both know that decisions about justice are made in human discussions only when both sides are under equal compulsion; but when one side is stronger, it gets as much as it can, and the weak must accept that. (v.89)[7]

The Athenians mean by this that justice is relevant only when both sides feel the force of law; when one side is more powerful, justice does not apply. The Athenians are not saying that might makes right, merely that might supersedes right when two parties are unequal. Forget about right or wrong, they are saying; the only issue to be decided here is whether you live or die.

The rulers of Melos warn the Athenians that they too might suffer if others follow their example and abandon justice:

> *Melians*: Well, then, since you put your interest in place of justice, our view must be that it is in your interest not to subvert this rule that is good for all: that a plea of justice and fairness should do some good for a man who has fallen into danger, if he can win over his judges, even if he is not perfectly persuasive. And this rule concerns you no less than us: If you ever stumble, you might receive a terrible punishment and be an example to others. (v.90)

The Athenians are unmoved. They believe that, as the stronger power, they have no choice other than to rule Melos:

> *Athenians*: Nature always compels gods (we believe) and men (we are certain) to rule over anyone they can control. We did not make this law, and we were not the first to follow it; but we will take it as we found it and leave it to posterity forever, because we know that you would do the same if you had our power, and so would anyone else. (v.105)

The Athenians are wrong, of course: They *do* have a choice. Other powers then and now have refrained from taking control of weaker ones. Trying to take control of everyone you can is a losing strategy because it leads to overreaching. Athenian victories over the Persian Empire gave them the belief they could conquer anyone and hold any empire. That was hubris. And, like the tragic poets, Thucydides knew that hubris always leads to a fall.

The rulers of Melos will refuse to surrender, and the Athenians will utterly destroy their people. Perhaps the people of Melos would have agreed with their rulers, that they would do better to lose their lives than join the Athenian empire. But no one asked the people. The rulers made the fatal decision. They made it selfishly, fearing for themselves. Had the island people given in to Athens, they would probably turn to democracy. That would mean exile for the oligarchs, pain and suffering, the loss of their personal wealth, and to fend off this danger, the oligarchs are willing to put everyone at risk of death or slavery.

A few years later, Athens will suffer a great defeat and will, in the long run, lose the war with Sparta. This is the story of two failures: The Athenians wanted a tribute-paying subject, but all they got was a desert they had to repopulate—and a reputation for cruelty. The people of Melos wanted to live and be free, but they lost everything. Neither the Athenian commanders nor the Melian rulers did right by their followers. There is no true leadership in this story.

What went wrong? I am aware of at least four ways of diagnosing the failure:

1. The fault lies with the unlimited ambition of the Athenians for power, along with their vast overconfidence. They think they will never be defeated, that they can rule anybody they want. This is hubris, and they will pay for it. That, I think, is Thucydides' diagnosis; he lays the blame on the leaders chosen by the Athenian democracy during the war.[8]

2. The rulers of Melos are to blame for their selfish preoccupation with staying in power. They were more afraid of losing their positions in Melos than they were of the destruction of their people by Athens. They were the wealthy few; they knew Athens would bring democracy to Melos if Melos surrendered, and that in a democracy they would have lost their power and probably their wealth as well. Fearing this, these rulers were afraid to ask the people of Melos whether they would prefer surrender to the risk of massacre. Rulers who put their personal interests ahead of their followers are not showing leadership. A leader never fears losing power.

3. The leaders of Melos are deluded idealists, like Billy Budd; they cling to justice at all costs and die for it, leading their followers to the same destruction. This too is a kind of selfishness. True leaders recognize their responsibility to the welfare of their

followers. They would never value their own moral perfection above the needs of their people.

4. The authorities on both sides lack guile:

    i. The Athenian demand is too blunt. Why not promise Melos freedom and prosperity? Their empire respects the laws of subject states and maintains the conditions in which trade in their area flourishes and islands prosper. The Athenians could even promise to keep the oligarchs in power. Of course, once Melos surrenders, they need not keep their promises. But they will, at least, have prevented bloodshed.

    ii. The response of the rulers of Melos is as simple and blunt as the demands of the Athenians. Why not surrender, promise to obey Athens, while waiting for a safe opportunity to rebel? Why not plan for secret operations against the Athenians after a nominal surrender? The time-honored strategy of people forced into servitude has always been to smile at your masters while spitting in their soup behind their backs.

Guile on either side would save the people of Melos. But is guile really the best option here? When Billy reads about the fate of Melos he should be challenged to think through the options, and he should be able to identify the relevant ethical factors, which include at least these:

- The obligation of leaders to look after the welfare of their followers
- Everyone's obligation to refrain from false promising
- Everyone's obligation to stand up for justice

In the situation that the Athenians have created for the rulers of Melos, no one could satisfy all of these obligations. Something has to give. Some obligation will be violated. For this cruel fact the Athenians are entirely to blame. They are atrocious; they have made themselves responsible for all of the death and destruction at Melos. But that does not mean that the rulers of Melos are off the hook: They faced an ethical dilemma and solved it badly. Whatever leaders do, they must not lead their people to destruction.

Thucydides is working toward a moral here in the grand scheme of his book: By behaving to allies and subjects with such cruelty, Athenians are sowing a bitter crop that they will reap when they face defeat at the hands of Sparta. He draws no moral for the rulers of Melos; we can do this on our own. History like this allows us to exercise our own moral imaginations; that is why Thucydides would make such good reading for Billy and his peers in our classroom. Without blaming the victims—and without risking anachronism—Billy can ask how he would think through a moral dilemma of the kind that arose on Melos. Other books may help. Let's start with Machiavelli.

MACHIAVELLI'S *PRINCE*

Two famous chapters from *The Prince* give Machiavelli's answer to this sort of dilemma. In short it is this: Do what you must to stay in power, but, whatever you do, make sure that people believe that you are good and trustworthy. Keep in mind that Machiavelli is writing about rulers, monarchs who maintain their positions by force. He is not writing about leaders as such. And yet Machiavelli does urge his rulers at least to exhibit the traits of leadership, whether they really have those traits or not.

Take Chapter 18, "How Far Rulers Are to Keep Their Word." Rulers who "know how to employ cunning to confuse and disorientate other men . . . have been able to overcome those who have placed store in integrity." You cannot survive as a ruler if you do not have the cunning of a fox:

> So you must be a fox when it comes to suspecting a trap, and a lion when it comes to making the wolves turn tail. Those who simply act like a lion all the time do not understand their business. So you see a wise ruler cannot, and should not, keep his word when doing so is to his disadvantage, and when the reasons that led him to do so no longer apply. Of course, if all men were good this advice would be bad . . . [9]

Even though men are often wicked, you must do your best to appear to be one of the good ones:

> It is essential to know how to conceal how crafty one is, to know how to be a clever counterfeit and hypocrite. So you should seem to be compassionate, trustworthy, sympathetic, honest, religious, and indeed, be all those things; but at the same time you should be constantly prepared, so that, if these become liabilities, you are trained and ready to become their opposites.[10]

In other words, be ugly whenever you have to, but wear heavy makeup.[11] Our Billy must ask himself whether this is a good strategy. How will he know when to be ugly? Would he be justified in being ugly merely to retain his position? What would justify ugliness? Perhaps nothing. Actions have consequences. Ugly actions may well make your soul ugly, especially if they become habitual. And, as history shows, they easily can become habitual. Rulers can gradually enter an accelerating spiral of lies and subterfuge from which they cannot easily escape. The problem with ugliness in the soul, as Plato pointed out,[12] is that you will probably have to live with it for the rest of your life—and, if your soul is immortal and remains unchanged, forever.

Still, if rulers are leaders, they have taken on an obligation to act to save their people. This obligation might, in some circumstances, be an ethical reason for telling lies or breaking promises. But Machiavelli does not trade in ethical reasons, at least not explicitly in the *Prince*. His recommendations are backed by just one sort of reason—the goal of retaining or expanding power. Whether pursuing this goal is good for the people, or right for the prince, does not bear directly on his arguments, although he does have the good of the Italian people in mind when he urges the unification of Italy for the defense of Italians against foreign invaders.

THE LIMITS OF GUILE (SOPHOCLES' *PHILOCTETES*)

The limit of guile is the need for trust. Leaders must aim to be trusted by their teams, and so if they use guile on their own people they must disguise it. But such disguises may wear off in the long run; or perhaps someone may see you without your makeup and recognize you for what you are. So guile at best leads to a fragile or temporary solution with the home team. As for the away team, you may need to fool them only once in order to save your own people from disaster, but your trick may never work again. The Trojan Horse is the most famous case of guile in our literary history; it was needed only once, and it ended the war with Troy forever (but not necessarily for good: the victorious Greeks mostly had terrible homecomings).

In Sophocles' play *Philoctetes*, a trickster and a young man are assigned to win over an especially valuable soldier whom the army had left behind earlier, marooning him on a deserted cape of an island. The soldier survived, but he is angry. And although he longs to rejoin the army, he trusts no one. The army is the Greek force at Troy; the trickster is Odysseus, and the marooned soldier has the ultimate weapon, the bow his friend Heracles left him at his death. The young man is the son of Achilles, who—everyone believes—has inherited his father's total honesty. The soldier will trust the young son of Achilles, they hope. So Odysseus teaches the young man to tell a series of whoppers, big lies, to bring the soldier back into the army as a volunteer. Only as a volunteer will he be a useful member of the army; since he has the ultimate weapon, no one could force him to fight on the right side or fight well.[13]

In fact, the boy quickly learns to lie, but then starts retracting lies out of compassion for the soldier. Even then, however, the soldier does not trust the army's leadership; they have practiced guile far too often. Even if he believes the boy, he will not trust himself to the boy's elders. But suppose the guile succeeds, and they get the man and his weapon to Troy. Will that work? Of course not. The soldier will be doubly suspicious of the army's leaders; he will not be the man they need. Once in the army, they could use force to keep him there, but an angry conscript is not a useful member of the team, and this one has a weapon with which he could wipe out the generals in a few minutes. Sophocles solves the problem by bringing the soldier's best friend back from the dead at the last minute; the soldier trusts him, and so all ends well for the army. But before the ending we have had ample time to reflect on the uses and limits of guile.

If you practice guile on your followers, in time you will lose their trust and cease to be a leader. In effect, guile is no better than force. To lie to your friends is to treat them as potential enemies—and they may actually become enemies once they find you out. A leader can no more safely rely on guile than on force to hold followers to the cause in a context of freedom. Guile takes people into a team unwilling and drops them into situations in which they can do great harm once they realize that they have been had. Then, guile leads to force. Once the members of your team learn you have deceived them, you may have to use force to keep them in line. Leadership calls for trust, and trust calls for character (Chapter 13).[14]

FACING EVIL IN ORGANIZATIONS: DEFEATING THE IMMUNE SYSTEM

Jimmy was brilliant, friendly, good-looking, and ambitious.[15] A National Merit Scholar, he was a top performer in my year-long course—at least in the first semester. Starting in January, however, he was dull, lackluster, and remote. He started failing his other courses. He knew me well enough by then to tell me what had happened over the vacation. He had found his father in bed with his sister. Everyone, including his mother, had refused to listen to him, and he was banished from his family. Heartbroken and confused at nineteen, he lost all focus. The family immune system had expelled him as a dangerous foreign body. Truly, he was dangerous to the family: His news stood to destroy them as they had been. He never recovered during the rest of his short life. I don't know what happened to the family.

Every community has an immune system that protects it from outside threats to its identity—and indeed from any changes that are felt as threats. This goes for families and also for great organizations. A series of commanders in the U.S. Marines attempted to eliminate brutal hazing by drill instructors in basic training. If anything, the hazing intensified, as the drill instructors' immune system kicked in. To them, apparently, the campaign against hazing was a campaign against the very soul of the Marines.

A recent investigation into the death of a recruit, Raheel Siddiqui, sheds light on the matter.[16]

About a year before the recruit's death, the commander of the training battalion involved was relieved of duty because of unfavorable reports from her subordinates.[17] The truth, apparently, was that many people objected to her attempts to cut down on hazing as well as to her actions to improve the success rate of women recruits. The organizational immune system had found a powerful weapon in the Marines' evaluation system, which includes a survey of each officer's subordinates—the Command Climate Survey. This is a laudable system, but commanders need to use it with care and make sure they understand the context. The base commander, who evidently did not have his ears to the ground, took the survey result at face value, unexamined. He asked no further questions.

How should a leader face an evil that is entrenched in an organization? Many attempts at organizational reform fail. The leader who tries to make such a change is either ignored or expelled. It's surprisingly easy to ignore a boss who wants to make changes: All we subordinates need do—instead of making the requested changes—is tell the boss that we are making those changes. Then, while doing nothing else, we start covering our tracks. We lie. We protect ourselves and our team from repugnant changes by pretending to go along—maybe even going along partway—while actually digging in. Because we humans like to feel good about ourselves, we have evolved advanced techniques for feeling that many of the worst things we do are good, or at least acceptable, because of the results they achieve.[18] So if an organization is morally evil, we should expect its loyal members to bolster its immune system with specious beliefs and arguments to make the evil appear to be good. In this way they feel better, while making no changes. This strategy is hard to defeat.

Industrial and military bosses, when they set out to make changes, usually do so from the top down. After all, they are at the top; how else can they proceed? The direct, honest approach is to announce the new policy and start to put it in effect with the usual tools of management—penalties and incentives. As the authorities uncover the web of falsehoods thrown up by the immune system, they may feel they have to sack and replace most of the middle management. But even this will not change the culture of the rank and file. Change is hard.

Leaders facing organizational evil will have to go beyond typical management tools. In order to defeat immune systems, reformers will have to find agreement with the proposed changes from members at every level. This will be especially hard in a multigenerational community such as a college fraternity or a military organization that has robust traditions. Generations of former members are beyond the current leaders' reach; they continue to pass their old values on to their children, grandchildren, and anyone else who will listen to them. The student leaders I have known who have tried to change attitudes in their fraternities from within, whether toward race or sex or hazing, have all failed in the long run.

If you are tempted to join an organization in order to reform it, take great care: It may change you more than you can change it. If it turns out to be strongly resistant to change, you may be wasting time while putting yourself in moral danger. You'd do better to start something new. And, if you ever have the authority to do so, you should shut down organizations that are resistant to change, as some colleges have done recently with fraternities.[19] In any case, try not to let an organization lead you to adopt values that you cannot honestly make your own. Ask yourself if the pleasure of belonging to a group is worth the cost of sacrificing ideals to which you have been committed, and which you have no good reason to abandon. As philosophers would say, maintain your personal autonomy.[20] That's not easy.

If your best choice is to try to reform an organization from within, study the situation carefully and read up on organizational change.[21] Changing an organization depends on changing people's minds, and that is one of the hardest things to do. You cannot change my mind by issuing commands to me or giving me lectures. Flattery and cajolery won't work either. Incentives and penalties fail. The inspiration of great leadership has the best chance of pulling this off.[22]

Before you try to change other people's minds, ask yourself what it would take to induce you to change your own mind on a point you care about. Here is a suggestion: Most people are endowed with an orientation toward what is good and right. Socrates drew on this to show that people who defend immoral actions are in conflict with themselves.[23] They can solve the conflict by adopting the higher ideal. In that case, they have not totally changed their minds; they have merely tweaked them into a more ethical consistency. So when setting out to change an organization, try to show how the change would fulfill the goals to which the members are most seriously committed. That's leadership.

Keep in mind that people won't follow you as a leader toward goals that you only pretend to support.[24] You must be truly committed in order to inspire your followers. With that in mind, before you face evil in others, you should do your best to face evil in yourself.

NOTES

1. Rupert Brooke (1887–1915), "Tiare Tahiti." See Appendix B for the larger context. Brooke had a great success as a poet while still quite young; his visit to Tahiti made a deep impression on him. He died on his way to battle in Gallipoli during World War I. The poem is published in many editions and can readily be found on the internet.
2. Ernesto Cortes, private conversation. Used with permission.
3. See Wootton's introduction (1994) to Machiavelli's writings.
4. Machiavelli, Chapter 18, 54.
5. Fischer 2000, 93–94.
6. The story is told by Thucydides, (1993, 102–109, v.84–v.116). Thucydides (460?–400? BCE) served as a general in the war between Athens and Sparta. He was banished from Athens as punishment for a defeat. During his exile, he wrote a history of the war (431–404 BCE) that was also an investigation into the way human nature varies with circumstance. His account of the war breaks off in 411, owing to his unexpected death.
7. References to Thucydides are by book and chapter; this is Book v, Chapter 89 (1993, 103).
8. Thucydides ii.65 (1993, 57).
9. Machiavelli, Chapter 18, 54. The image of the fox is drawn from Cicero's *De officiis*.
10. Machiavelli, Chapter 18, 55.
11. Outright hypocrisy is incompatible with leadership, but so is pure authenticity; leadership must be performed and this may involve a weak form of hypocrisy: presenting yourself as having qualities you are only striving for. See Chapter 11.
12. See Plato's *Crito*, where Socrates argues on this basis that life with a deformed moral character is not worth living. On the beauty or ugliness of the soul, see Chapter 13.

13. Sophocles' *Philoctetes* can be found in his collection of tragedies (Meineck and Woodruff 2007).

14. Thanks to Ernesto Cortes for teaching me the value of guile and the power of the Melian Dialogue as an illustration. Thanks also to Philip Bobbitt (2013) for introducing me to Machiavelli, to Maurizio Viroli (2014) for explaining to me Machiavelli's ambitions for the freedom of Italy, and to Douglas Biow for educating me about the world of Machiavelli in private conversations.

15. Jimmy: Not his real name.

16. Reitman 2017.

17. "In April 2015, less than a year after coming to Parris Island and 11 months before Raheel's arrival, Germano received the results of the battalion's annual Command Climate Survey, in which lower-ranking officers and non-commanding officers evaluate their commanders. In her survey, Germano's subordinates described her as 'hostile, unprofessional and abusive'." Though Germano maintains she was none of those things, Haas relieved her of her command." A familiar barrier to reform is the attitude of men toward women who exert authority over them, and that may have been a factor in this case. For a sample of the survey, see https://www.usmcsurveys.com.

18. Most of us tend to give ourselves moral assessments that are higher than we deserve. The point is well illustrated by Melville's account of Bartleby's boss: "To befriend Bartleby; to humor him in his strange willfulness, will cost me little or nothing, while I lay up in my soul what will eventually be a sweet morsel for my conscience" (1987, 15). The self-enhancement bias is well researched. See for example, Brown (1986) and Brown and Dutton (1995). The latter reports a survey showing that 70% of high school seniors taking college board exams rated themselves above the median in leadership ability (1995, 1290).

19. Bowdoin College banned fraternities in 1997. Results are mixed; these organizations are not merely hard to reform but also hard to eliminate. The obnoxious behaviors to some extent survived by moving off campus. See also Hechinger 2017. On Bowdoin, see Krantz 2017.

20. Personal autonomy: The concept was developed by Immanuel Kant (1785/ 2002, 58–59 and 68–69).

21. Kotter 2014 and Senge 2006 are good places to start for studying change in business organizations. Thanks to Aurora Winslade for bibliography and advice on this topic.

22. This is the main idea in Kotter 2014. Top-down change in a rigid hierarchy is difficult but not impossible; the Marines may well change the pattern of hazing at Parris Island by means of strict controls and frequent surprise visits from higher command.

23. For Socrates' treatment of people who are in conflict with themselves over value, see Plato's *Gorgias* 482b; he sums up his strategy at 509ab. For a modern

attempt to use the method, see Woodruff 2014, 251–255 ("Ask the Right Question").
24. On hypocrisy, see Chapter 11, "Performing Leadership."

WORKS CITED

Bobbitt, Philip (2013). *The Garments of Court and Palace: Machiavelli and the World That He Made.* New York: Grove Press.

Brown, Jonathon D. (1986). "Evaluations of Self and Others: Self-Enhancement Biases in Social Judgments." *Social Cognition* 4, 353–376.

Brown, Jonathan D, and Dutton, Keith A. (1995). "Truth and Consequences: The Costs and Benefits of Accurate Self-Knowledge." *Personality and Social Psychology Bulletin* 21, 1288–1296.

Fischer, Markus (2000). *Well-Ordered License: On the Unity of Machiavelli's Thought.* Lanham, MD: Lexington Books.

Hechinger, John (2017). *True Gentlemen: The Broken Pledge of America's Fraternities.* New York: Hachette Book Group.

Kant, Immanuel (1785/2002). *Groundwork for the Metaphysics of Morals.* Trans. and ed. Allen W. Wood. New Haven and London: Yale University Press.

Kotter, John P. (2014). *XLR8: Accelerate: Building Strategic Agility for a Faster-Moving World.* Boston: Harvard Business Review Press.

Krantz, Laura (2017, July 30). "Harvard Looks to Bowdoin as Model in Eradicating Frats, But Its Decision Had Mixed Results." *Boston Globe,* https://www.bostonglobe.com/metro/2017/07/30/harvard-looks-bowdoin-model-eradicating-frats-but-its-decision-had-mixed-results/1YSwSjkmUg6dPs2gxr860M/story.html.

Machiavelli, Niccolò (1994). *Selected Political Writings.* Ed. David Wootton. Indianapolis: Hackett Publishing Company, Inc.

Meineck, Peter, and Woodruff, Paul (2007). *Sophocles: Four Tragedies.* Indianapolis: Hackett Publishing Co.

Melville, Herman (1987). *Billy Budd, Sailor and Selected Tales.* Ed. Robert Milder. Oxford: Oxford University Press. Contains the 1962 edition of *Billy Budd* as well as "Bartleby the Scrivener: A Tale of Wall Street."

Reitman, Janet (2017, July 9). "How the Death of a Muslim Recruit Revealed a Culture of Brutality in the Marines." *New York Times Sunday Magazine,* https://nyti.ms/2uNv6yL.

Senge, Peter M. (2006). *The Fifth Discipline: The Art & Practice of The Learning Organization.* New York: Crown Business.

Skinner, Quentin (2010). *Machiavelli (A Brief Insight).* New York: Sterling.

Thucydides (1993). *On Justice, Power, and Human Nature: Selections from The History of the Peloponnesian War*. Ed. and trans. Paul Woodruff. Indianapolis: Hackett Publishing Company, Inc.

Viroli, Maurizio (2014). *Redeeming "The Prince": The Meaning of Machiavelli's Masterpiece*. Princeton, NJ: Princeton University Press.

Woodruff, Paul (2014). *Reverence: Renewing a Forgotten Virtue*. 2d ed. New York: Oxford University Press.

Facing Evil in Ourselves

Compassion and Justice

A brother noble,
Whose nature is so far from doing harms
That he suspects none.

> Edmund the Bastard, saying why he will succeed in his plot against his
> innocent brother, Edgar, in Shakespeare, *King Lear*, 1.3, 179–181

SEEING DANGER

Almost all leaders have a dark side. They have done wrong, or they yearn
to do something wrong. That is part of being human. If leaders understand
their own humanity, they will be better able to understand the humanity
of their followers—and of the greater community in which they lead. But
many of us are blind to our faults. Billy Budd was not blind. He had the
good fortune, or misfortune, to have landed on Earth with no moral faults.
Like Adam before the Fall, Billy could not imagine he would ever do anything wrong. If he asked his heart what it knew of evil intentions, he would
find nothing: He "had none of that intuitive knowledge of the bad which
in natures not so good or incompletely so foreruns experience."[1] This ignorance is fatal for him. He cannot recognize evil in Claggart, the man who
has set out to destroy him, because he cannot recognize any potential for
evil in his own heart. He needs experience.

To see evil in others, and so to protect themselves and their groups,
leaders need to face the dark side in themselves.[2] It helps to have a history

of moral failure, and pay attention to it, but the very young have little experience of moral failure. We can give them opportunities to fail by inviting them to lead, but a gap remains between the starry-eyed young and the veterans who are scarred by memories of their own failures and transgressions. Imagination may help fill the gap; so can the vicarious experience of failure through history and literature.

George Washington as a very young officer reportedly oversaw an atrocity against a French officer who had surrendered but was killed brutally while in the act of reading an official message to the British from the French. This was one of the triggers for the Seven Years War.[3] Much later, when in command of the Continental Army, Washington insisted that prisoners of war be treated well, even though the British did not reciprocate (although in one case he was unrelenting).[4] He was probably a better leader for learning a sense of how badly things could go under his command, and then carrying that knowledge with him, silently, through his career. The flaws and failings of great leaders should not be absent from our curriculum.

Leaders should know themselves. The younger they are, the less they have to know about their own potential for going wrong. Could education supply the need? It should. Knowing how imperfect are the great leaders of history should help young leaders appreciate their own flaws.

UNDERSTANDING YOUR OWN FAULTS IN OTHERS

> Go to your bosom,
> Knock there, and ask your heart what it doth know
> That's like my brother's fault.
>
> Shakespeare, *Measure for Measure*, 2.2, 136–138[5]

In Shakespeare's play, Isabella pleads for the life of her brother Claudio, who has been convicted of adultery for impregnating his fiancée before the wedding (which has been cruelly delayed). She asks Angelo, who is acting as judge, to examine himself: Could he not be tempted to go wrong in the same way? Angelo could, as we soon learn, and he knows he could.

He will, before the play is over, break the same law as Isabella's brother and sleep with a woman to whom he is not yet married. But he stands by his decision, without compassion. He would be a better judge if he knew himself better, especially if he knew how to use that knowledge.

A minor offense, committed under a temptation too strong for most of us to resist—that calls for understanding, not a death sentence. But in Angelo's Vienna, lax enforcement of the law had allowed the dukedom to become a sink of debauchery, pullulating with venereal disease. Angelo was given power precisely to correct this, and so he must do something about this infraction. He can't brush it aside, not if he is to stand up for the rule of law. But if he knew himself, he would know how easily he could transgress in like circumstances. Now he has the power to administer a light punishment—one that respects the law and, at the same time, fits the situation as he understands it. That would be an exercise of compassion.

In rejecting compassion, Angelo confuses it with clemency, and they are not the same. Clemency lets guilty people off the hook. Compassion takes human factors into account in measuring the extent of a person's guilt. Neither clemency nor compassion is the same as pity, which you can feel for criminals even as you condemn them to the utmost penalties.[6] In fact, you can feel pity at the same time for the victim of a crime and the criminal. "Yet show some pity," Isabella begs. Angelo is right in principle when he says that he does show pity in punishing wrongdoers:

> —I show it most of all when I show justice
> For then I pity those I do not know,
> Which a dismiss'd offense would after gall,
> And do him right that, answering one foul wrong,
> Lives not to act another.
>
> (*Measure for Measure*, 2.2, 100–105)

Clemency would let a transgressor off the hook entirely and make a mockery of the law. He must do something to punish Isabella's brother. But death? Perhaps for a serial homicidal rapist, but not for a young man jumping the gun on his wedding, with the young woman's full consent. Clemency is often wrong, but clemency is not the same as compassion.

COMPASSION

Suppose Angelo were asked to sentence a serial killer-rapist who targets women of color, and suppose also that Angelo is a terrible man who has similar homicidal motivations in his heart, waiting to be triggered. Such a judge should not fool himself about his longings to kill. Then he would have some measure of understanding, and indeed feel some compassion for the criminal. But the judge who understands must still do justice. The judge should not let knowledge of his own badness soften his heart. The penalty for murder must not be reduced because the judge feels that he himself could be a murderer. The judge who understands himself and others ought to face the evil in himself as honestly as he can, and let compassion rise in him. But if he faces the evil in himself honestly, then he sees how evil it really is. That is one reason why compassion does not entail clemency.

In the case of Isabella's brother, compassion would recognize mitigating circumstances—such as the brother's engagement and frustration at the postponed wedding. And compassion then would mitigate the penalty. The brother is not a lecher, and does not deserve a lecher's penalty; but the serial killer is a heartless, violent soul and deserves the full penalty for murder. Facing evil in yourself should make you a better judge, because you will be able to fit the punishment not just to the crime, but to the criminal. That's justice. And we now know that compassionate justice will make you a better leader—more respected by your followers and more effective in maintaining discipline.[7]

UNBLOCKING COMPASSION

Compassion is easy to lose, easy never to find in the first place. If you do not know yourself, if you are blind to your own capacity for failure, you will not find compassion for those who have done wrong. Reverence (I have said elsewhere[8]) is feeling aware of your own human limitations; that's why reverence is a source for compassion. Reverence too is a fragile virtue. Knowing yourself is hard, especially because it involves facing your own imperfections. Ignorance is a compassion blocker.

Compassion gives way to many things. Fear and anger, for example: A soldier who has lost a friend in combat may feel no compassion for civilians foreign to him; in a mania of anger and fear, he strikes out. Or peer pressure: Young men join their newfound fraternity brothers in hazing recruits, giving them pain and violating their dignity. Or the pressure of time: Busy travelers pass by a wounded man until finally a Good Samaritan happens by, whose compassion is not blocked by any of these things. Or the hardening of the heart that may come from the school of hard knocks: "I survived brutality of this kind; so can you."9

Leaders (I have said elsewhere10) are responsible for unblocking compassion in their followers. They must be able to recognize compassion blockers and deal with them. If you are in charge of a prison, you must know how easily prison guards can block compassion in themselves, and you must act to keep them in line. The command at Abu Ghraib failed atrociously in their leadership obligations.11 As a leader, you are responsible for all the fragile good qualities of your followers, especially compassion.12

Failures of compassion have terrible consequences. Judith Isaacson was offered a job as assistant *kapo* at Auschwitz.13 The lure was extra rations for her and her family. But she did not keep the job long. When she was told to whip her fellow prisoners into line—literally, with a bullwhip—she threw the whip down and rejoined the crowd of prisoners. Before she left for the camp, her high-school teacher had given her a text of Plato's *Gorgias*, with this sentence underlined: "It is worse to do wrong than to suffer it." Her teacher, when made a guard, forgot that truth and after the war soon drank himself to death. She, on the other hand, was able to live with herself after the war.

Leaders unblock compassion by setting good examples, by reminding their followers about what matters, by setting up guidelines for good behavior, and in every way by maintaining an atmosphere favorable to compassion and other virtues. Leaders take responsibility for their actions and the actions of their followers. They never say, "I had no choice." They never lay the blame for bad consequences on having to follow the rules.14 And they never say that justice blocked them from being compassionate. That would be nonsense.

JUSTICE AND SELF-KNOWLEDGE

Justice is the quality that prevents quarrels from tearing a community apart. Justice must be found in both leaders and followers. We also need justice between communities, so that two communities will not be in danger of destroying each other. Leaders are responsible for justice within the groups they lead, and also between their groups and outside groups.

A group needs justice in order to settle old quarrels and prevent new ones from breaking out. Agreement is necessary for justice; when leaders execute justice, they must convince their followers that justice has been done. That is one reason why leaders need good ears and strong voices: They need to listen to the sounds of discontent, and they need to be able to speak the golden words that will bring discontent to an end.

Leaders often become judges among their followers. Followers expect justice from their leaders and veer away from would-be leaders whom they perceive to be unjust. If their leaders appear to be cold-hearted and unable to show compassion for others facing hardship, then they are usually perceived as failing in justice. Compassion is central to justice, although it may run against fairness. Fairness can require you to treat all violators of the law in the same way, regardless of mitigating circumstances. If so, fairness requires you to set compassion aside. This is the main difference between justice and fairness, as I have argued in an earlier book.[15]

Fairness asks us to apply rules strictly across a range of cases, treating every case the same, without compassion. But justice pays attention to the particularities of each case. If your term paper is late because you just discovered that your boyfriend cheated on you, and you have just failed in a suicide attempt, fairness requires me to charge you the same penalty I charge other late students. The rules in the syllabus made no provision for such a case. But it would be compassionate for me to give you a break, and I think the class would agree that justice allows me (even requires me) to do this. After all, where in the syllabus would I put down all the possible circumstances that merit compassion?

This is one reason why leaders need to know their own faults—such knowledge is necessary for compassion, and compassion is necessary for justice. There is another reason that justice depends on self-knowledge, and this springs from the nature of justice itself. Justice is what keeps a quarrel from breaking a team in pieces. Quarrels often arise from faults on both sides, and sometimes leaders themselves are at fault. An old quarrel will go on tearing at a community until those at fault face up to their faults and do what justice requires.

Imagine that you screw up as a leader, and your team fails an important test. You are at fault, but you refuse to accept the blame. To deflect blame, you make excuses. In the worst case, you blame others. As the boss of the team, you may scapegoat one of your team members. The team knows better. They will not trust you ever again. They may accept your orders, but they will not be willing followers.

You may have had a leadership course that taught you always to radiate confidence in your own ability. And you may have been taught that to admit fault is to reveal a failure of confidence. But this is wrong. Why do we value confidence after all? We value confidence in leaders because that helps us trust them to lead us well. But if they do not admit fault, if they blame others for their failures, we will lose trust in them altogether. A confident demeanor will not make you a leader when everyone sees that you are a weasely liar.

Justice, compassion, and leadership all require self-knowledge. You must know your faults, and not merely know them, but face them honestly. If you can't do that, how can you face similar faults in the people who report to you?

FACING YOUR FAULTS IN OTHERS: BARTLEBY'S BOSS

When we see other people with faults like ours, what do we do? Are we especially lenient or especially harsh? Melville wrote a story about a lazy boss who is unable to face the laziness in his employees. In "Bartleby the Scrivener: A Story of Wall Street" we read a tale told by the boss himself, a lawyer who takes the easy way out of every situation. He luxuriates in a job that pays well and calls for very little work—a government-sponsored sinecure. He knows himself well enough to realize that he likes to take life easy: "I am a man who, from his youth upwards, has been filled with a profound conviction that the easiest way of life is the best."[16]

His employees take advantage of him, but, as he says, "I seldom lose my temper, much more seldom indulge in dangerous indignation at wrongs and outrages" (4). He employs two copyists—human photocopy machines, neither of whom works a full day. One drinks himself incompetent by midday and is worthless all afternoon. The other arrives with a hangover and is worthless during the morning. In one case, the boss gently suggests to an employee that he go to half-time work: "Being a man of peace, unwilling by my admonitions to call forth unseemly retorts from him, I took upon me ... to hint to him, very kindly" (6). But the employee stands up to him, and he backs down—just as he has always backed down in coping with his own laziness.

Rather than insist on a full day's work from his two copyists, he hires a third person to take up the slack—Bartleby, described as "a motionless young man" (10) who (we learn later) used to work in a dead-letter office. Bartleby soon begins refusing tasks assigned him, without any explanation. "I would prefer not to," he says again and again (11), and eventually stops work altogether. At first, the boss takes a compassionate line, feeling good about himself: "Here I can cheaply purchase a delicious self-approval. To befriend Bartleby; to humor him in his strange willfulness, will cost me little or nothing, while I lay up in my soul what will eventually be a sweet morsel for my conscience" (15).

But eventually he realizes that this is unjust to the other workers, who are at least doing something to earn their salaries (16). He tries to get rid of Bartleby, but Bartleby clings to him until he dies of a laziness so extreme he will not do what is needed to stay alive. Bartleby's boss, while aware of his own laziness, does not see it as a fault; indeed, he brags about it, never faces it, never tries to do anything about it.

The story invites different interpretations. See whether you agree with this one: This boss has an inner Bartleby, who would prefer not to do anything demanding. When he hires Bartleby he comes face to face with his own inner Bartleby and is at a loss. Bartleby is a mirror for what the boss does not want to deal with in himself. Simply put: If you can't face your own faults honestly, you can't face those faults in others. Yes, the boss knows he is lazy, but he fails to see that as a fault and fails to make any attempt to deal with it. How can he deal with Bartleby in the office when he can't even face his own inner Bartleby?

KNOW THYSELF

> They say best men are moulded out of faults,
> And, for the most, become much more the better
> For being a little bad.
> —Mariana, speaking of the villain Angelo, in Shakespeare,
> *Measure for Measure,* 5.1, 436–438

"A little bad": Much depends on the "little." She must mean: "Not so bad that he doesn't know that bad is bad, and not so bad that he doesn't know how bad he is." Angelo will be better for being a little bad if he recognizes the evil in himself and is prepared to guard against it. He will also be a wiser man.

In *Death in Venice,* Thomas Mann describes a famous author, Gustav von Aschenbach, whose writing is of such perfection that he has been given a title of nobility. Mann shows him sinking into the degradation of a passion for a young boy, losing control of himself, leering with "a rouged and flabby mouth":

> There he sat, the master: this was he who had found a way to rec-
> oncile art and honours; who had written The Abject, and in a style
> of classic purity renounced bohemianism and all its works, all sym-
> pathy with the abyss and the troubled depths of the outcast human
> soul. This was he who had put knowledge underfoot to climb so
> high . . . whose style was set for a model in the schools.[17]

The knowledge he has "put underfoot" includes what Socrates called "human wisdom"—the knowledge of one's own ignorance, in this case ignorance of oneself.[18] Aschenbach has deceived himself about the sort of being he is, imagining that his perfect style expresses his own perfec-tion. Mann's style too was set as a model in the schools, and Mann too was subject to passions that would have shocked his readers. But, unlike

Aschenbach, Mann understood himself, and in writing this little book achieved a kind of wisdom.

Let's list some reasons that you should know yourself, especially if you are a leader:

1. You will have to deal with similar faults in your followers, recognizing those faults and taking them into account as you work with them. The better you know yourself, the better you can help others who are like you. If you think you never had any problems mastering subjects as a student, you will not know how to help the slower learners in your class. Every teacher needs to have had trouble learning something—and recognize that.

2. You will have to live as best you can in view of your own faults, getting help from other people, asking for their understanding, and guarding against situations in which you are likely to go wrong. Angelo would have done better to make sure he was never alone with Isabella—as he would have done had he known himself better.

3. The group you lead may have a history in which you are now complicit, no matter how innocent you feel yourself to be. You have never been a racist, for example (you think), but the all-white brotherhood you have chosen to lead is not innocent, and, now, neither are you. You will have to face this and deal with it if you are to prevent future outbreaks of racism.

4. You need to appreciate your vulnerability to suffering and know how it will affect you in tough situations.

5. You need to assess your own ignorance and ask for help when you need it. Leaders who pretend to know the way out, when they do not, can lead their followers over a cliff. Washington, after the second battle at Trenton, wisely realized that he did not know the way out and asked for help. The result was one of the most impressive maneuvers of the war.[19] Had he pretended to have knowledge he did not have, and led his army the wrong way, he would have lost a large part of his army.

Ignorance is not an evil, but ignorance in disguise can lead to the greatest evil we can do. ΓΝΩΘΙ ΣΕΑΥΤΟΝ, "Know thyself," which the ancient Greeks inscribed at their most sacred site, meant "know that you are human, and recognize your limitations. Above all, be aware, and stay aware, of your own ignorance." This is no easy thing for leaders to do, as they grow older, learning and gaining wisdom, basking in the admiration of the young. Socrates said his one gift was for knowing that his wisdom was worthless, and he spent his life trying to give that gift to others. With Socrates at your side, or in your mind, you could not retain much pride in your understanding. His vital questions about how one ought to live were too hard even for him.

Knowing yourself—recognizing your limitations—is essential to every human virtue.[20] If you have too much confidence in your own judgment, you will not pay enough attention to the people on whom your judgment falls, and you are likely therefore to fail in justice or compassion.[21]

NOTES

1. Citations for *Billy Budd* are from the 1962 edition, in this format: chapter.print page/ms. page. This passage is from 16.171/86—that is, Chapter 16, p. 147 in the 1962 edition, p. 86 in the ms.

2. The Christ-like Prince Mishkin in Dostoyevsky's *The Idiot* seems to have no trouble recognizing evil in others and connecting with them and caring about them, anyway. How he does this is mysterious, but Dostoyevsky harps throughout on the humanity of Christ. Mishkin, though perfectly good, is painfully aware of his potential as a human being for evil, unlike Billy Budd, whom Melville identifies with Adam. The novel is a valuable counterpoint to *Billy Budd*, as, in Christianity, Christ is to Adam.

3. Sieur de Jumonville was killed either by a British soldier under his command (as the French alleged) or by the chief leading a detachment of Native Americans allied with the British. The scandal of this killing rocked Europe. See Anderson 2000.

4. As Washington wrote to British General Lord William Howe, "During this unhappy contest, there be every exercise of humanity, which the nature of the case will possibly admit of" (Fitzpatrick 1982, vol. 6, p. 101; cited by Doyle 2010, 11). The on exception was Major André, who was hanged rather than honorably shot by firing squad in retribution for Captain Nathan Hale's execution (Doyle 2010, 20). Whereas the British and Hessian POWs were returned in good health, the American prisoners were "often too sick for further service" (Doyle 2010, 31). Cf. Burrows 2008, 201; cited by Doyle 2010, 372n15.

5. Any edition of Shakespeare's plays is fine for most purposes. For scholarly work, I recommend the Arden series (multiple dates).

6. Woodruff 2011, 98–100.

7. Okonofua et al. 2016 showed, for example, that compassionate discipline by middle school teachers halved suspension rates for students, while increasing the respect in which students held their teachers. Middle managers I have taught in my classes report similar effects in the corporate world. Empathy and compassion come in various forms. For distinctions, see Batson 2009.

8. Woodruff 2014.

9. The experience of brutality can make you more compassionate or more brutal. Many bullies or abusers have been bullied or abused themselves and are passing the suffering on: "If I could take it, why can't you?" See Klein 2012, 38–41, and Mishna 2012. But knowing what it is like to suffer may help you to be compassionate, especially if you reflect on it. Reading about the effects of abuse is probably more helpful than direct experience for the growth of compassion. On this, see Appendix B on the value of the humanities.

10. Woodruff 2014, 196–198.

11. Ibid., 209–211.

12. "Once an army is involved in war, there is a beast in every fighting man which begins tugging at its chains. And a good officer must learn early on how to keep the beast under control, both in his men and in himself." Attributed to General George C. Marshall, spoken at an early age to a fellow officer, of atrocities committed by Americans in the Philippines. Sagan 2017 cites Mogelson 2011for this quotation; both articles illustrate the theme in horrifying ways. The principal biographies of Marshall report a similar sentiment (for example, Pogue 1963, 82) but not these words.

13. See Isaacson 1991, 11 for the story of her receiving the work of Plato from her teacher, and 79–80 on her experience as the *kapo*'s assistant.

14. Woodruff 2011, 189.

15. Ibid., 121–123. By contrast, John Rawls, the most important political philosopher of the twentieth century, is known for his theory that justice simply is fairness. His full theory is laid out in Rawls 1971.

16. Melville 1987, 3. Subsequent references in parentheses are to page numbers in this edition.

17. Mann 1963, 71–72.

18. Human wisdom is an important theme in Plato's *Apology* (2002), supposedly delivered in 399 BCE. The most famous failure of self-knowledge in literature is that of Oedipus (Sophocles 428 BCE/2000).

19. Fischer 2004, 313–315.

20. Kant says that the first command of all duties to oneself is to know oneself (1797/1996, 191); but self-knowledge remains an unreachable ideal "because

of the *frailty* (*fragilitas*) of human nature." He goes on to say "The depths of the human heart are unfathomable" (196).

21. For an opposing view, see Brown and Dutton 1995. They report that, according to their research: "Accurate self-knowledge is not necessary; in fact, optimistic self-evaluations have positive consequences" (1295). Moreover, "People rarely seek the truth about themselves when it comes to evaluative attributes" (1295). The positive consequences they find from self-ignorance are successes that would have been blocked in people whose pessimistic self-evaluations would prevent them from trying their hardest or even trying at all. They do not consider the ethical consequences of overly positive ethical self-evaluations. By contrast, Jaspers writes movingly of the importance of self-knowledge in response to German guilt in 1945.

WORKS CITED

Anderson, Fred (2000). *Crucible of War: The Seven Years' War and the Fate of Empire in British North America, 1754–1766*. New York: Alfred Knopf.

Batson, C. D. (2009). "These Things Called Empathy: Eight Related but Distinct Phenomena." In J. Decety and W. Ickes, eds. *The Social Neuroscience of Empathy*. Cambridge, Massachusetts: MIT Press, 3–15.

Burrows, Edwin G. (2008). *Forgotten Patriots: The Untold Story of American Prisoners During the Revolutionary War*. New York: Basic Books.

Dostoevski, Fyodor (1869/1963). *The Idiot*. Trans. Constance Garnett. New York: Bantam Books.

Doyle, Robert C. (2010). *The Enemy in Our Hands: America's Treatment of Prisoners of War from the Revolution to the War on Terror*. Lexington: University Press of Kentucky.

Fischer, David Hackett (2004). *Washington's Crossing*. New York: Oxford University Press.

Fitzpatrick, John C., ed. (1932). *The Writings of George Washington from the Original Manuscript Sources, 1745–1799*. Washington, DC: U.S. Government Printing Office.

Isaacson, Judith Magyar (1991). *Seed of Sarah: Memoir of a Survivor* Urbana, Illinois: University of Illinois Press.

Jaspers, Karl (1945/2001). *The Question of German Guilt*. Trans. E. B. Ashton. New York: Fordham University Press.

Klein, Jessie (2012). *The Bully Society: School Shootings and the Crisis of Bullying in America's Schools*. New York: New York University Press.

Mann, Thomas (1912/1963). *Death in Venice and Seven Other Stories*. Trans. H. T. Lowe-Porter. New York: Vintage Books.

Melville, Herman (1962). *Billy Budd, Sailor; The Definitive Text*. Ed. Harrison Hayford and Merton M. Sealts, Jr. Chicago: University of Chicago Press.

Melville, Herman (1987). *Billy Budd, Sailor and Selected Tales*. Ed. Robert Milder. Oxford: Oxford University Press. Contains the 1962 edition of *Billy Budd* as well as "Bartleby the Scrivener: A Tale of Wall Street."

Miller, Arthur. (1949/1975). *Death of a Salesman*. New York: Viking.

Miller, Arthur. (1955/2010). *A View from the Bridge*. London: Methuen Drama.

Mishna, Faye (2012). *Bullying: A Guide to Research, Intervention, and Prevention*. New York: Oxford University Press.

Mogelson, Luke (2011). "A Beast in the Heart of Every Fighting Man." *New York Times Magazine*, April 27.

Okonofua, Jason A, Paunescu, David, and Walton, Gregory M. (2016). "Brief Intervention to Encourage Empathic Discipline Cuts Suspension Rates in Half Among Adolescents." *Proceedings of the National Academy of Science*. 113(19): 5221–5226.

Plato (2002). *Five Dialogues: Euthyphro, Apology, Crito, Meno, Phaedo*. Trans. G. M. A. Grube, ed. John M. Cooper. Indianapolis: Hackett Publishing Co.

Pogue, Forrest C. (1963). *George C. Marshall: Education of a General*. New York: Viking Press.

Rawls, John (1971). *A Theory of Justice*. Cambridge, Massachusetts: Harvard University Press.

Sagan 2017. "The Changing Rules of War." *Daedalus*. Cambridge, Massachusetts: MIT Press. https://www.amacad.org/content/publications/pubContent. aspx?d=22457

Shakespeare, William. The Arden Shakespeare. https://www.amazon.com/s/?ie= UTF8&keywords=arden+shakespeare+complete+works&tag=googhydr-20&index=aps&hvadid=177117480875&hvpos=1t1&hvnetw=g&hvrand=1 4385857365801621547&hvpone=&hvptwo=&hvqmt=b&hvdev=c&hvdvcm dl=&hvlocint=&hvlocphy=9028283&hvtargid=kwd-90019781&ref=pd_sl_ 136c04bi79_b

Sophocles, *Oedipus Tyrannus* (428 BCE/2000). Trans. Peter Meineck and Paul Woodruff. Indianapolis: Hackett Publishing Company.

Woodruff, Paul (2011). *The Ajax Dilemma: Justice, Fairness, and Rewards*. New York: Oxford University Press.

Woodruff, Paul (2014). *Reverence: Renewing a Forgotten Virtue*. 2nd ed. New York: Oxford University Press.

Chapter 8

Facing Complexity

Leadership and Lying

We are used to hearing lies from politicians. We hate that, but we are not above telling harmless "white" lies to our friends. At least we would like to believe our lies are harmless. In *The Just Assassins*, a play by Camus, one conspirator expresses his discomfort to another: "Somehow I can't get used to lying," he says. His companion, Stepan, replies, "Everybody lies. What's important is to lie well."[1] What could it mean to lie well? You might save your life by telling a lie, but that same lie could corrode your life and destroy the possibility of friendship.

THE KNOCK ON THE DOOR

Osip Mandelstam, a poet, was arrested by Stalin's plain-clothed police in 1934 for the first time. David Brodski, a friend and poet, had come uninvited to spend the evening with Osip and his wife Nadezhda. Afterward, the couple realized that Brodski had been sent to make sure they did not destroy any incriminating poems before the police arrived. He was, unbeknownst to them, working for their enemies. Under Stalin, you could not trust your friends. To stay alive, you would have to lie to your friends, and they would lie to you. Soon after the arrest, Bukharin (another friend) asked Nadezhda:

"He hasn't written anything rash, has he?" I said no—just a few poems in the usual manner, nothing worse than what Bukharin knew of already. It was a lie, and I still feel ashamed of it. But if I had not lied we would not have had our Voronezh "breathing space" [a respite before the second and final arrest that led to Osip's death]. Should one lie? Is it right to lie? Is it right to lie in order to save someone? It is good to live in conditions where one doesn't have to lie. Do such conditions exist anywhere? I was brought up to believe that lies and hypocrisy are universal. I would certainly not have survived in our terrible times without lying. I have lied all my life: to my students, colleagues, and even the good friends I could not quite trust (this was true of most of them). In the same way, nobody trusted me. This was the normal lying of the times, something in the nature of a polite convention. I am not ashamed of this kind of lying and I misled Bukharin quite deliberately, out of a calculated desire not to frighten off my only ally.[2]

Stalin had created a world in which true friendship was almost impossible. A friend is someone I can trust with the truth about me (so says the philosopher Kant).[3] Nadezhda apparently had only one such friend, Anna Akhmatova. In Bukharin she was allowed to have an ally, but never a real friend, not under Stalin. Stalin had created a world in which leadership also was impossible. This was clever of Stalin: No one could lead a movement against him, because no one could trust anyone else long enough to start a movement. Trust is bedrock for leadership, as it is for friendship. Banish trust, banish leadership. Banish leadership and you leave only the iron hand of tyranny.

Nadezhda Mandelstam contradicts herself in this passage: First she says she is still ashamed, and then she says she is not ashamed, of her lying. Of course she had a perfect excuse for lying on this occasion, and she did the right thing, so she ought not to be ashamed of that. But she contributed to a general culture of lying, and at the same time she developed a personal habit of lying. These are both bad, and she had reason to be ashamed of them. Stalin had created a world in which anyone with a conscience would be ashamed to survive. And yet survive she must, to preserve the memory of her husband, and to keep the hope of freedom alive.

Imagine another knock on the door, almost ten years later, in France. You are a nursemaid caring for the baby of a couple who are away on errands. The SS soldier at your door asks whether your employers are Jewish. You say, "Don't be silly. Hold this chamber pot while I change the baby's diaper." You have told a lie (in effect), and, by so doing, you have saved three lives. Have you done anything to be ashamed of? The family trusted you, and you have been trustworthy. You don't owe anything to the soldier at the door. Should you be ashamed of deceiving him?

Now imagine you command an armed company in enemy territory. Your troops are all in danger, but you assure them they will be safe. At best, you are stretching the truth. Do you still deserve their trust?

Now try this story: Perhaps you are under orders to extricate your company from a dangerous situation, and you have no other orders. You have been moving your troops in conjunction with an allied unit. Both units, yours and the ally's, are in grave danger and will have to fight their way out against serious odds. You ask your ally to lead the way up a narrow defile and over a ridge in the face of the enemy, in the hope of surprising them. You promise that you will be right behind your allies. Then, while your allies advance and occupy the full attention of the enemy, you order a retrograde movement and take your people out of danger. The allied unit will probably be destroyed, but you expect to save your people by letting this happen. In effect, you will have used your allies as bait to distract the enemy.

Of course many things could go wrong with your plan: Divided, both units are easy prey, and the one that is in retreat is the more vulnerable. But suppose you carry out this plan, and it works. Should you be proud or ashamed of what you have done? Your first duty, after all, was to your own company. Had you gone up the defile with the others, you believe your company would have been destroyed as well; had both units stayed below or tried to escape, you believe both would have been destroyed. You broke a promise, used your allies as bait for the enemy, and saved two hundred lives. Good decision or bad?

In judging this case, keep in mind that commanders in combat rarely know precisely what is going on. You cannot be sure that your treachery will save your troops, and you cannot be sure that keeping faith with your allies would have meant both units would be destroyed. You will never know. Survivors may spend their lives afterwards wondering "what if." That is one reason why soldiers who survive combat often feel shame or guilt or both.

THE LEADERSHIP DILEMMA: HOME TEAM VERSUS THE WORLD

The Leadership Dilemma is this: Leaders should do what is right by other people—all other people. They have the same ethical duties that we all have when we are not leaders. But leaders have something more: They have taken on special responsibilities to the people they lead. These special responsibilities add complexity, because they may conflict with other ethical duties. What a leader owes to her people may conflict with what she owes to the world.

Remember the oligarchs who ruled Melos? They had a duty to protect their people, and they blew it. They could have fended the Athenians off with a treaty they fully intended to break, but they didn't have the guile. They had faced a choice between two wrongs—lying to an enemy, on the one hand, or beguiling their own people with false hopes and leading them to destruction on the other. Did they make the right choice?

Dilemmas of this kind are common. Business managers have a fiduciary responsibility to the people who have put up capital for their corporations—a group that may include widows, orphans, and aged pensioners. They—the managers—have taken on an obligation to do their best in the interests of this group. But doing their best may entail behavior that wrongs the outside world—colluding with unjust governments, polluting everyone's air or water, grinding down workers with hardship, danger, and low pay—as can be especially tempting when the workers are far away in very poor countries. This at least appears to be a dilemma: Doing right by one group, in such a case, seems to entail doing wrong by another.

Similar dilemmas face military commanders: They have a duty to protect their troops from harm, so far as is consistent with their mission. The mission is always supposed to come first in the military; you may have to take heavy losses in order to enable other larger units to survive or simply to bring the war to an end. At the same time, military commanders have a duty to do no more harm to the enemy than is proportional to the evil they seek to overcome. That follows from the theory of just war. On any theory it is wrong to kill innocent civilians, but military commanders often decide—wrongly—to save the lives of their own troops at the expense of civilian lives, or at a disproportionate cost in enemy lives. And in the fictional story I just told, a commander saved his troops at the expense of his allies.

Rulers, managers, and commanders face choices of this kind. You may have thought that these are not really ethical dilemmas at all, since they require choices between ethics and what you might call "pragmatism." If so, a true leader would always reject the pragmatic choice, because a true leader would inspire trust by being ethical. That would mean that true leaders would betray their people to the Athenians, bankrupt their widow and orphan shareholders, and take little heed for the safety of their soldiers in combat. But that is wrong: Ethical considerations fall on both sides of these choices. Betraying your people, bankrupting your shareholders, failing to protect your troops—all these are ethical failures, even if done for ethical reasons. People trust their leaders, and their leaders have willingly accepted that trust. Leaders have an ethical obligation to look after the interests of their followers. Leadership dilemmas are collisions between two kinds of ethical demands, not between ethics and something else.

How are leaders to choose between their responsibilities to the home team and their larger ethical duties?

Sometimes the choice is easy, though the execution may be hard. Sometimes the dilemma is only apparent. In the long term, doing right by the world may be right for the home team, though this may not seem so to the home team at the time of the decision. If so, you as a leader will have to persuade your team that you are doing right by them when you choose what is also right for the outside world. If you can't persuade them, they will replace you, and they should. Leaders have a responsibility to lead their followers in ethical directions—especially, as I have shown above, to lead them toward compassion for outsiders. But sometimes an ethical leader should put the team's interests first. Then the dilemma resolves in favor of the team: You may be right to lie to your enemy or even to your allies.

In some cases the dilemma is an artifact of simple-minded devotion to rules like "never tell a lie." These rules are not always right. When they are wrong, the ethical leader, if thoughtful, will be guided by something other than rules. What could that something be? Perhaps the moral universe is too complicated for rules—or, at least, for rules taken as absolutes.[4]

MORAL DILEMMAS

Our flawed world teems with moral complexities. Greek tragic poets made the most of these. For example, what is a young man to do if his mother has killed his father? If he does nothing to avenge his father, he violates his ethical obligation to his father. But if he takes action against his mother, he violates his ethical obligation to his mother. That is the dilemma of Orestes. In one play about him, he says, in effect, "I'm damned if I do, damned if I don't."[5] That seems an impossible choice, because Orestes is under conflicting obligations. It is impossible for him to honor both of them.

"That's life," the Greek poets thought. Human beings are always vulnerable to being thrust into traps that leave them no escape from doing something wrong. Orestes had to choose between honoring his father and honoring his mother. Greek culture put men first, before women, and so Orestes made the right choice, culturally speaking, in honoring his father at the expense of killing his mother. Aeschylus' play, *The Eumenides,* reaches that conclusion in a dramatic trial scene.[6] So the dilemma had a solution, but this solution does not leave Orestes unscathed. He has killed his mother, and he will never be free of that. He has made himself an orphan, and he has given himself a horrifying memory. He will be tormented by grief and guilt—even if he had no better choice than to kill his mother.

That is what I mean by a moral dilemma: a moral conflict from which you cannot emerge unscathed.[7] Any possible choice you make will leave you morally damaged—not just full of regret or remorse or guilt, but actually damaged. Moral damage or injury occurs when you take a step that will contribute to a bad habit. If you tell a lie, even if you have good reasons for believing that this is the best thing to do at the time, you are still falling into an easier way of lying. If you let your allies die, you fall into an easier way of accepting deaths that you cause. And the same goes if you are leading your own troops into a trap from which few survive. You are the worse for whatever you do to extricate yourself from a moral dilemma.

If our world had no flaws, then there would be no moral dilemmas. If, for example, parents never killed each other, then Orestes would never have to make the awful choice that is laid on him. But in our wicked world, parents often plunge children into dilemmas by quarreling. All too often, like the Athenians at Melos, powerful people limit our choices to ones that feel wrong to everyone.[8] This side of Paradise, people often meet "damned if you do, damned if you don't" scenarios. Choosing the best bad option is still a bad option.[9]

That's rotten. If you keep making bad choices when it seems necessary to do so, you will either smother your conscience altogether or throw yourself into tangles of guilt and shame. The moral complexity of war leaves many veterans feeling worthless through shame and guilt. In any case, making rotten choices may be habit-forming, and rotten habits are the ugliness of the soul. That is why the student leaders in our classroom must ask whether they can learn to be leaders this side of Paradise and still be good human beings. Could Billy Budd become an effective leader without shedding his real and visible goodness—the goodness that made him a natural (but ineffective) leader from the start?

This side of Paradise, we have war. One good reason against starting a war is that wars always lead to wrongdoing. You can't wage war without killing innocent civilians. We hide this under a business-like euphemism, "collateral damage." But call it what you may, war kills the innocent, and nothing makes that right—not even the rightness of standing by your obligation to your troops. Veterans of war do not emerge unscathed. Most of the toughest-looking dilemmas hit us in the context of war—or of anything at all like war. And yet we have war, and war does not seem likely to go away.

This side of Paradise, we have businesses in competition, which can be as effective as war in generating dilemmas. If I conduct my business with an eye to protecting the environment, and you, my competitor, do not, then you may put me out of business—leaving stockholders bereft, including widows and orphans. Competition can be regulated by government or by public opinion, but it will always introduce moral complexity. Still, competition has its value, and it is not going away.

So, yes, we could reduce moral complexity by moving closer to Paradise. If we could move all the way back to Paradise, we would wipe out moral complexity and live happily by simple rules. But don't fool yourself: In this world we will not always be able to follow the rules we lay down for ourselves. So we have to question the value and power of rules.

MACHIAVELLI: BREAKING THE RULES

Machiavelli wrote *The Prince* for rulers, not leaders, and he is most famous for urging them to break rules while pretending to be moral.[10] Should we allow our young leaders to read such a book? Will it corrupt them? I have often found students reluctant to expose themselves to the evil they expect to find in those pages, but I assign Machiavelli anyway. If my students do not face up to him, they will not face up to themselves. They may have made moral compromises already, but hidden them even from themselves. Machiavelli is ruthlessly honest; reading his work may lead us to honesty as well.

The rulers for whom Machiavelli wrote were always at war. To safeguard his own power, a prince at war may need to break promises and tell lies. And to safeguard his subjects, he needs to guard his own power safely. Machiavelli says this is fine for a prince, so long as the prince continues to *appear* honest and so long as the result is beneficial to the prince's subjects:

> Alexander VI [the Borgia pope] had only one purpose, only one thought, which was to take people in, and he always found people who were willing victims.
> ***
> A ruler . . . is often obliged, in order to hold on to power, to break his word, to be uncharitable, inhuman, and irreligious. So he should be mentally prepared to act as circumstances and changes in fortune require. As I have said, he should do what is right when he can, but he must be prepared to do wrong if necessary.[11]

Machiavelli's grand aim was the consolidation of Italy and its liberation from the great nations, France and Spain, which were competing to take advantage of Italy's being divided into small republics and princedoms. The Borgia pope he admires, along with his son Cesare, was engaged in securing papal power in the Romagna with that larger goal in mind. Although he is not explicit here, Machiavelli probably held that the deceit used by the Borgias in expanding papal power was excusable, in view of the goodness of the goal. But not every evil is excusable. A prince who is consistently wicked, and gives no benefits to his subjects, will not (and should not) stay in power. Machiavelli believes that cruelty can be used well or badly:

> Well-used cruelty (if one can speak well of evil) one may call those atrocities that are committed at a stroke, in order to secure one's power, and are then not repeated, rather every effort is made to ensure one's subjects benefit in the long run. . . . Those who use cruelty well may indeed find that both God and their subjects are prepared to let bygones be bygones.[12]

Be careful here. Machiavelli is saying that if the result is good, the evildoer will be excused. He is not saying that the end justifies the means. He is not saying that cruelty is justified; if it were justified, it would be just and not evil. But he points out clearly that cruelty remains evil and is therefore unjustified. He does not even say that the end excuses the means in all cases. The end has to be a really good one before God will let bygones be bygones.

This is the difference between a justification and an excuse: When I make an excuse, I admit that what I did was wrong, but deny that I am a bad person for doing that. I had no better choice, or I was terrified, or anyone would have done the same thing in my shoes—these are all excuses. When I justify my action, I show that it was the right thing to do after all: He attacked my family with lethal force, so I was right to kill him. That, if true, would justify what I did.

Breaking the rules may be right in some cases, and it may be excusable in others. But you can wear out an excuse. You may have good excuses for lying, but be careful not to use those excuses very often. No one will believe you if you do, and your lies will be wasted.[13]

FOLLOWING THE RULES

Machiavelli gives scant attention to the reasons why a prince ought to tell the truth and keep his promises. The most basic reason is built into the concept of leadership. The prince is not a leader if his subjects are not willing to follow him. We are most willing to follow leaders we trust. The people we trust most are those who (we think) tell us the truth and keep their promises to us. We trust them to follow the rules of honesty. More than that, we expect them to be honest people—that is, to follow the rules of honesty because they feel like following them; they like being honest.

Honest people enjoy being honest. That is why we trust them. We do not think they are honest merely out of strategy: that is, we do not think they do honest things merely to win our hearts or earn our votes. If we thought their honesty so shallow, we would be reluctant to follow them. Instead, we believe that their honesty is grounded in their souls. That, at least, is what we hope when we choose, willingly, to follow them. That is a pragmatic reason for a leader to develop the habit of truth.[14]

Sometimes you create conditions in which you ought to tell the truth no matter what—for example, when you take an oath or enter a formal competition. When you enter a formal competition you implicitly take on a special obligation to compete in a certain way, the same as the others. In sports, this is obvious, and we have regulatory agencies that aim to keep athletic competition fair by enforcing certain rules. Since early in the previous century, governments have been expected to regulate competition among businesses. But even in the absence of regulation, we have both ethical and pragmatic reasons to play fair—ethical, because in entering a competition we take on obligations to our competitors; pragmatic, because no one will play with us if we are known to play dirty. War too has its rules: All parties to a war expect each other to respect prisoners and the bodies of the dead, and this entails telling the truth about them. We don't need a referee to enforce such rules. Once the rules break down, both sides can suffer horribly as each side takes revenge on the other. To avoid that, reciprocity drives combatants to follow certain rules.

Leaders have ethical reasons as well. Lying is a form of disrespect: When you lie to me you assume that I am unable to cope with the truth; if you respect me you will tell me the truth and help me understand it. If you respect yourself you will believe that you have the power to tell the truth. Lying makes for an ugly and uncomfortable soul. For example, lying often means cowardice: You lie to me because you are afraid of the consequences. Courage—an admirable trait of leaders—is mostly (but not always) honest. So lying can be cowardly; it is often manipulative as well. When you lie to me, you block any chance I might have of facing the truth on my own terms. Lying violates my freedom to decide. Telling me the truth implies that you respect my mind, my judgment, my being an independent person.

What if I am not an independent person? What if I have given my mind to Hitler, sworn the Nazi oath of absolute obedience? In that case, your ethical reason for telling me the truth evaporates. I have given up whatever claim I might have had to your respect. Does the same thing happen if I am in too much pain to think, or have lost my mind to drink? If I suffer dementia? Or if I am a small child not yet able to think about the truth? Thirty minutes after a paroxysm of grief, my friend forgot his wife had died. Should I not join a conspiracy to keep up the fiction that she is in the next room? He will not remember that, either. If I tell him the truth every time he asks, he will be in constant grief. Why should I make him suffer? The rule does not apply here.

LIVING WELL WITH COMPLEXITY

Shallow thinkers want to chop their way out of complexity. They look for theories or commandments that will simply settle the matter of what you should do. You might say, "I choose to follow Kant. Never make a false promise." If you were the commander who was trapped by the enemy with your allies, and you held this view, you might lead your unit to a glorious and honest death alongside all those allies. But the relatives of your dead soldiers may well blame you for breaking your promise to your own troops. Kant would shake his head.[15]

If you had been trained differently, you might say, "I am on the side of John Stuart Mill. I will take the course that leads to the least pain and the most happiness. If I make the false promise to the allies, at least my troops will live; otherwise, all will be lost." But you are not looking ahead: The enemy will surely know about your betrayal and they may use it to pry your allies out of the alliance. If so, your larger army will suffer thousands of casualties that would have been prevented had you not betrayed the alliance. You would have failed to promote happiness. How could you have done better? You had no way to measure the costs of the possible outcomes. If you can't be sure of the outcomes, you can't rely on outcome measurement to justify your decision.

My military example (betraying the allies) is like what philosophers call a "trolley problem." Both are thought experiments designed to coax us into declaring our moral intuitions about certain outcomes.[16] An errant trolley is rushing down the tracks, bringing death toward five people; if you pull a switch it will change tracks and kill only one. Or if you dump a fat person off a bridge, that will stop the trolley and save the five lives. One for five looks like a good trade to many people. But the trolley problems are always simpler than real-life cases.

Trolley problems are unrealistic in that they present cases in which we know precisely the outcome that follows from each choice. Life is not like that. In facing a moral dilemma, you must take your ignorance into account. In the military case I set out, which could well be real, you simply do not know what will result from treachery in the long run, or from telling the truth. Trolley problems generally give you just two choices, and full information, but in real life you have more choices and less knowledge.

If you are the company commander in a tight spot, you need to be clear about the range of choices you have. Is surrender an option? If you join your allies, form a perimeter, and call for air support, are the two units likely to survive? Often courage will make you safer than treachery; might this work for you? You may not know the answers, but you should at least consider such questions. Even from a purely utilitarian point of view, it is generally safer to tell the truth than to count on treachery to yield the outcome you desire.

In combat, and everywhere in real life, we find ourselves in situations we cannot perfectly control. If you cannot control your situation, at least you can control yourself—and thereby influence your followers. You have the power to decide, after thinking things through, what you believe is right in the circumstances, and you have the power to stand for that. If you are persuaded by my points about truth and trust, then, unless you have a compelling reason to do otherwise, tell the truth and stand by your word. You need never be ashamed of that—even if it turns out you misjudged the outcome.

In Conrad's novel *Lord Jim*, the protagonist abandons a ship he believes is sinking, leaving the passengers to drown.[17] He was wrong to do so: The crew ought not to leave until the passengers are safe. "But there was only one lifeboat," you might say. He was still wrong, and he was wrong about the danger as well: The ship floated and the passengers lived. Would knowing more have helped him? Or should he have clung to the rules no matter what? The rules of the sea are clear: Stay with the ship until the passengers are safe. But can you be expected to throw your life away for that rule, even when you are sure nothing good could come to anyone by your staying with the ship?

Let's face it: Complexity is complex, and a theory that tells you otherwise is moonshine. In a serious dilemma, any solution may be defensible, but none of them would leave you entirely clean, morally speaking. If we professors have no solutions to offer, what can we teach that will help Billy and Joan decide when to lie, or when to make false promises? History, to begin with, so they learn how such scenarios are likely to play out. But also a certain approach to ethics—not the kind that promises it will tell you just what to do, but the kind that asks how to decide hard questions and then how to do what you decide to do. How can you decide bravely, compassionately, wisely, and then act in the same manner? This is adverb ethics, virtue ethics. We will come back to this in Chapter 13.

"Everybody lies," says Camus' Stepan. "What's important is to lie well."[18] I understand that to mean "to lie with virtue intact"—a tall order. Still more important, I would add, is to find a way to live without any temptation to tell lies. But whatever you do in a tough spot, do it well. That means do it thoughtfully, courageously, reverently, and with several other of these -ly words. Think: Can you courageously and reverently betray your allies? The answer depends on considering a detailed scenario. But whatever you are planning to do, if you can't do it well, don't do it at all.

NOTES

1. Camus, *Les Justes (The Just Assassins)*, 239.
2. Mandelstam 1970, 22.
3. Kant holds that moral friendship has this feature, that it satisfies our wish to reveal our opinions to another person in safety (1797/1996, 216 –217).
4. On these issues, see Dancy 2004.
5. Aeschylus, *Oresteia: The Libation Bearers*, lines 924–925 (Meineck translation 1998, 107). The *Oresteia* was performed in 458 BCE.
6. Aeschylus, *Oresteia: The Eumenides*, lines 566–777 (Meineck translation 1998, 140–150).
7. Many modern philosophers do not accept the concept of moral dilemmas. They defend the rule that "ought" implies "can." This means that whatever you ought to do, you are able to do; and if you are unable to do something, then you have no obligation to do it. If they are right, then Orestes has misunderstood his situation. He cannot have obligations to both parents, because it is not possible for him to meet both obligations. Since he cannot honor both his parents in his circumstances, he is under no obligation to do so. If it is better to honor his father, then that is what he is obligated to do. Therefore, there is no dilemma if a dilemma is a conflict of oughts and "ought" implies "can." But, as I argue here, following Hursthouse (1999), we do better to understand a moral dilemma as arising in a situation from which the agent cannot emerge unscathed by moral damage. For further reading on this topic, see the Study Guide (Appendix B).
8. The same logic from the previous note applies to the rulers of Melos. I said they were under three obligations, which they cannot satisfy together. But perhaps this is not true, and their only obligation was to make the best choice they could in the particular circumstances in which they found themselves. There are no real moral dilemmas if "ought" implies "can," as many philosophers have argued.
9. Rosalind Hursthouse calls these situations tragic dilemmas. A dilemma is tragic, she says, "not because the dilemma was irresolvable, but because, resolving it correctly, a virtuous agent cannot emerge with her life unmarred" (1999, 77).
10. On the moral dilemmas facing the prince or the politician, see Walzer 1973. But keep in mind that everyone faces such issues—not just people in politics.
11. Machiavelli, Chapter 18 (Wootton translation 1994, 54–55).
12. Machiavelli, Chapter 8 (Wooten translation 1994, 30).
13. On lying, see Bok 1978. On excuses, see Woodruff 1982.
14. On rules and roles, Betty Sue Flowers has shown me in private conversation that there's also the issue of role—to some extent, Vere has to be the embodiment of the law, and to apply it equally, even when a good man will be hanged. He is, after all, wearing the "king's buttons." The role of a leader within a constitution, set of laws, or rules of a game is interesting. Alexander the Great was not bound in this way.

15. Kant's actual views on lying are more nuanced than is generally recognized, though he gives powerful moral reasons against lying even when it is beneficial. See the "casuistical reasoning" sections in his *Metaphysics of Morals* (1797/1996. 184).

16. The trolley problem was first introduced by Philippa Foot (1967) and then analyzed further by Judith Jarvis Thomson (1976).

17. Conrad 2012, 104–105. In Chapter 10 I discuss the incident in more detail as it bears on courage.

18. Of *The Just Assassins*, Camus writes: "I tried to achieve dramatic tension through classical means—that is, the opposition of characters who were equal in strength and reason. But it would be wrong to conclude that everything balances out and that, in regard to the problem raised here, I recommend doing nothing. My admiration for my heroes, Kaliayev and Dora, is complete. I merely wanted to show that action itself had limits. There is no good and just action but what recognizes those limits and, if it must go beyond them, at least accepts death. Our world of today seems loathsome to us for the very reason that is made by men who grant themselves the right to go beyond those limits, and first of all to kill others without dying themselves. Thus it is today that justice serves as an alibi, throughout the world, for the assassins of all justice" (1958, x).

WORKS CITED

Aeschylus (1998). *Oresteia*. Trans. Peter Meineck. Indianapolis: Hackett Publishing Company, Inc.

Bok, Sissela (1978). *Lying: Moral Choice in Public and Private Life*. New York: Random House.

Camus, Albert (1944/1958). *The Just Assassins* in *Caligula and Three Other Plays*. Trans. Stuart Gilbert. Preface by the author trans. Justin O'Brien. New York: Alfred A. Knopf.

Conrad, Joseph (2012). *Lord Jim: A Tale*. Ed. J. H. Stape and Ernest SullivanII. Cambridge: Cambridge University Press.

Dancy, Jonathan (2004). *Ethics Without Principles*. Oxford: Oxford University Press.

Foot, Philippa (1967). "The Problem of Abortion and the Doctrine of the Double Effect." *Oxford Review* 5, 5–15.

Hursthouse, Rosalind (1999). "Irresolvable and Tragic Dilemmas." In *On Virtue Ethics*. Oxford: Oxford University Press, 63–87.

Kant, Immanuel (1797/1996). *The Metaphysics of Morals*. Ed. Mary Gregor. Cambridge: Cambridge University Press.

Machiavelli, Niccolò (1994). *Selected Political Writings*. Ed. David Wootton. Indianapolis: Hackett Publishing Company, Inc.

Mandelstam, Nadezhda (1970). *Hope Against Hope: A Memoir*. Trans. from the Russian by Max Hayward. New York: Athenaeum.

Meineck, Peter (1998). *Aeschylus: Oresteia*. Indianapolis: Hackett Publishing Company, Inc.

Molière (1965). *The Misanthrope and Tartuffe*. Trans. Richard Wilbur. New York: Harcourt Brace Jovanovich.

Sartre, Jean-Paul (1948/1955). *Dirty Hands (Les Mains sales)*, in *No Exit and Three Other Plays*. Translated from the French by Stuart Gilbert. New York: Alfred A. Knopf.

Thomson, Judith Jarvis (1976). "Killing, Letting Die, and the Trolley Problem." *The Monist* 59(2), 204–217.

Walzer, Michael (1973). "Political Action: The Problem of Dirty Hands." *Philosophy and Public Affairs* 2, 160–180.

Woodruff, Paul (1982). "Justification or Excuse: Saving Soldiers at the Expense of Civilians." *Canadian Journal of Philosophy*, Supplementary Volume VIII, 159–176.

Chapter 9

Facing Fear, Showing Courage

*I want to learn from you who is courageous—not only in infantry, but
also in cavalry and in every sort of military force, and not only in the
military, but in danger at sea, or in the face of disease or poverty or politics, and not only in the face of pain or fear, but in the face of desires or
pleasure, whether standing fast or in retreat—for I suppose there are
some who are courageous in such circumstances.*

—*Socrates in Plato's* Laches 191c8–e2.[1]

FACING ENEMIES

The Athenian general was sick that day. His kidney ailment had flared up, so
he stayed behind at the Athenian camp—the oval camp—while his army
went out to continue its work. They were extending siege lines around
Syracuse, which were now far from the camp. That day, the enemy took
advantage of the situation, attacked the oval camp, and almost overran it.
But the general rose from his sickbed, took command, and saved the day
by a brave tactic. He rolled supply wagons into the area that the enemy had
breached and set them afire. That was enough.[2]

Leaders need courage because their followers need courage. If you
follow a coward, you may never have a chance to show courage or even
practice it. If the leader runs away, and you alone stay to fight, you are
showing stupidity, not courage: You will be killed to no purpose. If, on
the other hand, you are able to bring order to the retreat, you may become
the *de facto* leader, bringing the unit to safety or even to making a stand
together that would save the mission. But the same soldier who runs away

following a bad commander may stand up courageously with a good one. Leadership makes a difference everywhere, but especially in danger.

Much later in the same campaign the enemy grew so strong that the Athenians had to abandon camp and march into a very dangerous hinterland. Their best hope of survival lay in keeping panic at bay, marching in good order, staying together. Our general led one of two divisions. The other division succumbed to panic; it was soon divided and destroyed. But our general's division held out longer, until it sustained heavy losses and was eventually rounded up by the enemy. The general was executed on the spot.[3] His name was Nicias, and his courage had been infectious on many occasions. At the time, in 413 BCE, he was an old man.

"Of all the Greeks of my time," wrote the historian Thucydides, "he was the least deserving of such misfortune, because his entire way of life had been governed by aiming at virtue."[4] Nicias was certainly brave in war. The soldiers who followed him were lucky in that. But he was not brave in everything. The defeat of his army, in the end, was due to his cowardice in failing to stand up for his troops to the authorities at home. Athenian assemblies were notoriously changeable. Had Nicias been honest with the people at home about the state of the war, he might have persuaded them to order the army to withdraw from Sicily. But he might well have failed to persuade them. Fearing failure, he wrote to the assembly saying that he needed an addition of as many more troops as had been sent at the start. He was hoping they would call the troops home rather than send a second armada, but they took him at his word and doubled the troops at risk.

Then, things went from bad to worse. After a major Athenian defeat at the Great Harbor, Nicias should have agreed with his co-commander to withdraw immediately, but he held back out of fear. Nicias was afraid that if he retreated without permission from home, he would be taken to court on his return and executed by a people outraged at defeat. In any case, he had the power to send the army to safety—if he were willing to put his personal safety at risk by angering the assembly. He wasn't.

Compare him to a commander of our time. In 1967 General Victor H. Krulak had finished a tour commanding the Marines in Vietnam and was slated to be the next Commandant of the Marine Corps. He was a small man, but feisty. He went to the White House and confronted President Lyndon B. Johnson in the Oval Office.[5] He complained that his Marines were being asked to spend their lives on useless missions in Vietnam. Krulak knew of better ways to conduct the war. Johnson ushered Krulak out the door of the Oval Office—a towering president forcing out a diminutive, but highly spirited, general. Krulak had failed to change the president's tactics; but, for the sake of his troops, he did what he could. Later (apparently) Johnson nixed Krulak's promotion. Facing Johnson for the sake of his troops, at the expense of his own career, took courage on the general's part. That was leadership. This protest cost General Krulak the promotion he had counted on, but like any true leader, he had the courage to put the good of his followers ahead of his career.

Nicias showed courage in the oval camp, but he would not have followed Krulak on his mission of protest to the Oval Office. When he realized that the army he led was losing lives to no purpose, Nicias had been afraid to lead them to safety when it was still possible.[6] The historian tells us Nicias was honest about this with his troops, telling them, in effect, that "for his part he knew too much about the nature of the Athenians to want to be killed unjustly by them on a dishonorable charge. If he had to die, he'd prefer to do so at the hands of the enemy—a risk he'd be taking on his personal initiative."[7] This brave general was more afraid of his fellow citizens than of the enemy. That is a serious failure: Leaders owe it to their troops to show courage against their mutual enemy, of course, but also against civilian authority when that endangers the troops. After all, civilian authorities are the enemy of troops they send on a fruitless but dangerous mission. Your people's enemies may be at home or abroad, but wherever they are, you must have the courage to face them. That is a leader's job.

FACING FRIENDS

Leadership calls for special reserves of courage among friends. Are you brave enough to listen to criticism? To admit you have things to learn? To offer love and respect to people who may despise you? To leave, to turn over your leadership to someone else when the time comes?

Courage is the quality by which you are able to persevere in doing the right thing in spite of fear or danger. You may have courage and still be beset by many fears, but you will not have a chance to develop courage in yourself unless you have some fears to work against. We have many opportunities for fear: fear of disease, fear of death, fear of losing your job, fear of the enemy, fear of rulers or bosses, fear of failure. And then there is fear of what people will think about you.

Teaching is a profession that calls for leadership. Successful teachers have influence on their students that goes well beyond what they can achieve by carrots and sticks. Carrots and sticks will not make a student curious or even interested. Passion for learning does not spring from fear of a ruthless teacher. It takes courage for teachers to give students the freedom in which they can grow best. In what follows, I will base much of my case on examples from the classroom.

LISTENING

In war, fear of the enemy is obvious, and so is fear of bad commanders who may lead you to a meaningless death. Less obvious is fear of your own followers, in any situation. If you have ever been a leader or authority figure, you have felt the clutch of fear in your belly when someone begins to say something that might be critical of your leadership. It takes courage to listen to criticism. And it takes courage to admit that you still have things to learn. But if you are human, you do have things to learn; and this will be true all your life.

Leaders or teachers who present themselves as omniscient are cowards. Teachers must be willing to learn from their students. At the college level, I am often delighted to find students who know more than I on some topic on which I touch. They deserve respect.

Above all, teachers need to take the trouble to learn what is in their students' minds—what they know and understand at a given moment in the classroom, what topic needs further explanation, what is boring to them, what is exciting. Listening for this from a group is hard, but can be done, albeit imperfectly. A quiz (using modern classroom response technology) can show instantly that 40% of the class does not understand a concept. Well, then, the other 60% may be able to do a better job than the teacher did in making the thing clear.[8]

The best approach for a teacher is listening one on one. How can you help a student improve the argument of her paper if you do not listen to what she wants to say? This may take courage. She may be trying to build an argument in favor of the death penalty, but even if you detest the death penalty, you must listen to her and patiently help her build a better argument. If you blow her away with your own superior arguments against the penalty (so you think), you will lose a precious opportunity. Good arguments rarely change people's minds. She will declare you hopeless and learn nothing except that you are a typical academic liberal, and all communication between you will come to an end. But if you don't shut off communication with her, you might leave a question in her mind that would plant a seed of doubt, or she in yours. Go for that.

Good listening takes time as well as courage; even if you listen by way of the latest technology, you must take time to listen to individuals, if you are to be a good teacher. Your time is expensive. If you are in a research faculty you enjoy a high salary, and you have a monumental workload of research, which you must put aside to listen to your students. If you are not a research professor, you are underpaid and overworked, with too many students and no assistants to help with grading. So listening is threatened by economics either way.

Can one-on-one listening continue to have a place in education? I will return to this in the chapter on communication, where I argue that listening is the cornerstone of communication.

LOVING

Cowardice is evident in many authority figures, but especially in tyrants. Tyrants are so fearful of overthrow that they will do anything to stay in power. They strike fear into the hearts of their people. This, says Machiavelli, is a good thing. In the previous chapter, I agreed with Machiavelli that rulers have an obligation to protect their people, and this obligation may trump other ethical considerations. Do leaders also have an obligation to be kind or compassionate to their followers? For this too Machiavelli has an answer:

Is it better to be loved than feared, or vice versa? My reply is that one ought to be both loved and feared; but, since it is difficult to accomplish both at the same time, I maintain it is much safer to be feared than loved, if you have to do without one of the two.[9]

Remember that this advice is for rulers who are afraid of losing power, but one of the marks of true leaders is that they have no fear of this kind. They are always ready to step aside rather than resort to force when their followers seek new leadership. Fear is a mark of tyrants: Terrified of losing power, they fall into the habit of keeping their subjects in line by means of terror. Machiavelli knows that terror on both sides is the greatest pain tyranny brings.[10]

Tyrants are afraid because they have earned the hatred of their subjects. They predict (usually correctly) that if they step aside they will be killed ignominiously. Think of the exits forced on Mussolini, Khadafy, Ceausescu, and many others—all disgraceful, humiliating, fatal. But if you have done little wrong, and you have the courage to face the risk of new leadership, then you do not need to make your followers fear you. Do you need to have your followers love you? That is a lot to ask of them. As Machiavelli contends, you may have the power to make people fear you, but you cannot have the power to make them love you. He concludes that it is wiser to aim at making them fear you, if you have to choose between fear and love. If that is your only choice—whether to aim at being feared or at being loved—then Machiavelli is right, but only if you really do have the power to make yourself feared.

Fear is among the most powerful of motivators, as Thucydides pointed out two millennia before Machiavelli.[11] But Machiavelli is wrong on an important point: You cannot control the responses other people will have to you. You may make yourself lovable, and no one may love you; you may make yourself fearful, and everyone may still laugh at you, if they have courage, or if you are pompous. Other people's fear and love are not under your control. You may, however, have some control over your own feelings and how they affect you. The wise leader does not fear her followers—or, if she fears them, she does not act on those fears.

You have real choices when it comes to yourself. Machiavelli overlooks these. Why focus on the feelings of other people, which are hard to influence, when you have some power over your own feelings? What attitudes should you take to your followers? Machiavelli has missed a third alternative: You have the power to offer your own love and respect to those who follow you, and you can do this without relaxing discipline.[12]

A wise teacher can be stern and loving at the same time. Students may treat you with scorn, but that should not deter you. If you can give a student a bad grade, while at the same time showing respect and even love, the message that grade carries has a better chance of coming home: the student will know that the grade is not about him, but about the work he did, which he should do better next time.

Must you then be kind and loving in every case? If you should, should you never punish anyone? A leader who is also a commander must be willing to punish those who do wrong; in an army or navy, that means punishing those who disobey. Machiavelli is right about this:

> Every ruler should want to be thought of as compassionate and not cruel. Nevertheless, I warn you to be careful about being compassionate.[13]

People follow a leader more readily if they see the leader as compassionate. But we must take care about this. Compassion can lead us astray. It is not the same as clemency. Compassion is a kind of understanding, which does not entail letting criminals off the hook.[14] He is right again here:

> It is more compassionate to impose harsh punishments on a few than, out of excessive compassion, to allow disorder to spread, which leads to murders and looting.[15]

Good advice. Machiavelli points to the rebellion of a Roman army against a brilliant general who was too lenient; and Melville's Captain Vere is eloquent on the need to maintain discipline on a ship of war—with the emphasis on war.[16] In peace, the cost of leniency drops; and in Paradise, it drops to nothing. In Chapter 13, "Becoming Magnetic," I will try to show why a leader can be loving and compassionate without letting wrong go unpunished.

When I began my career in administration, a former student sent me a copy of *The Prince* and asked me to decide whether, as department chair, I thought it better to be feared or to be loved. I had no answer at the time, and I soon found out that I had the power to bring neither of these to pass. An academic chair does not have the power to be feared; such power resides in deans and committees. But as a chair, I represented unpleasant policies coming from above me, over which I had no control. It was hard in such times to be a lovable chairperson. Now I would tell my former student: "Take back your question. The important thing for me as chair is not to fear my colleagues (who are mostly senior to me), and next in importance is for me to conduct my affairs in such a way that I can continue to love and respect them."

LEAVING

Today I am reading news of a number of heads of state who are trying to change the constitutions of their fragile democracies to allow them to serve longer terms. Some of them seem to want to rule their nations forever. Generals who have won independence for their nations seem especially hard to dislodge.[17] In U.S. history, however, we have a model of the courage to leave: George Washington. Read his Farewell Address; it is one of the most valuable documents in history. Although the words are not his, the sentiments are.

To leave a position of power, you must have the courage to face two kinds of attack: Those who come after you may attack you personally, and they may also attack (or simply lose by fumbling) what you have accomplished. You may see your dreams crumble after you hand them on to a successor.

In a stable democracy, we have a remedy for the first fear. Unless you have done something illegal, you should have nothing to fear from your successor, so long as the rule of law obtains. In fact, in U.S. history, we have given presidents even more protection than the law requires. Presidents and ex-presidents generally do not criticize each other, and they have offered each other (and their subordinates) amnesty for minor peccadilloes in office. I think we should rejoice in this: We should allow nothing that would make people in power believe they must cling to office for their own safety.

As for the second fear—that your dreams will collapse if you are not in power to shore them up—ask yourself this: Are your dreams so impractical that they will not find support after you are gone? If they are, nothing will save them in the long run. If there is good in them, they will probably survive—unless conditions are so bad that even you could not save them. Do your best, and leave what you have done to the next generation of leaders. You can do a lot to groom successors, though you may not have the power to choose them, and you can set up your organization in such a way that it has strong potential for survival.

Even if you cling to a position of power, you must still expect to leave your life. As you prepare to leave, you must know that your children, biological or adopted, will not live as you have done, will not carry out all of your dreams or keep all of your projects alive. The books you have written will be remaindered, the books you own will be sold or turned to pulp, your papers recycled, your ideas forgotten. Your legacy may be meaningful for a time, but it will eventually be forgotten. Your great-grandchildren will not know your name. Be brave, pass on what you can to the next generation, but don't burden them with any false hopes you may have for the future. Your grandchildren too, after all, will be forgotten in the long run. Knowing this takes courage.

As I moved from one position of authority to another, I saw some of my dreams realized and maintained and others destroyed by my successors. I mourn the dreams that have been destroyed, but I do not know that I could have saved them. A leader should have dreams, but never care too much about them. When the time is right, a leader must leave. Leaving shows courage.

SHOWING COURAGE

A leader stands up to enemies and friends. A leader listens, a leader loves, and, eventually, a leader must leave. In all of these actions, a leader must show courage in order to do what a leader must do. We also have a different sort of reason for showing courage as leaders. Remember that if you are a leader, people follow you because they want to, not because they have been forced to, not because of other things they want, not because of things they fear. There are no carrots or sticks in leadership. The question that remains, then, is why should anyone *want* to follow you?

Machiavelli is right that you can't rely on people loving you. And love does not lead to following in all cases: I adore my small grandchildren, but I do not follow them or accept them as leaders—yet. But Machiavelli is wrong in implying that the only alternative to love is fear. I have just written of a third alternative—offering love and respect to your followers. Now consider a fourth alternative—character. As a leader, you must have some power to draw people to you, and this power must come from something you reliably control. And the only thing you can control reliably is yourself, your own character.

Pericles led Athens successfully because he was admired and trusted for his fine character. At the center of a fine character is courage, for an obvious reason. Without courage, you are likely to waver under pressure, and you will have no firm character for others to admire. Ulysses Grant commanded an extraordinary degree of loyalty from his troops; one reason for that was his steadfast courage. A private was overheard to say, in admiration, "Ulysses don't scare worth a damn."[18] You should want to be that kind of leader, one who is admired.

You will never have the power to make people love you; you will never have the power to make brave people fear you; you will never even have the power to make people admire you. But you do have the power to offer them something to admire. George Washington made a palpable effort to develop an admirable character, and, apparently, it worked. How did he do that? Where does courage come from? And what should we do for our students to help them nourish courage in themselves and others? Those questions are the subject of the next chapter.

NOTES

1. My translation. For the context, see Plato 1973, 33.
2. Thucydides vi.94–105 (Woodruff translation 1993, 129).
3. Thucydides vii.80–86 (Woodruff translation 1993, 148–152).

4. Thucydides vii.86 (Woodruff translation 1993, 152).
5. The account of their meeting is based on Krulak's own words (Coram 2010, 312–315).
6. Later, Nicias was deterred from leaving by soothsayers who found a bad omen in a lunar eclipse (Thucydides vii.50). But it is his fear of the Assembly that concerns us here.
7. Thucydides vii.48 (Woodruff translation 1993, 135).
8. This principle underlies the "peer instruction" method outlined in Mazur 1997. For the use of technology in the classroom, see also Bruff 2009.
9. Machiavelli 1994, 51–52 (Chapter 17).
10. Bobbitt 2013, 134.
11. Thucydides i.88 (Woodruff translation 1993, 29).
12. Little has been written on the love of a leader for followers, but some writers from the First World War took on the theme, insofar as it can be separated from the homoerotic writing popular in the period. On this see Fussell 2013, 164–165. On friendship in combat units, see Gray 1998, 88–95, who brings out clearly how war affects our proclivities for love and friendship.
13. Machiavelli 1994, 51 (Chapter 17).
14. See Chapter 7.
15. Machiavelli 1994, 51 (Chapter 17).
16. Machiavelli 1994, 53 (Chapter 17). Melville 1962, 109–113.
17. See Bershidsky 2014, Filkins 2016, and Martin 2014.
18. Quoted on Keegan 1987, 210. Grant found early on that he was not afraid in combat. Of this lesson, Keegan writes: "This confidence in his physical courage—discovery of his moral courage would come later—was the foundation of his future generalship" (1987, 183).

WORKS CITED

Bershidsky, Leonid (2014, December 29). "2015: The Year of the Putin Dictatorship." *Bloomberg View*.

Bobbitt, Philip (2013). *The Garments of Court and Palace: Machiavelli and the World That He Made*. New York: Grove Press.

Bruff, Derek (2009). *Teaching with Classroom Response Systems: Creating Active Learning Environments*. San Francisco: Jossey-Bass.

Coram, Robert (2010). *Brute, the Life of Victor Krulak, U.S. Marine*. New York: Little, Brown and Company.

Filkins, Dexter (2016, March 31). "Erdogan's March to Dictatorship in Turkey." *The New Yorker*.

Fussell, Paul (2013). *The Great War and Modern Memory*. New York: Oxford University Press.

Gray, J. Glenn (1998). *The Warriors: Reflections on Men in Battle*. Lincoln, NE: Bison Books.

Jones, Roger (2015, February 24). "What CEOs Are Afraid of." *Harvard Business Review*.

Keegan, John (1987). *The Mask of Command: Alexander the Great, Wellington, Ulysses S. Grant, Hitler, and the Nature of Leadership*. London: Penguin Books.

Machiavelli, Niccolò (1994). *Selected Political Writings*. Ed. David Wootton. Indianapolis: Hackett Publishing Company, Inc.

Martin, Rachel (2014, February 23). "Hero Or Dictator? Mugabe After 34 Years at Zimbabwe's Helm." *NPR*.

Mazur, Eric (1997). *Peer Instruction: A User's Manual*. Upper Saddle River, NJ: Prentice Hall, Inc.

Melville, Herman (1962). *Billy Budd, Sailor: An Inside Narrative*. Ed. Harrison Hayford and Merton M. Sealts, Jr. Chicago: University of Chicago Press.

Plato (1973). *Laches and Charmides*. Trans. Rosamond Kent Sprague. Indianapolis: Bobbs-Merrill Company, Inc.

Spalding, Matthew, and Gentry, Patrick J. (1996). *A Sacred Union of Citizens: George Washington's Farewell Address and the American Character*. Lanham, MD: Rowman and Littlefield Publishers, Inc.

Thucydides (1993). *On Justice, Power, and Human Nature: Selections from* The History of the Peloponnesian War. Ed. and trans. Paul Woodruff. Indianapolis: Hackett Publishing Company, Inc.

Chapter 10

Finding Courage

Fear is natural to us and many other creatures. We are born with some fears, though we learn others. Courage is our response to fear—our ability to do what we should when we are afraid, or when other people would be afraid. Courage is almost as natural as fear; everyone who has grown beyond infancy must have found some way of forging ahead in the presence of danger. Our students do not start at zero, then. They have already found some courage—although they probably do not know it. Courage is a paradox: If you are confident that you have it, you probably do not. Courage is not the sort of thing you can simply have. And if you think you know what it is, you are probably deceiving yourself. It can't be simply understood, either. But, whatever it is, most of us know we want it. Tim O'Brien's captain spoke for many of us when he said suddenly:

> "I'd rather be brave . . . I'd rather be brave than almost anything. How does that strike you?"[1]

What is courage? What sort of thing is it? That's not an easy question. Courage baffled Socrates and his companions in the *Laches*; it remained a mystery to William Ian Miller, who devoted a large book to it:

> We know roughly what courage is, because we so desperately seek it and admire it and love to hear it told about. But then we aren't always sure when we have it, even those fortunate enough who are clearly blessed by it. Our sincerest modesty comes when we have to judge the quality and quantity of our own courage. Our fear, our self-doubt make us suspect that we just got lucky when we managed

to do okay; but we have no great confidence that we will do very well when the dragon comes again.[2]

Is it even possible to recognize courage in ourselves or others? We ought to investigate this mystery with our students. In the previous chapter we saw how important courage is to a leader in different kinds of situations. Now we must ask what courage is in these situations, where it comes from, and how it can be sustained. Working out what we think courage is—that has to be a large part of the project of becoming courageous.

Finding courage is not like digging up a treasure. It is not like taking a vaccine against moral failure. It is a lifelong project. Finding and maintaining courage is more like practicing a musical instrument than it is like being six feet tall: You will never be perfect at courage, and you will grow worse if you do not keep it up. If courage calls for different actions in different situations, then you need to ponder these differences, to prepare for new situations as best you can.

WHAT SORT OF THING IS COURAGE?

Courage is usually listed as a virtue,[3] so we could start by asking what the virtues are. But this can take us back to courage, as it is usually said to be a clear example of a virtue. If it is, we could learn what virtues are by finding out what courage is. On this point, we have enough questions to ask:

- Is courage the ability to do what you ought to do when you might be deterred by danger or fear? (That looks like a good start on the question, but it leaves a lot unexplained.)
- What would we mean by *ability*?
- How should we know what we ought to do?
- Are there things you need to know in order to have courage?
- What counts as danger?
- Must you be aware of danger to be courageous?
- Must you feel fear in order to be courageous, or merely be aware of danger?
- Must you show courage *every* time you encounter danger, in order to be courageous?

Our students should wrestle with questions like those.

All human beings apparently have courage at some level unless they are oblivious to danger; if they didn't have some courage they would be unable to act in the presence of danger, and danger is always with us. Some people seem to have more courage than others. When asked what we want in our leaders, courage is usually on the list—as it should be, for the reasons I gave in the previous chapter. If you are too susceptible to fear, and have a position of authority, you may well become a tyrant.

Even those who are notably courageous may show some lapses. General Krulak did not let fear (if he felt it at all) prevent him from doing what he should in battle, or in facing his president at home. But he was afraid all his life to be honest about his Jewish roots.[4] No one is perfectly courageous. Even for the best of us, there is probably a situation that will defeat courage.

Courage takes a kind of wisdom—the wisdom to judge what you should do in a given circumstance, along with the wisdom to evaluate the various dangers you face. Which is the greater danger—dying or being responsible for thousands of innocent deaths? That may be an easy question, but others are harder. No one can be perfect in this kind of wisdom; that is why no one can be perfect in courage. But, with the help of our friends, we can improve.

Part of the wisdom we need for courage is the wisdom to recognize that we are all vulnerable to failures of courage. Behind this wisdom lies the wisdom to know that our wisdom cannot be perfect. That is what I call Socratic wisdom, because it was the one sort of wisdom that Socrates claimed to have.[5] What I know about myself I can predict for others: The bravest person I meet will probably not be perfectly reliable. That is one reason we should help each other sustain our courage.

What I say about courage in this chapter goes for all the virtues— reverence, justice, compassion, and so on. They are all to be found and refined in roughly the way we find courage and refine it. All our virtues are vulnerable to lapses, often due to situations we cannot handle—when fears or temptations may overpower our moral defenses. So part of the wisdom courage requires is knowing what situations you cannot handle and avoiding them or else getting help from your friends when you cannot avoid moral danger.[6]

Moral danger affects others, too. As a leader, you need the wisdom to know what situations create moral danger for those who follow you. For example, you need to know that prison guards are in danger of abusing inmates, and you need to work with them to prevent that.[7] Leaders are responsible for the behavior of their followers, and they must learn to set a moral climate that is favorable to courage and compassion and justice. Leaders cannot rely on their own courage or the courage of their followers in every situation. They must plan to avert failure.

At this point I imagine you waving your hand in class and blurting out, "If I can't rely on my own courage or the courage of others, then there isn't any real courage anywhere; courage must be an illusion."

"Not so fast," I will answer. "I never said that courage had to be perfect."

"But if it's not perfect, then what is it?" you ask.

"Slow down," I say. The first question to ask is not what it is, but what sort of thing it is.

Courage is a lifelong project requiring a serious commitment. Humanly speaking, you are a courageous person if you seek to develop courage and maintain it in yourself and others, find friends and companions who make similar commitments, and take joy in success, pain in failure. The clearest sign of courage is the pain you feel when you give way to fears that should not have swayed you—or the joy you feel on finding that you have come through a trying situation without a serious lapse. The same goes for all the virtues. They are all, in essence, commitments. Virtues in human beings are not fixed traits that always result in virtuous behavior.[8]

Is a commitment to courage good enough? What if you fail again and again? That is a question for us to discuss. Plainly, you cannot claim to have a commitment that never influences your action. What does it mean to be committed to courage? If you practice singing daily but rarely hit the high note, are you committed to music? [9]

COURAGE WITH OTHERS

Courage takes a community.[10] In order to practice courage, you have to be connected to other people who are, like you, zealous for courage. Imagine you are in a unit of cowards. Faced with danger, they will all turn tail, or perhaps turn on each other. You may of course try to do the thing that ought to be courageous. You might advance alone upon the enemy while your comrades flee. But you would be stupid to do so. Courage is not stupid. Solitary actions—with no social support—will kill you. Getting killed is not a way to practice courage, or anything else.

Nicias did not trust his people, the Athenians. He was afraid that they would not have the courage to accept defeat and move on without lashing out at the man they had put in command. His cowardice was part of their cowardice: Their cowardice made them dangerous to him and so fostered his cowardice. In a more courageous community, a general such as Nicias could have safely admitted defeat.

Victor Krulak, by contrast, was part of a community of Marines that were trained to give each other the strength to speak truth to power. When I discuss Krulak with Marines today, they say, "That is what a Marine does."[11] Hiding his background to make himself look better in the eyes of other Marines—that too is something a Marine does.

In Conrad's *Lord Jim* a young sailor faces a challenge for which he is not prepared, and he does so in the company of cowards.[12] A ship loaded with Muslim pilgrims is foundering. There is only one lifeboat. The white English officers quietly take the lifeboat and slip away to safety, leaving the pilgrims to drown. Jim follows the officers, and regrets that for the rest of his life. Would he have felt the same regret if the matter had not come to be known? Did he, on his own, feel pain at moral failure, or only when found out? A gap had opened between his actions and his commitments—and that gap opened, as so often happens, under the influence of others. How much is he to blame for his actions? Should his captain, who led him astray, bear the blame for what Jim did? How much courage can we expect from individuals who are isolated, morally speaking? Can we reasonably expect to be heroes, when we are alone with our commitments to courage?

Courage, for most of us, takes a community of a certain sort: A courageous community is respectful and allows for independent judgment. A courageous community is one you can trust—you can trust them to respect your judgment. Leaders must take this to heart, because they set the tone for the communities they lead.

FALSE COURAGE

If you cannot trust your community to respect you, then you will have incentives to try to prove yourself to them—to follow their judgment blindly, or to do something stupidly fearless to gain their admiration: to drive too fast, to snort drugs or inject them. These are all examples of false courage. Bravado is no way to practice courage. The first step in finding courage is to identify qualities that look like courage but are not—qualities like bravado and fearlessness. These qualities are stupid and courage is not; they undermine courage.

You show courage (we thought at the beginning) when you are not deterred by danger. But what if you are too stupid or too ignorant to be aware of danger? Surely, in such a case, you have false courage at best. Joan of Arc and Billy Budd do not show courage. They may do the right thing in the presence of danger, but they never know what danger they are in,[13] and so they have not developed the ability we call courage. Adam had nothing to fear in Eden, and neither did Billy Budd before arriving on the ship of war. These children of Paradise have never known danger, so they have never had a chance to practice courage—that is, to practice not being deterred by the fear that danger can cause. And courage, like any ability, has to be developed. Courage takes practice.

There are many ways to be a coward. Some are obvious, like being weak, finding yourself unable to think or act because fear has disabled you. Your best chance of escaping such weakness is practice—making fears familiar enough that you can live with them. That is what military training does, and we know it works up to a point. It works so long as the trainees are faced with dangers that have been predicted by their trainers. An unpredicted danger may throw trained soldiers for a loop, even if they are well trained otherwise.

Training can produce true courage only if it faces the most important causes of cowardice. These include the ones I mentioned earlier: disrespect, separation from community, loss of independent judgment. Add to them the mistaken belief that fearlessness or bravado is courage. Such mistakes will stymie your attempts to develop true courage. Then there is the cause of cowardice that is the most terrifying: tyrannical behavior.

Every tyrant makes himself a coward, living in fear of his subjects, and every cowardly tyrant tries to make his subjects into cowards too. Some, like Stalin, are terrifyingly successful at that. If you want to develop courage, be a leader who is willing to step down, not a tyrant who lives in terror of being overthrown.

FALSE COWARDICE

"Come on, don't be a wuss. Try it out!" It might be heroin or cocaine or simply a stiff drink. It might be leaping off a cliff into a pool of water. "Scaredy-cat!" Someone dares you to pass a slow-moving truck on a curve: "You drive like an old lady!"

Now you are grown up and dealing with your company's policy on emissions. "In this line of work," your boss says, "we have to have the courage to bend the facts a little in our favor." Or you are in the military, and you find reason to think your unit is putting innocent people into detention camps. "You're too sensitive," says your commander. "Be a man, toughen up, remember that this is war and war is hell."

Or now you are very old, and you know you will die soon. Your doctor wants you to try another expensive and painful treatment that you fear will prolong your agony and the agony of your loved ones. "You are a fighter," says Dr. Strong. "Be brave and whip this thing. Don't wimp out on me and refuse treatment."

All these people are abusing you by making improper requests and threatening to call you a coward if you refuse. But those who stand up to such threats are not cowards. Refusing a dare could be the bravest thing you ever do, though it may look like an act of cowardice to some—"false cowardice," I call it. "Only the defeated and deserters go to the wars, cowards that run away and enlist," writes Thoreau in the concluding chapter to *Walden*.[14] There he also extols the courage that it takes to explore oneself, as Socrates urges everyone to do. Socrates believed he would be a coward if he surrendered his mission as a philosopher for fear of death. Death, he firmly believed, is not the greatest danger, because we cannot know whether it is a bad thing. The greatest danger, he believes, is to fall into wrongdoing. But he has good reasons to believe that he is innocent, and that his mission is the best thing that has happened to Athens.[15]

We are all vulnerable to dares—to being made to feel like cowards for not doing something stupid or wrong. But that would be false cowardice. Finding the difference between false cowardice and true cowardice is a challenge for us all, from small schoolchildren to old people in nursing homes.[16]

FAKING IT?

You have led your troops into the forest, your GPS has failed, your map is unclear, and you are totally lost. Do you admit this to your troops and ask for their help? Or do you put on a show of confidence and lead them somewhere, not knowing whether you should go forward or backward? Or try this: You and your troops are trapped and pinned down by a larger force, and you are terrified. Do you let the troops see your fear, or do you make a show of confidence?

In military training I was taught that an officer never admits he is lost, never shows the slightest crack in his confidence (we were all men in those days). That was wrong. If you are lost, your followers may be able to help you. There are times for leaders to ask for help from their followers. How you ask for help and use it makes a difference; you may still radiate the confidence that the team will find its way out. And there are times when leaders should show far more confidence than they feel. Confidence, by itself, can make up for being outnumbered, as has been shown in countless battles (though General Custer's confidence did nothing to save his men). Even when the situation is dire, you must know you will make it worse if you or your followers fly into a panic. So even if panic pulls at your entrails, and you feel your bowels loosening, must you, for the sake of your team, fake confidence? Or should you validate the fears of your team members by showing that you share their fears?

It takes courage to admit that you are lost or afraid, when that is the right thing to do. And it takes courage to fake confidence, when that is the right thing to do in the face of danger. It is tempting to say that it takes courage to fake courage, but that would be wrong. If you can radiate confidence while your heart is sinking, when that is what your followers need, you are showing a true sort of courage. You can fake confidence, but you cannot fake courage. Does that make sense?[17]

TRUING COURAGE

> The Master said, "How could I dare to lay claim to either sageliness or Goodness? What can be said about me is no more than this: I work at it without growing tired and encourage others without growing weary."
>
> —Confucius, *Analects* 7.34

We said that true courage would be the ability not to be deterred from doing what you should do by fear or danger. If that is correct, then, in order to have true courage, you must know what you should do. That is a tall order for a mere human being. If you had a moral compass, then you would always know what direction to go. But the moral landscape is not so simple, as we have seen. A bad compass might point steadily in a stupid direction. The best moral compass will have a needle that spins around and won't settle when decisions are tough. Then you will have to use your own judgment—then you will need moral wisdom.

Part of moral wisdom, as we have seen, is knowing yourself—knowing your own weaknesses, your vulnerability to moral failure. Another part of moral wisdom is a combination of a moral sense with good judgment— the ability to decide where you should be going when the compass they gave you in Sunday school seems to point wrong or does not point at all. Your courage won't be perfectly true, but it will be the best you can manage.

SOURCES OF COURAGE

Where does moral wisdom come from? Where has your courage come from? (You must know by now that you have always had some courage.) How much of this list rings true to you?

- Good examples of courage in your family, your teachers, and the other people who show leadership around you
- A community that is willing to become more courageous as a community and will not block the advance of its more courageous members
- Opportunities to practice courage, including opportunities for leadership at an early age
- Observing the human landscape and learning to appreciate the hidden courage of people around you
- Learning to communicate well, both listening to those around you and speaking in order to achieve the consensus that leadership in courage requires
- A classroom that gives you opportunities for independent thinking and courage
- Exploring questions about courage in philosophy
- Reading about courage and cowardice in the real world (e.g., O'Brien [2014], or Grant's memoirs) or in fiction that is based on real-world experience (e.g., Conrad)
- Practicing to know yourself, to gain the self-knowledge that yields a modest understanding of your own moral vulnerability.

SOURCES OF FAILURE

> The Master said, "That I fail to cultivate Virtue, that I fail to inquire more deeply into that which I have learned, that upon hearing what is right I remain unable to move myself to do it, and that I prove unable to reform when I have done something wrong—such potential failings are a source of constant worry to me."
>
> —Confucius, *Analects* 7.3

What are the sources of moral failure? What is it that saps courage, undermines it, or distracts us from the demands that courage makes? If I am right that we all have some courage, then this is the most important question for us to keep in mind. Above all, this question calls for self-knowledge. When we fail, why do we fail?[18]

Drawing on the sources we listed for courage, we can start a list of the sources of failure:

- Cowardly elders setting bad examples
- A cowardly community
- Temptations that strain human goodness
- False notions of what courage is
- Overconfidence in your own courage.

Of these the most insidious is the last, because it is the least expected. If you think you cannot fail to be courageous, you are more likely to put yourself in tight spots, or in bad company, where your courage is most likely to fail you. And if you think you know what courage calls for, you may not consider how easily you could go wrong. If someone dares you to show that you don't care about physical danger, you might fail to notice the moral danger that hides behind such a dare. And then you won't find the moral courage that you need to resist the dare.

We would do well to read tales of heroism, but we would do even better to read tales of moral failure, such as Conrad's *Lord Jim*. Courage may be hard to find, but, like all the virtues, it is even harder to maintain. Good character slips through the fingers of those who think they have it made.

NOTES

1. Captain Johansen in O'Brien 2014, 134.
2. Miller 2000, 282.
3. The theory of virtue underlying this chapter is developed at greater length in Woodruff 2018.
4. Coram 2010, 30–31, cf. 45–47.
5. Read Plato's *Apology* with special attention to 23ab (Reeve 2002, 44).
6. John Doris gives the example of avoiding the candlelit dinner with a flirtatious colleague that might tempt one into marital infidelity (2002, 147–148).
7. Zimbardo 2007; cf. Woodruff 2014, 207–212.
8. Supposing that you have virtues as fixed traits is dangerous (Doris on "ethical brinksmanship," 2002, 146–153); supposing that other people have fixed vices is dangerous in another way, as it can lead to violence (Harman 1999).

9. Commitment may be merely necessary, and not sufficient for virtue. See Miller (2000, 283) on the gap between character or will and courageous action. The Civil War soldier who ran away in every battle but put himself in the front line again and again was known as the good coward. He was never punished for cowardice, because, I surmise, he had truly committed himself to courage. On the good coward, see Miller 2000, 2ff., and 46. See also O'Brien 1987, 31ff.

10. Thanks to Reuben McDaniel for the following point made during conversation: "Courage is an emergent property in a community with respectful interaction." To show courage in bucking social trends, it helps to be confident that others will respect our choices.

11. Krulak himself downplays the incident in the Oval Office and says nothing about its effect on his career (1984, 202).

12. Conrad 2012, 104–105.

13. On ignorance of danger, see Miller 2000, 282.

14. Thoreau 1854, 344–345.

15. Plato, *Apology*. Read the whole of it, with special attention to the magnificent ending (Reeve 2002).

16. On moral courage to say no to a dare, see Miller 2000, 261–262, on Grant.

17. See the next chapter on hypocrisy and performing leadership. See also Miller 2000, 90–91. Fear is contagious (Miller 210); that is a reason for pretending you do not have it. You would be faking fearlessness, but not courage, if you did a courageous thing when you are not committed to courage. Courage is hard to fake, but easy to lie about. A hilarious example of lying about courage is provided by Shakespeare's Falstaff in *Henry IV Part 1*, Act 2, Scene 4.

18. In teaching ethics, philosophy needs to pay attention to psychology, learn the causes of moral failure, and address them. A good example of this approach is the set of brief, sharply focused videos in "Ethics Unwrapped" at the University of Texas at Austin, developed by Cara Biasucci and Robert Prentice (http://ethicsunwrapped.utexas.edu).

WORKS CITED

Aristotle (1989). *Nicomachean Ethics*. Trans. Martin Ostwald. New York: Macmillan Publishing.

Confucius (2003). *Analects*. Trans. Edward Slingerland. Indianapolis: Hackett Publishing Company, Inc.

Conrad, Joseph (2012). *Lord Jim: A Tale*. Ed. J. H. Stape and Ernest SullivanII. Cambridge, UK: Cambridge University Press.

Coram, Robert (2010). *Brute, the Life of Victor Krulak, U.S. Marine*. New York: Little, Brown and Company.

Doris, John M. (2002). *Lack of Character: Personality and Moral Behavior*. Cambridge, UK: Cambridge University Press.

Grant, U. S. (1886/2017). The *Personal Memoirs of Ulysses S. Grant: The Complete Annotated Edition*. Ed. John F. Marszalek et al. Cambridge, Massachusetts: Belknap Press/Harvard University Press.

Krulak, Victor H. (1984). *First to Fight: An Inside View of the U.S. Marine Corps*. Annapolis, MD: Naval Institute Press.

Miller, William Ian (2000). *The Mystery of Courage*. Cambridge, MA: Harvard University Press.

O'Brien, Tim (2014). *If I Die in a Combat Zone, Box Me Up and Send Me Home*. New York: Broadway Books.

Plato (1992). *Laches* in *Laches and Charmides*. Trans. Rosamond Kent Sprague. Indianapolis: Hackett Publishing Company, Inc.

Reeve, C. D. C. (2002). *The Trials of Socrates: Plato, Aristophanes, and Xenophon*. Indianapolis: Hackett Publishing Company, Inc.

Thoreau, Henry D. (1854). *Walden*. Boston: Houghton, Mifflin and Company.

Woodruff, Paul (2014). *Reverence: Renewing a Forgotten Virtue*. 2nd Edition. New York: Oxford University Press.

Woodruff, Paul (2018). "Growing Toward Justice." In *Justice*. Ed. Mark LeBar. New York: Oxford University Press, 13–37.

Zimbardo, Philip (2007). *The Lucifer Effect: Understanding How Good People Turn Evil*. New York: Random House.

Chapter 11

Performing Leadership

"I'll tell you what, Dan," said Sir Hugo, "a man who sets his face against every sort of humbug is simply a three-cornered, impractical fellow. There's a bad style of humbug, but there's also a good style— one that oils the wheels and makes progress possible. If you are to rule men, you must rule them through their own ideas . . . there is no action possible without a little acting."

[So says Sir Hugo Mallinger, trying to interest his adopted son, Daniel Deronda, in politics. The young man responds]:

"I can't see any real public expediency that does not keep an ideal before it which makes a limit of deviation from the direct path. But if I were to set up for a public man I might mistake my own success for public expediency."[1]

Early in my military training, I was taught to look and sound like a commander. A command voice and an erect posture are essential, I was taught. Never show any sign of weakness or failure. I was not good at these things. I knew how to be loud and bossy, but that is not enough; I was an inveterate sloucher; I had poor posture and, when I was confused, I liked to tell people that I was confused. Would it have been right for me to start pretending—to try to look and sound like someone I wasn't? Or did I need to learn to be a different person—to grow into the command posture and the command voice? Or would I be a better leader if I made no change at all, went on slouching, mouthing off in civilian fashion, and confessing my failures? May a leader, like an actor, perform a part? The eminent military historian John Keegan observed that acting ability was indispensable to a famous conqueror:

> Alexander [the Great], it is clear, was an actor of the most consum-
> mate theatrical skill. His courtly upbringing, first at the knee of his
> histrionic mother, then at the saddle-bow of his equally sensation-
> alist father, amounted to a complete thespian apprenticeship.[2]

Our students need to ponder who they are now, whom they wish to be mistaken for, and whom they wish to become as they mature. Will playing a part help them toward their goals?

PERFORMING LEADERSHIP: GEORGE WASHINGTON AT NEWBURGH

In March 15, 1783, Washington gave the greatest performance of his ca-reer in order to head off a conspiracy that might have led to military gov-ernment. The Congress of that day was hardly more competent than the Congress of our own. They would not vote the funds to pay the officers, and the officers were fed up. Many of the officers wanted to overthrow Congress; some wanted Washington to take over as a monarch of some sort. Washington got wind of this and managed to take control of a meeting the conspirators had planned near Newburgh, New York. His stature was such that he could have the meeting postponed while he penned an ex-traordinary speech. Either before or during the speech, we are told that he took out a pair of glasses—which no one had ever seen him wear before. "Gentlemen," he said, "you will permit me to put on my spectacles, for I have not only grown gray, but almost blind in the service of my country."[3] This piece of theater brought tears to the eyes of some of the officers. It probably had a deeper effect on his audience than the content of his speech, which was strong and heartfelt, as we shall see in the next chapter.

The danger of civil war between Congress and the army was real, but with this theatrical gesture and this speech, Washington won over the army. Great threats call for great theater, but great theater can adorn great truths. This showman was truly sincere; he really did believe in freedom and in the subordination of the military to the people. And although he had always had magnificent ambitions, he knew where ambitions might lead if they are unbridled—to a tyranny that would destroy the freedom he had been fighting for. And so he restrained his ambitions and buried them behind the face of leadership.[4]

WEARING THE FACE OF LEADERSHIP

A *hypocrites*, in ancient Greek, is a spokesperson, one who answers for another. The word came to mean *actor*, and from that it came to mean what we mean by "hypocrite." Ancient Greek actors wore masks to represent the characters for whom they were speaking. You, as a leader, may need to wear a mask. Keegan has written a book with a revealing title: *The Mask of Command: Alexander the Great, Wellington, Ulysses S. Grant, Hitler, and the Nature of Leadership*. The most effective leaders have put on a face that is not exactly their own—and then they have tried to grow into it.[5]

George Washington would not make Keegan's list or any list of great military leaders. He was not especially good at most of the things military commanders do; he was no master of military tactics, and he was not especially good as a writer or speaker.[6] But he was a great leader for all that—"a self-made man feverishly striving to become a self-made hero."[7] According to Joseph Ellis, an historian who has written extensively about the founders of the United States:

> It seemed to me that Benjamin Franklin was wiser than Washington; Alexander Hamilton was more brilliant; John Adams was better read; Thomas Jefferson was more intellectually sophisticated; James Madison was more politically astute. Yet each of these prominent figures acknowledged that Washington was their unquestioned superior.[8]

Toward the end of his book on Washington, Ellis turns to the eulogy delivered by Gouverneur Morris, which emphasizes how Washington kept self-control over the tumultuous passions which accompany greatness, and frequently tarnish its lustre. With them was his first contest, and his first victory was over himself. So great the empire that he there acquired, that calmness of manner and of conduct distinguished him through life. Yet, those that have seen him strongly moved, will bear witness that his wrath was terrible; they have seen boiling in his bosom, passion almost too mighty for a man; yet, when just bursting into act, that strong passion was controlled by his still stronger mind.[9]

Washington's famous aloofness and silence were, Ellis remarks, "in all likelihood protective tactics developed to prevent detection of the combustible materials inside."[10] A few chapters back, I called attention to the courage Washington showed in his famous decisions to relinquish power. Morris thought these were signs that Washington had conquered ambition, but Ellis disagrees: Washington, he writes, knew "he could no more trust people to behave virtuously than he could trust his own instincts to behave altruistically. . . . He fully realized that all ambitions were inherently insatiable and unconquerable. He knew himself well enough to resist the illusion that he transcended human nature."[11] As a result, on Ellis's view, Washington's career was a lifelong struggle, in which he achieved power over himself while extending his power over others. Keeping up the face of leadership was a project that occupied him all his life. In this, apparently, lay his superiority over the others. Could any of them have refused to be a dictator, if the opportunity beckoned? Declined to run for a third term as president? No such national hero elsewhere in the world, before or since, has had such strength. Apparently Washington drew real strength from the mask he worked so hard to maintain.[12] He quite deliberately built a myth around himself and did his best to live up to it. The myth served his purpose as a leader, but it has bedeviled historians ever after.[13]

HIDING FAULTS

Washington was undoubtedly a leader in our sense, because, as his eulogists pointed out, many people followed him eagerly, even when they were not compelled to do so.[14] And yet Washington had many faults, which he strove to conceal. He was rapacious in his pursuit of wealth and dishonest in trying to cover up his failures. He accepted an assignment as a supreme commander, although he had a limited grasp of tactics and military engineering. And he knew all this about himself.

Students of leadership should make themselves aware of the faults of leaders they admire, and then they should debate the merits and risks of concealment. Those who think about Washington's leadership must resist the tendency that dominated early histories of the man—they must stay away from worshipful hagiography. He was above all a man with a good front who knew how to wear a uniform and sit a horse. He looked and acted majestic, as the newborn country needed in its leader.

How honest must we be about ourselves as leaders? How much of our flaws should we reveal? How much should we be willing to uncover in order to maintain our integrity? Can the cost of integrity be too high for a successful leader?

HYPOCRISY: TARTUFFE AND ALCESTE

> Do you trust my pious face?
> Ah, no, don't be deceived by hollow shows;
> I'm far, alas, from being what men suppose;
> Though the world takes me for a man of worth,
> I'm truly the most worthless man on earth.
> —Tartuffe, in Molière's *Tartuffe*, 3.6[15]

Let's be honest about hypocrisy. We are none of as good as we like to appear. And that is not a bad thing: Society would be a mess if we revealed our true feelings on every occasion. In his play *The Misanthrope*, Molière shows a man, Alceste, who is so devoted to the truth that he insists on revealing his feelings in social situations in which they are not appropriate. Realizing that he cannot be true to himself and survive in the social whirl of Paris, he decides to leave society altogether. Here are his last lines, spoken to friends who prefer the gentle falsehoods that smooth their way in society:

> May you be true to all you now profess,
> And so deserve unending happiness.
> Meanwhile, betrayed and wronged in everything,
> I'll flee this bitter world where vice is king,
> And seek some spot unpeopled and apart
> Where I'll be free to have an honest heart (5.8).[16]

In this play, Molière is complaining that the French court at the time (1664) is not comfortable with honesty, but he is also showing that common courtesy depends on a little hypocrisy. Even Alceste contains his feelings on occasion: Earlier he has urged the woman he loves to "Pretend, pretend, that you are just and true,/And I shall make myself believe in you" (*The Misanthrope*, 4.3).[17] There is a middle course between the false flattery Alceste despises and the brutal honesty he affects.

The most odious hypocrite in literature is Molière's Tartuffe, a penniless crook posing as a puritanical man of religion. He has become the bosom friend and adviser of a wealthy man who has signed over all his property to Tartuffe. In the play it seems absurd of him to do this, but in our own time we see some religious teachers rolling in the wealth they have cozened out of their followers.

In the speech with which I opened the section, Tartuffe is telling the truth, but ironically. His victim's son has accused him of hypocrisy; instead of denying the charge, Tartuffe affirms it in tones of injured innocence. By this double hypocrisy he convinces his victim that he is truly as good as he seems. The victim disinherits his son and drives him from the house. This is a very disturbing scene: The victim would be doomed, if not for the godlike intervention of the king.

In real life, could a man at the French court survive while telling others what he truly thinks of them? Hypocrisy may be a necessity for survival in such a court. That is one of the lessons Molière must want us to take away from *The Misanthrope*. But surely, if true, that would be a sign that the French court is a terrible environment for a human being. Hypocrisy can go too far, as both plays show. We are better off if we can declare our thoughts and feelings to each other without fear. Indeed, friends (as Kant says) are those to whom we may safely tell the truth about ourselves.[18] And we need friends. Molière is implying that the French court is no place for friendship, but only for false courtesies.

Shakespeare's King Lear is no friend to his daughters. He will not let them say what they think and insists that they declare their love for him. His older daughters tell him what he wants to hear, but his youngest, Cordelia, tells the truth: She loves her father, but she expects she will love her husband more. Lear punishes her and rewards her sisters. The case is extreme, but the pattern is familiar enough: People in power bask in the warmth they feel from fawning hypocrites—so long as they do not detect the hypocrisy. If you hold power, and are wise, you will try not to push people into hypocrisy. Lear suffered terribly for doing this, when his other daughters revealed their true feelings toward him.

We have two ways to live a lie, active and passive. We can actively spin webs of deception (so long as we keep our lies consistent) or we can let people continue to believe nice things about us that are not strictly true. The latter is not necessarily any better than the former. In *Old School*, Tobias Wolff presents a teacher who lives a passive lie, allowing the students and younger teachers to believe that he had been friends with Ernest Hemingway. When a visit from the great author is imminent, the truth comes out. Living a passive lie was a disaster for this teacher: He should have spoken out when he heard that he had this reputation.

DEFINING HYPOCRISY

Hypocrisy is the vice of conmen and swindlers, slimy politicians and false prophets. It is a perennial danger to religious teachers and philosophers like me who write about ethics. Hypocrisy (in a general sense) is pretending to live by standards that are not yours. This could mean a number of things.

Courtly hypocrisy occurs wherever courtesy comes between our beliefs and our behavior. "I am so glad to see you," I say, when I wish you had not interrupted me.

Tragic hypocrisy is found among those who fail to live by ideals to which they are sincerely committed. Religious figures may be tragic hypocrites if they are truly committed to abstinence from sex but fail to find the strength or wisdom to abstain. Tragic hypocrites compound their hypocrisy if they preach on behalf of ideals they do not live by. But don't be confused: Hypocrites need not be false prophets; their sermons may be true (even if the sermonizers are not) and their ideals may be worth following. And don't confuse tragic hypocrisy with the criminal version.

Criminal hypocrisy is the vice of Tartuffe. Criminal hypocrites take advantage of others by preaching ideals to which they themselves are not committed. They most often do this for money. The problem with criminal hypocrites is not merely that they do not live consistently by the high ideals they preach; consistency is hard for everyone. The problem is that they preach ideals for profit, while having no genuine commitment to them. Their practice is a kind of theft.

Most admirable is what I will call heroic hypocrisy. This is the hypocrisy of the leader who builds an image for herself and then tries to grow into it. As in the case of tragic hypocrisy, the image of the hypocrite is better than the person, but the direction of flow is reversed: The tragic hypocrite is backsliding from her image, while the hero is using her image to help her live a better (though never perfect) life.

LOOKING AS GOOD AS YOU TRY TO BE

Now, in 2018, I am writing a book on leadership—this book. Am I letting my readers believe I know what leadership is? That I have been a successful leader? I have been in positions that called for leadership, and sometimes I have risen to the call. Other times I have failed. Am I a hypocrite for writing the book you are now reading? By writing this book, am I pretending to be an expert on a subject on which my success has been spotty? Not if I confess my self-judgment, as I have just done. We are all human. We do not always succeed even where we are experts worth listening to.

In 1998 I had the idea to write a book on reverence, but I came close to setting the idea aside: "Only a truly reverent person should write such a book," I said to myself, "and I am not truly reverent." Fear of hypocrisy almost deterred me from writing a book that now gives me joy and has been helpful to many readers. But I overcame the fear, and I am glad I did. I learned by writing the book, and I am a better person for having articulated the ideals it expresses. Even though I have not lived up to these ideals, the writing of them made me a better person. I was surely right to try. Perhaps we may be permitted to take on the appearance of the virtues we are striving for.

The ancient Greeks had a useful word, *spoudaios*, for a person who is earnest and zealous of being good. Aristotle uses the word for the imperfect but noble characters who are most impressive on the tragic stage.[19] We admire such people for their earnestness, and we pity them for their failures. In writing about courage, I said that courage is not something you achieve as a human being, but something you make a commitment to work on—a project. The best we can humanly be, I think, is *spoudaios*.

Leaders need to look a little better than they are. You should not reveal everything bad about yourself. Wear makeup as needed, but don't let your success with makeup entice you to try to get away with real ugliness. Wearing makeup does not by itself make you a Tartuffe, though it can tempt you in that direction. Tartuffe really is bad through and through. There is a more honest kind of hypocrisy, which you may use as a leader to bring out the beauty that you honestly seek to make your own. The analogy with cosmetics helps: Makeup can make genuine beauty more visible. A goddess would not need makeup, but then none of us is divine, and so, perhaps, all of us can use a little makeup.

Keep in mind, however, that there is a kind of hypocrisy that undermines trust. Never lie about the ideals to which you aspire. Tartuffe's criminal hypocrisy is a lie about his intentions. A leader's performance should always represent him as he is honestly trying to be. Tartuffe is disgraced when he is found out. You need not be disgraced if you conspicuously fail to live up to your ideals. You can try harder. And you can help others avoid whatever traps you have fallen into.

Whatever you do, don't lose the trust of those above you; that could be fatal to your followers. And don't lose the trust of your followers; that could be fatal to you—they may stop following you or even shoot you in the back. You must tread a delicate line between the honesty that is offensive or discouraging and the dishonesty that drives people away.

The crucial point is this: As a leader, you should project good qualities to your followers, set a good example, and urge them to do the same. Project these good qualities even though you cannot possibly have them in perfect form. No human being is truly a saint. Never forget that you are human; never forget that you will inevitably stray at times from the values you preach. But you must truly be striving to live by those values and to help others do the same.

For a healthy society, we need to approach those values as closely as we can, and therefore someone has to preach them. Why not you? You have enough life experience, or enough book learning, to know how much good can come from people who try to live by these values; and you have seen the evil that can come from those who do not. Do not back away from values for fear of being a hypocrite, though in a hard case you may need to back away from your values in order to save lives. Leaders who do not know when to lie, as Machiavelli warns us, can cause irreparable harm to their followers. But leaders must wear the face of leadership, as Machiavelli also understood.[20] And the face of leadership is a mask of good character.

HARD QUESTIONS

You have a friend who shyly shows you his precious poetry. Do you tell him how awful it is? Alceste got himself in serious trouble because he believed that every truth must be told, and so he told his friend how bad his poetry really was. Would he have done better to find a tactful way to advise his friend, the would-be poet? In responding to your friend, why don't you look for a few good lines you can point to, in hopes he will write more lines of that sort? And perhaps you can direct him to a poet who would be able to give him further advice.

Leadership presents special problems for you if you are committed to avoiding the passive lie. Suppose you are a company commander in combat. You are trembling inside with fear over the coming battle, and your bowels are coming loose. Should you act confidently in the hope that your troops will think they have nothing to fear? That would be a passive lie. Or should you confess your fear to your troops? If you do, will you set them trembling too? Or will you give them the comfort of knowing that it's all right to be afraid? Or will you tell them that if they are not as scared as you, then they don't know the situation they are in?

Or suppose you hear your troops mouthing off against your battalion commander, and you agree in your heart that the colonel is an idiot. Do you say this to your troops? Or do you tell them to shut up and get on with the mission?

Now suppose you must send one of your platoons out on a mission. You are afraid your young lieutenant may not be up to the job, but there is no one else you can send, and you have to make the attempt. Do you admit your fear to her or to her people? Do you express confidence in her ability to succeed, even though your heart is sinking, so as to boost her morale and theirs?

Now put yourself in her place. Suppose she knows she is not up to the job; no matter what you say to her, she will believe that she will fail. Will she hide this from you? Or will you have built a relationship with her such that she can tell you, without fear, that she cannot do what you have asked? And then what do you do? Invent an alternative? Tell her to do it anyway?

Suppose your unit is in trouble. You must extricate your company from its defensive position, but you are not sure you have a good plan for doing this. Do you ask your subordinates to brainstorm a solution with you? Or do you pretend you know what to do and move ahead with your plan? Washington was in such a position after the second battle of Trenton in January; he asked for advice, took it, and saved the army.[21]

I was taught as a young officer never to admit I was at a loss, but always to pretend I knew what I was doing. Military doctrine is more permissive now on this point, but it would still oppose any kind of collaborative decision-making by a commander. The general is supposed to listen to the reports of her staff, request information as needed, and then make a decision. Has this worked well in recent wars? Would Washington-style consultative decision-making have been more effective than the method we used in Vietnam and Iraq?

We can ask a similar question about teachers. Suppose that, as a teacher, you suddenly find yourself on uncertain ground. A student asks a question you cannot answer. Do you pretend to be omniscient, so that your students will respect your authority? Will your students believe in your omniscience for very long? Would you really want them to be so credulous? Or do you model self-knowledge—and, therefore, humility—and curiosity? I think it best for teachers to model the behavior they hope to see in their students—like Socrates, recognizing their own ignorance, proclaiming it, and seeking a remedy.

How truthful must a teacher be? On weekends, you lounge around in ragged shorts and a tank top. "This is the real me," you think. To be truthful, should you dress like that in class? Or do you think you should show respect for your students by dressing better than they do? Reverse the question: Suppose you wear makeup on your public face. Does honesty compel you to wear it in private as well?

Suppose you are afraid your students will think that you never sowed any wild oats in your early days. Should you confess to them all the sins of your youth? Or some sins and not others? Counseling a troubled student, do you have good reason to speak about your own troubles as a young person?

Are you lying when you take responsibility for the failures of others? Washington urged Nathaniel Greene to evacuate Fort Lee at the end of the losing battle for New York. Greene was sure his troops could defend the place, and Washington reluctantly acquiesced in Greene's plan. The event proved Greene wrong and Washington right. After the troops in the fort were massacred, Washington wept—and then, as I think any fine leader would do, he took full responsibility for the failure. He did not cling to the truth of "I told you so."[22] Greene went on to many successes, sharing hard-earned trust with his commander. As a leader you are often responsible for the failures of your subordinates. Not every truth needs to be told.

INTEGRITY

Most people agree that leaders must have integrity, and also that integrity is a good thing. But if leaders must perform—if they must deliberately put on the face of leadership—then how are they to maintain their integrity? This is a thorny problem. Much depends on what we mean by "integrity."

Does integrity require that your public self be fully transparent, revealing your inner core? I hope not, because then integrity would undercut leadership in many situations.

Does integrity require that you be at peace with yourself? Again, I hope not, because many great leaders have suffered internal torments. Kant understood that our desires are naturally at war with our duties;[23] a state of perfect inner peace is not likely to occur in a human soul, though many spiritual leaders have pretended to it. Washington was neither transparent nor at peace with himself.

Lastly, does integrity require that all of your actions be consistent with your beliefs and with each other? If so, integrity would not always be a good thing, since a psychopath could be consistent in this way. In addition, leaders should be free enough from consistency that they can exercise wisdom and compassion to bend rules in special cases. Leaders must be flexible.

So let's rule out those three definitions. Integrity is not transparency or internal peace or perfect consistency. As an alternative, I suggest that we think of integrity as faithfulness to our ideals. An ideal is, by definition, something a human being cannot perfectly achieve, but it *is* something a person can faithfully strive for. Insofar as you can approach an ideal at all, you can do so in different ways, from different directions. So you can be faithful to an ideal without being perfectly consistent in how you approach it.

The real world can be cruel to those who pursue ideals. Sometimes, circumstances can require a leader to set aside a cherished goal, temporarily, in order to achieve it in the long run. For example, Abraham Lincoln, who was deeply committed to democratic processes, was nevertheless willing to take subtle undemocratic actions to end slavery.[24] Slavery is blatantly inconsistent with democracy. By contrast, the subterfuges of political processes in real life—such as Lincoln used—are not blatant and need not be destructive of democracy—unlike the practice of slavery. Democracy could recover from what Lincoln did, but it could not have survived if slavery were the law of the land. So, in ending slavery the way he did, Lincoln was pursuing a democratic goal by means that were not democratic. In doing this, was he compromising his integrity? That's a good question to discuss with your friends or your class. Did Lincoln suppose that the end justifies the means, or is the issue more complicated?[25]

If integrity is faithfulness to your ideals, then integrity won't make you good, unless your ideals are good and you find good ways to approach them. But goodness calls for integrity. Any virtue must be accompanied by integrity, because every virtue is an ideal. I have said that good character is a lifelong project, not a fixed trait. If this is right, then you can have integrity without being transparent or consistent or at peace in every moment. Have you learned to appear courageous in tough times? Even when your heart quakes? Even when you know that you have quietly fled from danger on some occasions in the past? If you are serious about cultivating courage, you are showing integrity even now, even wearing the face of courage that you have not completely earned— a face that you will never completely earn.[26]

Consider this crisis. You have just been told that a substantial force is preparing to overrun your position. You feel a spasm of fear. Perhaps you owe it to your followers to wear the confident face that will help them face danger, rather than setting off a contagion of panic. In Shakespeare's *Henry V*, the young king of England, facing a vastly superior French force at Agincourt, tells his troops he does not wish for one man more. He assures them that they are about to win a glorious victory. Why ask for more troops? If they had more troops, they would have to share their glory with a greater number. Shakespeare stages this speech as the cause of Henry's victory. That works brilliantly on stage, but I doubt it would work on a field of battle: In history, Henry won through superior tactics and the cold-blooded murder of hundreds of prisoners who had surrendered.[27]

On a real battlefield, troops would probably not believe a speech like the one Shakespeare's Henry gives. As a leader in a tight spot, you might help your troops more by letting them know it is OK to be frightened. You are quaking yourself, so there is nothing wrong with your troops, nothing wrong with their fear. Now you must all help each other get through this crisis. Do you tell them this, make your plans calmly, show them how your plans can work, and summon whatever help you can? That would be faithful to the ideal of courage, but it is not the only way. Instead, you might put on a false face of courage and inspire your troops to victory. That also would be faithful to your commitment to courage. Think about this now, before you are in a tight spot. What should you do?

NOTES

1. Eliot 1901, Chapter 33, 397–398.
2. Keegan goes on to suggest that Alexander's mask hid a ferocious savagery, and that the consequence of Alexander's successful performance as self-forgetting was "to ennoble savagery in the name of glory" (1987, 90, 91).

3. Chernow 2010, 434–436. The remark about the spectacles is variously reported. Different versions of the story place the incident at different points in the performance; one version puts it as Washington was preparing to read his speech, another puts it during the speech, before he read a letter he had received from members of Congress. Here I follow the interpretation of Ellis 2004, 144. For the evidence, see Fitzpatrick 1938, volume 26, 222n88: The remark is quoted from a Col. David Cobb from someone named Ford. The story is good enough that readers should be warned that it may not be true. See also Fleming 2007, 271.

4. Washington himself was a great lover of theater, much to the chagrin of a more puritanical Congress. Brookhiser writes that the stage naturally appealed to Washington as someone "made for stardom" (2008, 74).

5. "Leaders must be able to put on a show . . . put on the face of a leader" (Pfeffer 2015, 86–87). On this topic see also Goffman, 1959.

6. Washington's tactical ineptness is clearly apparent in his defeat on October 4, 1777, at Germantown: His plan was simply too complicated to succeed. Ellis 2004, 103; cf. Chernow 2010, 308–311.

7. Ellis 2004, 273.

8. Ibid., xiv.

9. Morris 1800, 44–45.

10. Ellis 2004, 273.

11. Ibid., 274.

12. In this period, as Washington knew, a leader had to bring value to the office. He had to be presidential before the presidency could become an institution to be admired (Suri 2011, 1–2). As Higginbotham notes, in Washington's America "the man by his character and performance gave dignity to the office; the office was less likely to give luster to the man" (1985, 16); cf. Higginbotham's Chapter 2 on Washington's transformation into a leader of men.

13. Compare Washington's control of emotion with what Keegan says about Wellington: "He did indeed succeed, between the ages of thirty and forty-five, in banishing feeling from his personality." And like Washington, Wellington tamed his feelings because of the reasonable fear that such feelings lead one to seek tyrannical power (Keegan 1987, 162–163).

14. Morris 1800, 44.

15. Molière 1965, 260.

16. Ibid., 152.

17. The French urges the hypocrisy indirectly. It reads: "Efforcez-vous ici de paraître fidèle,/Et je m'efforcerai, moi, de vous croire telle" (lines 1390–1391; ibid., 117).

18. Kant 1797/1996, 216. Moral friendship (as distinguished from friendship based on feeling) is the complete confidence of two persons in revealing their secret judgments and feelings to each other, as far as such disclosures are

consistent with mutual respect. With others, one finds oneself "constrained *to lock up* in himself a good part of his judgments (especially about other people)."

19. Aristotle 1987, 3 (*Poetics* 48a25–28).

20. See Chapter 6, "Facing Evil, Learning Guile."

21. Washington's consultative style as a commander is striking by comparison with today's military doctrine. In early days, his councils ended with a vote; later he saw to it that they ended in consensus, although no one doubted that Washington was in command throughout each meeting. For accounts of his councils, see Fischer 2004, 100 (decision to abandon Long Island); 264–266 (decision to recross the Delaware; "a remarkable and very instructive success for Washington's maturing style of quiet, consultative leadership"); and 313–316 (decision to move toward Princeton).

22. Fischer 2004, 113–114. Similarly, Eisenhower was prepared to accept all of the blame should the invasion of Normandy have ended in defeat, going so far as to draft remarks announcing his failure (Eisenhower 1986, 252).

23. Because our inclinations are always threatening our moral choices, we need to have a kind of virtue that is always growing in power: "if it is not rising [it] is inevitably sinking." "Virtue can never settle down in peace and quiet with its maxims" Kant 1797/1996, 167.

24. Consider the passage of the 13th Amendment. In addition to personally lobbying for the amendment, Lincoln knowingly misled Congress regarding the status of peace talks with the Confederacy to ensure the amendment's passage (Luthin 1960, 572–575).

25. Machiavelli is often said to have taught that the end justifies the means, but that is clearly a mistake about him; see p. 99.

26. On integrity, my view may be similar to that of Cheshire Calhoun (1995). For a substantial discussion of philosophical work on this topic, see Cox, La Caze, and Levine 2013.

27. On Agincourt (about which we have eyewitness reports from both sides) read Keegan 1976, 78–116.

WORKS CITED

Aristotle (1987). *Poetics*. Trans. Richard Janko. Indianapolis: Hackett Publishing Company.

Brookhiser, Richard (2008). *George Washington on Leadership*. New York: Basic Books.

Calhoun, Cheshire (1995). "Standing for Something." *Journal of Philosophy* XCII: 235–260.

Chernow, Ron (2010). *Washington: A Life*. New York: Penguin Books.

Cox, Damian, La Caze, Marguerite, and Levine, Michael (Fall 2013). "Integrity." In *The Stanford Encyclopedia of Philosophy*. Ed. Edward N. Zalta.

Eisenhower, David (1986). *Eisenhower: At War*. New York: Vintage Books.

Eliot, George (1901). *Daniel Deronda*. In *The Personal Edition of George Eliot's Works*. New York: Doubleday, Page & Co.

Ellis, Joseph J. (2004). *His Excellency: George Washington*. New York: Alfred A. Knopf.

Fischer, David Hackett (2004). *Washington's Crossing*. New York: Oxford University Press.

Fitzpatrick, John C., ed. (1938). *The Writings of George Washington from the Original Manuscript Sources*. Washington, DC: U.S. Government Printing Office.

Fleming, Thomas (2007). *The Perils of Peace: America's Struggle for Survival After Yorktown*. New York: Smithsonian Books/Collins.

Goffman, Erving (1959). *The Presentation of the Self in Everyday Life*. New York: Doubleday Anchor Books.

Higginbotham, Don (1985). *George Washington and the American Military Tradition*. Athens: University of Georgia Press.

Kant, Immanuel (1797/1996). *The Metaphysics of Morals*. Trans. Mary J. Gregor. Cambridge, UK: Cambridge University Press.

Keegan, John (1976). *The Face of Battle*. New York: Penguin Books.

Keegan, John (1987). *The Mask of Command: Alexander the Great, Wellington, Ulysses S. Grant, Hitler, and the Nature of Leadership*. New York: Penguin Books.

Luthin, Reinhard H. (1960). *The Real Abraham Lincoln: A Complete One-Volume History of His Life and Times*. Eaglewood Cliffs, NJ: Prentice-Hall, Inc.

Martin, Clancy W. (2015). *Love and Lies: An Essay on Truthfulness, Deceit, and the Growth and Care of Erotic Love.*. New York: Farrar Strauss and Giroux.

Molière (1965). *The Misanthrope and Tartuffe*. Trans. Richard Wilbur. New York: Harcourt Brace Jovanovich.

Morris, Gouverneur. (1800). "An Oration." In *Eulogies and Orations on the Life and Death of General George Washington, First President of the United States*. Boston: Blake.

Pfeffer, Jeffrey (2015). *Leadership BS: Fixing Workplaces and Careers One Truth at a Time*. New York: Harper Business.

Rowling, J. K. (2007). *Harry Potter and the Deathly Hallows*. New York: Scholastic Books.

Shakespeare, William (1995). *Henry V*. New York: Washington Square Press.

Suri, Jeremi (2011). *Liberty's Surest Guardian: American Nation-Building from the Founders to Obama*. New York: Free Press.

Wolff, Tobias (2003). *Old School*. New York: Vintage Books.

Chapter 12

Good Ears, Strong Voices

For forth he goes and visits all his host;
Bids them good morrow with a modest smile,
And calls them brothers, friends, and countrymen.
Upon his royal face there is no note
How dread an army hath enrounded him;
Nor doth he dedicate one jot of colour
Unto the weary and all-watched night;
But freshly looks, and over-bears attaint
With cheerful semblance and sweet majesty;
That every wretch, pining and pale before,
Beholding him, plucks comfort from his looks;
A largess universal, like the sun,
His liberal eye doth give to every one,
Thawing cold fear, that mean and gentle all
Behold, as may unworthiness define,
A little touch of Harry in the night.

—Shakespeare, *Henry V*, 4.1.33–48

The situation is terrifying. Henry's army is outnumbered by the French. Drenched by incessant rain and exhausted by long marches, they find the French occupying high ground, blocking their path to safety. Thus far, history and Shakespeare agree. In history, Henry is a brilliant tactician who will lure the French into a constricted killing field, massacre them, and so win the day. Shakespeare's Henry is a brilliant communicator. The night before the battle, he visits the soldiers in disguise and listens to them, gauging their morale. Then, on the morning of the battle he speaks to them, delivering the most famous motivational speech in literature. After we win our great victory, he tells his army, we shall all be remembered, to the ending of the world:

> We few, we happy few, we band of brothers;
> For he today that sheds his blood with me
> Shall be my brother; be he never so vile.
> This day shall gentle his condition;
> And gentlemen in England now abed
> Shall think themselves accursed they were not here.
> And hold their manhoods cheap whiles any speaks
> That fought with us upon St. Crispin's day.
>   —Shakespeare, *Henry V*, 4.3, 62–69

It's not true. Henry will not treat his soldiers as brothers after they win the battle. Yes, they will be remembered for winning against the odds, but they will also be remembered for having slaughtered their prisoners in violation of the laws of war and the traditions of the era. In Shakespeare, Henry's rhetoric wins the day, as it has done before. His rhetoric won the siege at Harfleur and will win the heart of the French princess.[1] This play is about the power of communication, of listening and speaking.

True leadership, I have said, occurs only in the context of freedom. Leadership is evident only when people cheerfully and freely do, in concert, what they are not required to do. If people follow you beyond what they absolutely have to do, you must be showing leadership. Concerted action is based on shared goals and agreed-upon means to those goals. The agreement that leadership needs depends on communication. For true leadership to occur, this communication must lead to agreement that is wholehearted and long-lasting. Once Henry's soldiers wake up after the battle and see that their king will not treat them as brothers, they will not be so willing to put their lives on the line for him again. A leader cannot go far by means of such deception or phony rhetoric.

Most of the power of a leader grows through communication. What can our students do to acquire this power, and what can their teachers do to help them along the way? Communication is the most important of the skills that leaders-to-be must learn, by experience or in the classroom, and it is a skill that colleges and universities are well situated to teach.

What follows in this chapter is not a manual for teaching communication. It is, instead, a reminder of the many elements of communication that a future leader should consider learning—like everything in this book, it is about goals. If teachers took all the goals of communication seriously, they would change the way they teach. If they did that, students would have a better time, because they would connect better with what they are asked to learn; after all, few leaders will be called upon to write academic papers with citations in MLA format. In any case, there is more to leadership communication than merely writing and speaking—there are images, for example, which recent technology has made easier to use. But writing and speaking and image-making are no use unless you know your audience. The foundation of communication is the art of listening. How many college teachers are teaching that?

GOOD EARS

Leadership starts with listening—an essential element in communication.

"Turn your megaphones into hearing trumpets," wrote William Stafford.[2] Only those who listen can speak for others, and only those who speak for others can lead them where they—the whole team, including the others—want to go. Of Billy Budd, the handsome sailor, Melville wrote, "Ashore he was the champion; afloat the spokesman; on every suitable occasion always foremost" (1.8/44). Spokespersons must understand the people they are speaking for. Leaders listen carefully enough to give voice to others, often to those who, by reason of oppression or poor education, have trouble finding voices on their own.

In discussions I am often no better than my students. Instead of listening to others, I am forming in my own mind the important thing I want to say next. But then, when I say this important thing, it falls on deaf ears. Not knowing what others are thinking at that moment, I fail to connect with their thoughts, and so I fail to connect with them. I might as well have come from another planet. Perhaps the students think I did: Some loving students once designed a T-shirt depicting me as a space alien.

Listening is hard but essential. As a lecturer, I find I must know where my students are in their minds in order to make a connection. Teachers should put a lot of thought into how to get on the same planet with their students—to listen to them, to read what they write, to give them time (or even require them) to ask questions. Teachers are wasting their breath when they speak unless they know how much their students understand, and how much they don't. I ask students to write weekly blog posts or journal entries with their thoughts or complaints about the material; I do not grade these on style or content but give students full credit if they write these pieces before class discussions. I find that those who journal or blog before a class always have something to say when they come to class.

Teachers can reward good listening in student discussions. Insist that when students speak, they address what another student has said earlier and don't just say "I agree with Wendy, but what I think is . . ." My grades for participation are based on students' attentiveness to each other. Teachers can also give students assignments to listen outside of class. For example, they can ask them to take oral history from relatives or neighbors, or (without making judgments) to ascertain people's reasons for living or voting as they do.

Good listening is not purely passive. The challenge to the listener is to participate actively in a conversation without taking it over, so as to make the speakers feel that they are truly being heard.

Leadership (as I have often said in these pages) requires an alignment of goals within a team. A leader must know what goals people have in order to pull them into a team. A leader must also give voice to those on the team who cannot speak for themselves, so that the members of the team may understand each other.[3]

Amateurs of the subject often assume that a leader must be an extrovert, but many successful leaders have been introverts. Introverts, apparently, are naturally good listeners, and their talent for listening works to their advantage in leadership.[4] Indeed, we can find so many different ways to be a leader that almost any set of natural talents can be used in leadership. Anyone can learn to listen well, however, and those who wish to lead should begin early to practice the art.

STRONG VOICES

Speaking and writing go together, and students need help with both.[5] If you present your ideas to your classmates before you start to write, you will find that your writing comes more readily; after you have answered your peers' questions, you have a better idea of what your main point will be. Teachers can build this into any writing assignment. Every act of communication has an audience. In a classroom, this audience should be your fellow students, not your teacher. As leaders, your students will not be leading folks from other planets such as their professors; they will be leading people like their peers, so students should speak to them and write for them. Professors should ask for that.

For a leadership course, teachers may ask students to address their teams on a leadership or management issue—such as a reduction in staff, the distribution of bonuses, or the changing mission of the team. Then ask speakers to follow up with a brief memo to the team. For both the speech and the memo, ask students to offer advice to each other; that is, to "workshop" the memo and the speech. If possible, give them a chance to revise their work.

Speeches should be clear and brief—one to two minutes long. Outside academe, short talks ("elevator speeches") are often the most effective. Writing assignments will be most useful to students if they too are short. Again, in the real world, students will write very brief texts, tweets, website copy, or memos. Only those who go on to graduate school will write anything like an academic paper after they leave college.

Assignments

I have overseen courses that teach writing and speaking, and I have found that students do best when responding to the best assignments. Writing is a process (for most writers), and good assignments carry students through the process. Digital learning platforms easily allow for an assignment that is articulated into steps such as these: First propose a topic; then, if it is approved, find good sources and submit a short annotated bibliography. After that, write a draft and receive feedback from a teacher, a peer, or both. Then revise and submit a final version.

Teachers need to know that students make little use of comments unless they are asked to revise, and that students make better use of oral than of written comments. Commenting on final or terminal papers is generally useless for the teaching of writing. A paper that is turned in without process at semester's end gives students useful practice in writing, but it does not give the teacher an opportunity to coach students on their writing. Students have no compelling reason to read the professor's comments on a terminal paper—why should they?—so they rarely do.

Coaches are expert at helping students carry out repeated actions better. In communication, teachers are coaches, and the actions need to be repeated. Coaches are also expert at motivation; the pregame speech and the halftime speech are famous. Can teachers do anything in the classroom to help students develop the power to motivate others?

Motivation

History and literature are larded with speeches given (or supposedly given) before battles. Two of the most famous are to be found in Shakespeare's *Henry V*: "Once more unto the breach" (3.1.1–37) and "we few, we happy few" (4.3.21–69). These are useful texts to read and discuss. Thucydides is the first historian to report on pre-battle speeches; the ones he gives us are numerous and fascinating.

Among the most powerful speeches of literature is Mark Antony's in Shakespeare's *Julius Caesar*, "Friends, Romans, countrymen, lend me your ears!" (3.2.72–107). This speech is worth studying, especially for its clever use of irony. Antony wins over a hostile audience partly by indirection, partly by appealing to justice, and partly by appealing to their material desires. From the first word to the last it is calculated to draw in its audience, please them, and incite them to rage against Caesar's enemies.

Contrast that with the brilliance of Coriolanus' speeches, which reflect contempt for his audience and lead to his downfall. He has told himself that it is "better to die, better to starve, than crave the hire which first we do deserve" (*Coriolanus* 2.3.113–114). He believes that he has earned public office by his valorous deeds on the battlefield, and that he would besmirch his honor if he spoke to the people or their tribunes in a diplomatic way. Later, when he is in danger of execution as a public enemy, he says: "I would not buy their mercy at the price of one fair word" (3.3.90–91). And he is utterly incapable of masking his feelings, as his mentor explains: "His heart's his mouth; what his breast forges, that his tongue must vent" (3.1.255–256).

Coriolanus is unfit to be a leader of the Romans because he is deeply out of sympathy with their values. He would have to lie to win them over, and he is too honorable for that. Mark Antony believes in the cause for which he speaks, so he can infuse his speech with honest passion while still using rhetorical devices that distort the truth. He disarms opposition by saying, "I speak not to disprove what Brutus spoke" (3.2.100), but that of course is exactly what he is doing.

Rhetoric is a powerful tool. A great speaker can manipulate an audience, but only if the audience members do not know they are being manipulated. Rhetoric is therefore a self-effacing art. Leaders should know something of the use and abuse of this art.

Leaders need to know, however, that speeches are not the strongest motivators. Remember Melville's Bartleby?[6] Bartleby would prefer not to do anything he is asked to do. Nothing the boss says will change his attitude. At the same time, Bartleby's fellow employees are doing less than they are asked, and no speech is going to change that. The fundamental problem in that office is that the boss is lazy. If the boss does nothing, why should anyone else?

Disaffected employees and team members will shrug off a motivational speech. "Yeah, yeah," they may say to themselves as the boss or commander or coach mouths off. "What's this to us?" Carrots and sticks have some effect, but they cannot change a team member from unwilling to willing. Grudging obedience is not the goal of a leader. When the halftime speech works, it works because the coach and the team share a goal: They all want to win, and they all believe they can do it. If they receive the speech as mere flimflam or false optimism, it will make no difference to them. If they all share the goal at the outset, however, the speech may help to convince them that they can achieve this goal. But the team captain may be more effective simply by modeling confident behavior.

Nothing communicates motivation as powerfully as a good example.

Vision

Henry's speech before the battle implies a narrative. He imagines a future scenario centered on the memory of the battle they are about to fight: "Gentlemen in England now abed shall think themselves accursed they were not here." But he could do much more to give his soldiers a vision of the future that their victory would create. Leaders can use narrative to help their followers feel that they are part of a meaningful story. Poet and visionary Betty Sue Flowers writes, "One of the tasks of a leader is to imagine and articulate these connections between daily activity and purpose—to paint a picture of the cathedral to the laborer so that the answer to the question 'What are you doing?' is not 'Laying bricks,' but 'building a cathedral.'"[7]

Bartleby's boss is unable to motivate his employees for the same reasons he is unable to motivate himself. They are all laying bricks, but to no purpose. There is no cathedral to be built by their labor. It is all meaningless work designed to support the boss in his sinecure. A leader has to be able to envision and communicate a future worth working for.

In the American war in Vietnam, hardly anyone was left by 1969 who had a vision of a victory worth fighting for. The older officers were striving for medals and promotions (or so it seemed to me), and the younger people mostly aimed simply to finish their year of duty safely and go home. Yes, a fiction about the future of Vietnam had brought us into the war, but that fiction had become hard to believe. You won't fight for a future unless you can imagine it.

The present, however, is always with us, and when there is horror to be found in the present we are moved to change it. In the years leading to the Civil War, the abolitionist movement had little traction until Harriet Beecher Stowe published *Uncle Tom's Cabin* in 1851–1852. The first chapter alone of this piece of fiction was enough to enrage the non–slave-holding public against slavery. Imagine an African American who is at least equal in intelligence to the white man who thinks he owns him, and is superior in virtue as well. His name is Tom, and he is the farm manager, trusted and trustworthy. Now imagine that he is going to be sold down-river to pay the debts of the elegant man who thinks he owns Tom. That could happen in 1851. Outrageous! And there is worse to come in this fiction. That story was one of the most effective motivators for soldiers engaged in the war on the Union side.

Or consider the horror of communism, as depicted in Orwell's fable *Animal Farm* (1945), which helped fuel enthusiasm for the Cold War. Good leaders use narratives to show how the present is broken and how the future might be better, should their followers share in that vision. Do not underestimate the power of fiction to expose present horrors, or the power of vision to draw us toward a better future.

Songs

In the Vietnamese civil war, the communist-led Viet Cong were far better motivated than the defenders of the U.S.-backed regime, even though most of them had no interest in communism as an ideology or as a practical economic system. One reason for this is that the Viet Cong were able to present themselves as the defenders of Vietnamese independence. Another reason was that the Viet Cong had a cadre of writers producing songs designed to sustain morale. On the U.S.-backed side, which I advised for a year, there were no fight songs that I heard.[8]

Songs are powerful. A good song, once heard, lingers in the mind. The tune and the words make each other memorable. If well composed, a song can lift the spirits of a crowd and bring them together. Nothing does more to help people feel solidarity with a group than singing such a song together. Nietzsche was right when he claimed that music (the domain of Dionysus) dissolves individual differences.[9]

"The Battle Hymn of the Republic" helped muster the troops that won the Civil War. Julia Ward Howe was brilliant in many ways and deserves to be famous for other achievements as well, but her lyrics for this song are unforgettable, and they changed our world. A century later, "We Shall Overcome" became an anthem of the civil rights movement. Songs or chants also bring together supporters of a football team, as we learn on campuses on Saturdays in the fall.

Poems are almost as effective as songs, if they are written to lodge in the memory. In today's culture, the prevailing poetry is rap lyrics—rap being mainly poetry supported by strong rhythm. Many college students aspire to write songs, and their teachers can encourage this by accepting songs in fulfillment of some requirements. Good songwriting is harder than many students think, so the more practice the better.

If you want to influence others, think about how you might do this through song, and then practice the art.

TECHNOLOGY: BEYOND WORDS

Communication in the twenty-first century has changed, owing to the development of social media, which favor the use of very short texts along with images and videos. At this point in the revolution, students often know more than their teachers about the latest forms of effective communication, which change almost monthly. Students should be willing to teach each other, and professors should be willing to learn. Teachers, for their part, would do well to be open-minded about the kind of work they accept for assignments. Also, close attention to the use of technology in current political campaigns should be welcome in today's classrooms.

OVERCOMING DIFFERENCES

The student we interviewed was superb in every way but one: When he spoke to us, he cast his eyes down to the table. We debated whether to recommend him for a Rhodes Scholarship. We knew he would fail to impress the next round of committees if he did not learn to engage people with his eyes, but we also knew that casting his eyes down was his way of showing respect for us—the way he learned from his Chinese parents. We taught him to look us in the eyes; he took the lesson to heart and won the scholarship. But perhaps we would have done better to leave him as he was and teach the committees to recognize the respect in his way of speaking to them.

If you lead a diverse team, you must learn to communicate across the barriers that differences raise among us. There are many kinds of difference besides those due to cultural heritage. How is it best to listen to a person who is deeply shy? How best to speak to someone who is so sure of himself that he rarely stops talking and almost never listens? What difference

does gender make to communication? Sexual identity? A leader's education should consider questions like these.

CHARACTER: THE FINEST EXAMPLE

Your words will have the most powerful effect if your character backs them
up. The character you show in composing and presenting a speech is essential to its success.

Remember Newburgh? The freedom for which George Washington
has led the Continental Army is in peril, even as victory over the British
Empire is at hand. Congress is gridlocked, unable to vote on funding for
the army. Some officers of high rank have proposed to overthrow Congress
and to set up a military government, perhaps farther west. They have
planned a meeting, which they expect will be packed with sympathizers.
They do not expect Washington to attend, but they may well call on him to
take the new nation's reins as a military dictator.

News of this comes to Washington, who has always had good ears.
Somehow he causes the meeting to be postponed for three days, during which
he writes a speech—the most important speech in American history. This was
the speech that established the principle of civilian rule over the military.

No one expects him to attend, or to give the speech he will give. He
gains their attention and sympathy at the start, by means of his famous
gesture with his spectacles. Then he goes on to make his goals clear—goals
that were the same as theirs:

> If my conduct heretofore, has not evinced to you, that I have been a
> faithful friend to the Army, my declaration of it at this moment wd.
> be equally unavailing and improper. But as I was among the first who
> embarked in the cause of our common Country. As I have never left
> your side one moment, but when called from you on public duty. As
> I have been the constant companion and witness of your Distresses,
> and not among the last to feel, and acknowledge your Merits. As
> I have ever considered my own Military reputation as inseparably
> connected with that of the Army. As my Heart has ever expanded
> with joy, when I have heard its praises, and my indignation has

arisen, when the mouth of detraction has been opened against it, it can scarcely be supposed, at this late stage of the War, that I am indifferent to its interests. But, how are they to be promoted?

Then Washington goes on to show how the plan they were considering would undermine the goals they shared, replacing one tyranny with another. He then brings the speech to this dramatic conclusion:

> And let me conjure you, in the name of our Common Country, as you value your own sacred honor, as you respect the rights of humanity, and as you regard the Military and National Character of America, to express Your utmost horror and detestation of the Man who wishes, under any specious pretences, to overturn the liberties of our Country, and who wickedly attempts to open the flood Gates of Civil discord, and deluge our rising Empire in Blood.[10]

The would-be rebels listened to his words, but, more important, they were moved by his example—the example of a man they believed to be devoted, single-mindedly and without ambition, to freedom, a man who would turn down any offer of absolute power. Washington's language was rough; he was not a great writer, and he had penned this speech himself. But he was sincere, and they saw him as their champion. By this he saved the nation. Soon after, at his insistence, the officers were paid. That was leadership.

His words were well chosen, but the character behind them was essential for their effect. More skillful speakers might have seemed less trustworthy—precisely because of their skill. Aristotle rightly emphasized the importance of character to rhetoric.[11] No level of skill will save you as a communicator unless your audience trusts you. Trust hangs on character, and character is the subject of the next chapter.

NOTES

1. At Harfleur, he urges on his troops with a speech as famous as the "happy few" speech he gave before Agincourt: "Once more unto the breach, dear friends,

once more" (3.1.39). On being repulsed, he promises the French mayor of Harfleur that if he does not surrender, "The gates of mercy shall be all shut up" (3.3.10). And he warns any resistant denizens of Harfleur, "Your naked infants [shall be] spitted upon pikes" (3.3.38). The scene in which he woos Princess Katherine is 5.2.

2. Stafford 2003, 36.
3. On the need to speak for members of the team: What I call the Ajax Dilemma arose partly because the leader failed to speak for different members of the team, so that Odysseus and Ajax did not understand each other's goals or each other's values. On this, see Woodruff 2011, 195–197.
4. Cain 2013, 53–63.
5. For teaching the art of speaking, I recommend Reynolds 2011 and, for writing, Trimble (2011).
6. Melville 1962, 1–41; cf. Chapter 7, "Facing Evil in Ourselves."
7. Flowers, unpublished manuscript (no date). For the cathedral anecdote, which is widely quoted, see for example Kukolic 2016. Coker (2012) attributes it to Christopher Wren and, with his fellow authors, builds a textbook on leadership around the idea.
8. How do I know this? I served as an adviser in Chau Doc Province from June 1969 to June 1970. The troops I worked with were dedicated to their cause against the Viet Cong; after all, the Viet Minh (same group as the Viet Cong, really) had killed their great religious leader, Huynh Phu So, and minced his body into small pieces (Buttinger 1967, 410). But our side had no songs. In 2002, on a return visit, I met the man who wrote the most effective fight songs for the Viet Cong, a man highly honored for his service.
9. Nietzsche 1872/1999, 21, 98–104.
10. The Newburgh Address is readily available online and can be found in the original manuscript version. It is short and repays careful reading in full.
11. Aristotle, writing in his *Rhetoric* in the fourth century BCE, introduced the idea that character (*ethos*) matters in public speaking (1.2.3–4; 1926, 17): "There are three ways to make a speech convincing: the first is by the moral character of the speaker, the second by putting the listener into a certain disposition, and the third by the argument itself, through proving its point or seeming to prove it—by character when the manner of speaking makes the speaker worthy of being believed" (my translation). Greek theater had already made much of this theme: Odysseus, for example, was far too clever with words to be believed, and so, in the play I mentioned in an earlier chapter (Sophocles' *Philoctetes*), he needed a young unskilled person to speak his words for him. But in that play, only a tried and true friend is to be believed, a man of sterling character—Heracles.

WORKS CITED

Aristotle (1926). *The "Art" of Rhetoric*. Trans. J. H. Freese. Cambridge, Massachusetts: Harvard University Library.

Buttinger, Joseph (1967). *Vietnam: A Dragon Embattled*. London: Pall Mall Press.

Cain, Susan (2013). *Quiet: The Power of Introverts in a World That Can't Stop Talking*. New York: Broadway Books.

Coker, Greg (2012). *Building Cathedrals: The Power of Purpose*. With Terry Daniels, Dave Tatman, and Skip Wirth. Louisville, Kentucky: Clark Legacies.

Flowers, Betty Sue. *Destiny*, Chapter 15 (in manuscript).

Kukolic, Siobhan (2016). "Are You Laying bricks or Building a Cathedral? *Huffungton Post* 10/18/2016. https://www.huffingtonpost.com/siobhan-kukolic/are-you-laying-bricks-or-_b_12387634.html

Melville, Herman (1962). *Billy Budd, Sailor, and Selected Tales*. New York: Oxford University Press.

Nietzsche, Friedrich (1872/1999). *The Birth of Tragedy and Other Writings*. Ed. Raymond Geuss and Ronald Speirs. Cambridge: Cambridge University Press.

Reynolds, Garr (2011). *The Naked Presenter: Delivering Powerful Presentations with or without Slides*. Berkeley: New Riders.

Stafford, William (2003). *Every War Has Two Losers: William Stafford on Peace and War*. Ed. Kim Stafford. Minneapolis: Milkweed Editions.

Trimble, John R. (2011). *Writing with Style: Conversations on the Art of Writing*. 3rd Edition. Boston: Prentice Hall.

Woodruff, Paul (2011). *The Ajax Dilemma: Justice, Fairness, and Rewards*. New York: Oxford University Press.

Chapter 13

Becoming Magnetic

A breathtakingly handsome teenager has just shown up. Socrates reports the reaction of those present, adults and children:

No one—not even the smallest children—looked at anyone else. They all looked at him as if he were a sacred idol. Then Chaerephon yelled at me, "How does the young man strike you, Socrates? He has a good looking face, doesn't he?"

"Exceptionally so," I answered.

"But if he were willing to strip," said he, "you wouldn't think he had a face at all; that's how beautiful his body is."

Then everyone agreed with what Chaerephon had said.

But, as for me, I said, "Heracles! No one could match him, that is, if he has just one small thing in addition."

"What's that?" said Critias.

"If his soul's nature turns out to be good. It ought to be, considering that he is from your family, Critias."

"Oh," he said, "in that respect too he is *kalos* and *agathos*—fine and good."

—Plato, *Charmides*, 154c6–e4[1]

Good looks, if you are lucky enough to have been born with them, will make you a magnet for people's eyes, but they will not make you the sort of magnet that people will follow into battle, not by themselves. You can be ugly, and you can still be a magnetic leader. But you can be drop-dead gorgeous and yet fail to gather willing followers around you. To be a leader, you must have the character of a leader and know how to make it shine.

In the opening of Plato's dialogue *Charmides*, Socrates has just been introduced to a strikingly handsome young man, a magnet for the eyes of all. But Socrates' eyes are not glued to the lad; instead, he is watching everyone else gazing at the young lad. Socrates will not be impressed by good looks, unless they are a sign of good character; good character—the soul's nature—is what he cares most about. That's what he looks for, but the soul is hard to see. How can we tell whether a person's character is good? How can I tell in my own case?

Critias calls the lad *kalos* and *agathos*—fine and good, an expression used in ancient Greek for aristocrats. The two words mean almost the same thing, "good," but with this slight difference: *kalos* may also be translated "beautiful." Goodness and beauty ideally go together. A good body is healthy and strong; physical beauty is often a sign of health and strength. Good character is like health and strength in the soul; if your character is not only strong but beautiful, then people can see how strong it is.

Beauty of soul: I mean by that whatever makes good character shine out so that others are aware of it. That, I think, is what makes leaders magnetic when they are magnetic: They have a kind of psychic strength or health that they make evident to those around them.

Leaders look for good character in their followers, and followers look for good character in their leaders. On both sides, we need to have good character in the soul. But hidden goodness is not good enough: We need to make our goodness evident to others. If we wish others to take us seriously, we must take care of our physical appearance. That's obvious. We wash ourselves, exercise regularly, and dress with care. But we also need to be morally attractive. How do we manage that?

In a leadership situation it's no use hiding your good qualities. It's worse, however, to try to show them off, or to pretend that you are radically better than you are. We don't trust showoffs, and for good reason. If you try to show off your wisdom, you are a fool like Shakespeare's Polonius. Wise people do not show off. And if you try to show off your courage, you are a daredevil and a fool as well. Courage is unassuming. Still, you need to bring your good qualities into the open, so that your leaders and your followers are aware of them. How do you show your good qualities without showing off? I have no easy answer to this. The best advice I can give is to act with integrity, in all things small or large.[2] And look for models in history. How, for example, do you think George Washington did it?

VIRTUES, OR BEAUTIES OF THE SOUL

On his front were enthroned the virtues that exalt, and those that adorn the human character. So dignified his deportment, no man could approach him but with respect—None was great in his presence. You all have seen him, and you all have felt the reverence that he inspired; he was such, that to command, seemed in him to be an ordinary function, while others felt a duty to obey, which (anterior to the injunctions of a civil ordinance, or the compulsions of a civil code) was imposed by the high behests of nature.

—Gouverneur Morris, Eulogy on George Washington, 1800, 44

People trusted Washington. He was not a golden-tongued orator or a gifted writer. He was not a brilliant tactician. But he knew how to look good in a uniform, especially on a horse. And he was notably courageous. That was easy enough to see from his behavior in battle. He also made it clear that he had no interest in power for its own sake. That he made clear in many ways, almost daily in his councils of war. In councils, he listened to others and did not always insist on having his own way. He had colossal self-control—which he needed in order to hold down his equally colossal temper. His associates knew all this, because they had seen him on those rare occasions when he did lose his temper.

We are naturally drawn by the magnet of good character. We want the same qualities in both leaders and followers because we want to be able to trust them to act well in a variety of circumstances. Trustworthiness is not an independent virtue—rather, it is the product of all the virtues working together. Can you trust me to do the right thing in danger? Yes, if I have courage. Under temptation? Yes, if I have self-control. Can you trust me when I have untrammeled power over you? Only if reverence keeps me from hubris—the vice that leads to overreaching. Can you trust me to do right by you in disputes? You can if I have justice engrained in me. Can you trust me to stand by you when you fail? When you are in trouble? Yes, if I am as loyal to you as I expect you to be loyal to me.

If you say "yes" to all of these, then you have found a leader you can follow with joy. In the same way, if you are the leader and you find someone about whom you can say "yes" on these points, then you have found a follower to whom you can give a delicate mission without detailed supervision.

WHAT LEADERS MUST BECOME (AND FOLLOWERS TOO)

What qualities do you think make a leader magnetic? Leaders-to-be should think about these and come up with their own lists. Here's my list, however, with brief notes about why I think each one matters for a leader or follower. I have written in detail about only one of these, courage, in earlier chapters. Leaders-to-be can work on understanding the others using that as a model.

Courage. Leaders must stand up to every kind of danger and every kind of fear. They must not be deterred by fear of the enemy, or even by the fear of their friends and superiors. They must have the courage to listen to opposing points of view; and, when it is time to step aside and give up power, they must have the courage to do so.[3]

Self-control. Leaders should not be easily swayed by desire or passion. Desire could excite a leader to forget self-control and harass a subordinate sexually; passion could drive a leader to make bad decisions out of anger or jealousy.

Reverence. Reverence is the quality that helps us avoid hubris, arrogance, or overweening pride. If you have power over others, and no one is watching you, you are in danger of hubris. If not checked by reverence, you may do outrageous things to other people, knowing that you can get away with it. We shouldn't trust you with much power if you are not reverent. If you have a great success, you fall into danger of hubris. You may think you earned your success, and if so you are likely to become overconfident in your ability to win against the odds.[4] Then hubris might cause you to lead your followers into a disaster. Or drive you to make yourself a tyrant.[5]

Compassion. Groups are dangerous if not well led. They can gang up on outsiders (or new members) and do great harm. Leaders need to endow their teams with compassion. You are likely to be in need of compassion yourself, either from your leader or your followers. We are all vulnerable, as reverence teaches us.[6]

Justice. Injustice may tear a team apart, and when this happens, leaders are to blame either because they have failed to resolve quarrels among the team, or because they have taken unfair advantage of their positions. They may violate justice by being cruel, or they may put personal interests ahead of the goals of the team. As a follower, I may put my life on the line for a cause that I share with you, my leader, but I will not put my life on the line so that you can earn a promotion. Leadership cannot happen between us unless you and I have a goal in common. Followers rely on their leaders to resolve quarrels in accordance with justice. Justice is what keeps a team working together in peace.[7] Justice goes beyond simply following rules or enforcing them; it requires wisdom.

Loyalty and Independence. Loyalty runs both ways between followers and leaders: Loyal followers obey instructions, while loyal leaders ensure those instructions don't put their followers at undue risk. Loyal leaders and followers stand by each other in time of need.

Independence is the capacity to act without instructions—or even in disobedience to instructions—when it is best to do so. Leaders and followers alike should have both of these, along with the wisdom to balance them.

Creativity, Honesty, Reliability. Creativity is the ability to find solutions no one has yet considered as well as to share a vision of what a team can accomplish. A creative leader should be able to tell an inspiring story, to situate followers in a narrative that they wish to be part of. Leaders can use fiction well, but to do this they must use fiction to light up the truth. There can be honesty and dishonesty in fiction; leaders need the wisdom to understand that. Honest leaders do not torment their followers with impossible dreams.

Reliable leaders stay on course and do not shift with every changing breeze. Their followers need to know what direction the team is going. As a creative leader, you will be unpredictable, but you should not be so unpredictable that others cannot rely on you. Again, balance is needed.

Leaders and followers need the wisdom to weigh creativity against relia-bility and choose a course that is clear enough to be followed.

Wisdom. In the last analysis, all of the good qualities I have listed so far call for practical wisdom. This begins with self-understanding and extends to understanding other people.[8] If you understand yourself, you recognize what you are doing as you do it, you call it by the right name,[9] and you know why you are doing it. Understanding others is similar: Know what they are really doing, and why. Wisdom endows those who have it with the capacity to appreciate other people for what they are, enabling you to extend love and respect beyond boundaries.

Wisdom also includes *good judgment*, which requires you to know what factors are relevant to a decision, to pay attention to them, and to listen well and recognize good advice when you hear it.

CHARACTER WITH COMMITMENT

If you think you are wise, you are a fool. If you expose yourself to temp-tation believing that you have perfect self-control, you are in grave moral danger. You may be confident in your own courage, after surviving many battles, and still crumble from fear of your superiors. If you are self-aware, then, you will know you are human, and you will not forget that humans are vulnerable to moral error, no matter how good they have been in the past.[10]

Character is not something I can hold and carry with me. It is not like a diploma or a PhD degree or even like having a certain blood type. It is not like being your grandfather. If I am your grandfather today, I will al-ways be your grandfather, alive or dead, come what may. But being wise is different: Even if I am wise in some fashion today I may well be foolish tomorrow.

So let's use words carefully. *Being* wise is not a reasonable goal for a human being. *Becoming* wise, on the other hand, is a good project for the whole of a human life. I have said that the virtues are not fixed traits. They are projects that call for wholehearted commitment. If your goal is courage, then you will practice courage in large things and small, when people are watching and when they are not. And the same with all the other goals of character.

MAKING CHARACTER SHINE

To make your compassion shine, you must at least demonstrate your commitment to becoming compassionate. The same goes for all the magnetic qualities I listed above.[11] Two reasons for this: First, no one can be expected to demonstrate perfection in compassion or any other virtue; a clear commitment to getting compassion right can make up for a number of the mistakes you will inevitably make. Second, if you aren't committed to compassion, and if you aren't motivated by that commitment, then it does not matter how often you get things right and appear to be compassionate. We won't trust you enough to follow you if your commitment does not shine through your actions.

Suppose you appear unfazed by danger in battle after battle, but this is not due to any commitment to courage: You are out of your mind with drink or drugs. That is false courage. So your commitment to courage has to be the source of your courageous behavior, and you must somehow make this clear. For you to be our leader, you need to show us that you are not getting things right by accident, but that you are succeeding out of a commitment to develop and maintain that kind of character. On the few occasions when you do fail, you must take responsibility and set about making the changes you need in order to avoid a second such failure. That takes commitment, and it will shine.

Your followers will be watching you closely, whatever you do. They will be quick to catch inconsistencies in your actions—and of course there will be some of these. To become magnetic, you need to be just as quick to catch yourself. As I said in an earlier chapter,[12] you can be inconsistent and still display integrity, so long as you are visibly faithful to your commitments.

You will be judged on small matters as well as large ones. You will be watched when you are exhausted as closely as when you are well rested, as closely when you are rushed as when you have time to ponder, as closely when you are afraid as when you are confident. That degree of watchfulness is hard to face. How can you act with integrity under the stress of leadership? That is your challenge.

Of course, commitment is not enough. Remember the soldier who kept running away? The one who would try again and again to get courage right?[13] He was committed to courage, all right, but we would not trust him to lead us in battle. So you need to show us some measure of success, beyond commitment.

CHARACTER IN COMMUNITY

Developing character and making it shine: These are things you cannot do alone; they are like learning and using a language. You cannot develop language skills all by yourself. Language is shared. So is the sort of behavior that goes with good character. We have languages of behavior, which we can learn only when we are among people with whom we share our language. Take reverence, for example. Different cultures express reverence differently, and the same goes for respect. You can't develop the capacity for respect without expressing respect, and you can't express it unless you are among people who have respectful ways of interacting. Start by learning how to show respect. Do we shake hands here? Salute? Doff our hats?

I have shown earlier how much courage depends on community.[14] You cannot grow courage alone. The same is true for growing any of the beauties of soul. We all tend to rise or fall with the expectations of those around us. Leaders and followers should expect the best of each other. This is most obvious between teachers and students. As students, we learn best around teachers who expect the best from us. As teachers, we are at our best around students who have high expectations for us. The same goes for athletes and coaches, and for soldiers and their commanders. The expectations of others matter, and that is why community matters, to becoming magnetic.[15]

CHARACTER AND DIVERSITY

Different cultures expect different things of their leaders, and in today's world many working teams are diverse, culturally and in other ways. Gender, sexual identity, cultural heritage, personality type—all these make differences that leaders must recognize. Reverence will not permit leaders to believe that only their culture is correct.[16] Education for leadership should introduce students to diversity so that they will not be surprised by it. Formal teaching in the classroom about diversity is probably not as helpful as it is to have diverse contacts outside class, whether with friends or enemies. That's one reason why a diverse residential campus is valuable, and why segregated social groups can be harmful.

Students would do well, however, to think in the classroom about how best to work in a diverse team—recognizing its diversity, allowing for it, but not calling undue attention to it. People should never be required to speak for some group to which they are perceived to belong, although they should feel free to do so. There is a delicate balance in treating diversity in a diverse classroom. On the whole, today's students understand this balance better than their elders.

What does diversity mean for the study of culture? I have argued that virtues such as courage and justice and reverence are human necessities. We all are subject to fear, thanks to evolution. Fear saves lives, but it also can deter us from doing what we need to do. Hence the need in every human culture for some kind of courage. We all need to live in communities, and communities (as the Greeks realized in ancient times) all require some sort of justice and some sort of reverence. But not the same sort everywhere.[17] Different cultures express justice and reverence in different ways, and leaders must be educated to understand this—to be able to see the essential virtue behind the veil of language and expected behaviors.

WEI WU WEI (SILENT LEADERSHIP)

Sometimes, even this side of Paradise, we need to think about the ideal, about perfection. People often want to know what a leader must *do* in order to be a good leader, but such emphasis on action is often misplaced. In a perfect world, perfect leaders would not need to do anything but shine like a star to give us a point of goodness by which we could steer ourselves.

Compasses point to the north because they follow the Earth's magnetic field. In Confucian philosophy, the ideal emperor would need to do nothing but sit on his throne and face south,[18] like the pole star, shining out so that his subjects could align themselves along the same axis, drawn by the magnetism of the emperor's goodness. The magnet and the emperor act on others without action on their own part, peacefully and quietly. "Act-Non-Act" is the meaning of *wei wu wei*, an important doctrine in both Confucian and Taoist teaching. The ideal emperor does not rule by force, and he does not even rule by enforcing law. Heaven rules Earth, but heaven has no need to speak,[19] and neither does the emperor. He rules by character alone—by becoming magnetic.

NOTES

1. My translation. For the context, see Plato 1973, 59. Critias will later turn out to be the brutal leader of a group known as the Thirty Tyrants, who terrorized Athens after its defeat at the hands of the Spartans, driving out supporters of democracy, executing their enemies, and appropriating their wealth. Charmides will grow up to be little better.

2. On integrity, and the difference between that and consistency, see p. 144.

3. See Chapter 9, "Facing Fear, Showing Courage," and Chapter 10, "Finding Courage."

4. Consider the warning in Ecclesiastes (9.11): "Speed does not win the race nor strength the battle. Bread does not belong to the wise, nor wealth to the intelligent, nor success to the skillful; time and chance govern all" (*New English Bible*, 1970).

5. Here I am using "reverence" in a special sense, for which see Woodruff 2014.

6. On compassion, see Chapter 12 in Woodruff 2014; cf. the brief discussion in Chapter 7 of this book.

7. See Woodruff 2011.

8. See Chapter 7, "Facing Evil in Ourselves," on justice and self-knowledge; cf. Woodruff 2011, 177–184.

9. Confucians call for something known as the "rectification of names." This entails avoiding self-deception by using the right words for what you are doing. On this see Confucius 2003, 13.3, 139–140; cf. Xunxi 2014 (Chapter 22), 236–237.

10. See Doris 2002, 147.

11. I am grateful to William Gibson for a fine conversation about commitment.

12. Chapter 11, "Performing Leadership," p. 144.

13. See Chapter 10, "Finding Courage," or Miller 2000, ix–xi.

14. Chapter 10, "Finding Courage," pp. 122 and 128.

15. I owe the point about expectations to Baker Duncan, whose wisdom grew from his experience as headmaster of a school. From my own headmaster, Canon Martin of St. Albans School, and from many gifted teachers, I see that this has been true in my own case.

16. As I have argued in Woodruff 2014, 150–155.

17. Protagoras, a fifth-century BCE teacher, appears to be a source for the idea that human survival depends on justice and reverence. See Woodruff 2014, 51–54, with 264–265 and Plato's *Protagoras* 322a–d.

18. Confucius 2003, 15.5, 175.

19. Confucius 2003, 17.19, 208; Lao Tze 1993, 5 and 23.

WORKS CITED

Confucius (2003). *Analects*. Trans. Edward Slingerland. Indianapolis: Hackett Publishing Company, Inc.

Doris, John M. (2002). *Lack of Character: Personality and Moral Behavior*. New York: Cambridge University Press.

Ivanhoe, Philip J. (2000). *Confucian Moral Self-Cultivation*. 2nd ed. Indianapolis: Hackett Publishing Company.

Morris, Gouverneur (1800). "An Oration." In *Eulogies and Orations on the Life and Death of General George Washington, First President of the United States*. Boston: Blake.

Lao Tze (1993). *Tao Te Ching*. Trans. Stephen Addiss and Stanley Lombardo. Indianapolis: Hackett Publishing Company, Inc.

Miller, William Ian (2000). *The Mystery of Courage*. Cambridge, MA: Harvard University Press.

New English Bible (1970). Oxford and Cambridge, UK: Oxford University Press and Cambridge University Press.

Plato (1973). *Laches and Charmides*. Trans. Rosamond Kent Sprague. Indianapolis: Hackett Publishing Company, Inc.

Woodruff, Paul (2011). *The Ajax Dilemma: Justice, Fairness, and Rewards*. New York: Oxford University Press.

Woodruff, Paul (2014). *Reverence: Renewing a Forgotten Virtue*. 2nd ed. New York: Oxford University Press.

Xunzi (2014). *Xunzi: The Complete Text*. Trans. Eric L. Hutton. Princeton, NJ: Princeton University Press.

PART III

CHANGING HOW WE TEACH AND LEARN

Every teacher teaches leadership. Every teacher teaches ethics. Professors need to pay attention to their effect on students. Tyrannical teaching breeds tyrants, not leaders, and there is too much of that on most campuses. Some teachers encourage ethical failure directly or by omission. Even those who teach subjects directly related to leadership, such as ethics or history, often do so in ways that cause moral injury to students. My final chapter calls for a revolution in and out of the classroom. All courses should promote the independence of students, improve their communication skills, and help them model themselves on great leaders. Many courses can give students opportunities to lead their teams to success.

Chapter 14

Tyrant Teaching

THE LESSON: BE SILENT

In Ionesco's 1950 play *The Lesson*, the professor insists on taking control of his students. One by one he kills them, while his compliant housekeeper arranges for the disposal of the bodies. After killing a student on stage with a knife, he insists: "It's not my fault. She didn't want to learn! She was defiant. She was a bad student! She didn't want to learn!"[1] In the original production of Ionesco's play, performed five years after World War II, the housekeeper assures the professor that he will be safe so long as he wears his Nazi armband. That line was dropped in subsequent productions.

But professors need not be Nazis to kill students—at least to kill their desire to learn—and get away with it. This professor's teaching method is simple. He teaches one on one, and he requires little of the student: "Button your lip. Stay seated and don't interrupt" (74). The one student we see in the play came to him with a desire to learn. That is not surprising; every human being is born with curiosity. But what students want to learn may be quite different from what professors want to teach them. This professor pays no attention to the goals of his student. His goal is power, and so he pays no mind to his students' anguish:

> Harmless at the outset, the Professor becomes more and more sure of himself—nervous, aggressive, and dominating—until he controls the Student, who becomes helpless in his hands. Naturally, his voice, which was thin and reedy at the beginning, becomes stronger and stronger until it rings out like a clarion call, whereas

the Student's voice becomes virtually inaudible after having been so clear and true at the start. (53)

This lesson is a nightmare. But is it so far distant from waking reality? How often do professors put students down so firmly that they cannot rise again? That they learn to hate the subjects the professor teaches? Or that they learn craven obedience to authority? Or that they learn to cheat in order to survive? Yes, academic dishonesty is often learned in the classroom.

None of us who teach think of ourselves as tyrant teachers, and yet the story is partly true of all of us. We have authority over our students, and we are free from most constraints in the classroom; academic freedom makes sure of that. We revel in our freedom, and we do not always use it wisely. Satires like Ionesco's can teach us a lot. "Why are you laughing?" the satirical poet Horace addresses his reader. "I changed the name, but the story is about you" (*mutate nomine de te fabula narrator*)[2]—meaning that you should be able to see something of yourself in the absurd figures of satire. That is part of facing evil in ourselves. Even if none of us is a tyrant teacher overall, many of us let tyrannical behavior creep into our teaching. Tyrant teaching is one way of teaching ethical failure. We will see that there are others.[3] Tyrant teaching saps students' independence and pushes them to pursue false goals such as pacifying the tyrant; it also makes accomplices of our housekeepers—as does Ionesco's professor, whose housekeeper discreetly disposes of the bodies of his students.

We do not play tyrant without help from others. University administrators—like Ionesco's housekeeper—sometimes enable professors to get away with murders of the mind. Students also are complicit when they allow themselves to be silenced. All three groups are tempted to slide toward tyranny—doing it or accepting it—because it so often seems the easiest way to go. But they all need to change.

If we care about learning, we should want to banish tyrant teaching. Equally, if we care about leadership, we should do our best to take the tyranny out of teaching. For one thing, tyrant teaching sets a rotten example for students to follow; for another, it deprives them of opportunities to practice leadership in the classroom. If we want our students to graduate with creative, independent minds, we must keep tyranny out of our engagements with them.

MIND-MURDER: THE ACCOMPLICES

Change begins with seeing what goes wrong. We who are real-life equivalents of the figures in Ionesco's nightmare need to recognize ourselves. After we do that, we can try to steer a safer course. I begin with the students, not because I wish to blame the victims, but because they have an opportunity to learn something by reacting against tyrant teaching. They have an opening for practicing leadership.

Students

Students find it all too easy to sacrifice themselves. After all, most high schools have taught them habits of silent obedience. In any case, silence is the easiest course to take in the presence of a loud-mouthed professor—a professor who appears (to students) like an alien from another planet. To make matters worse, the professors who most need to hear from their students are the ones who are least likely to listen to them. They might silence students with a stare or drown the students' voices out with their own loud ones; they might miss office hours, refuse to respond to emails. If you as a student can speak to tyrant teachers privately, when they will not lose face in front of the class, you might have a better chance of being heard. But at eighteen you may well be afraid to confront an older person without the support of your friends. If you gang up on such a person, however, the response may be worse.

Still, if a heroic student were to stand up and insist on telling the truth, what a difference it might make:

> "We can't hear you in the back of the room."
> "We can hear you all right, but we have no idea what you are saying."
> "Why do you want us to learn this material?"
> "Your stories about sex are repellent to me. Can you use some other
>   kind of example to make your point?"
> "None of us know what you want us to do in this assignment."

Even if students have no such complaints, they might well want to challenge what they have been told:

> "On page 33 at the top the book says the opposite of what you
> just said."
> "I have thought up a better way to solve that problem."

A mind that is alive will be full of questions, and you as a student should want your mind to be alive. So should your professors, but they may not realize that.

In Sophocles' *Antigone*, an experienced ruler, Creon, is confronted by his young son, Haemon.[4] We in the audience know that if Creon would only listen to his son, he would escape the coming tragedy. He is poised on the edge of an abyss, and his son could save him. His son knows this, but Creon will not listen. When I teach this play, I ask my students why the younger man should speak up to the older, when he admits that the older man knows so much more. To sharpen the point, I ask my students why they should speak up to me about the *Antigone*, a play about which they know nothing, but on which I am an expert. This is a challenge: Students need to know why they should not button their lips even when told to do so. Their mental lives depend on speaking up and asking questions. True, if they speak up to a tyrant teacher, they may make no difference; old farts are not good listeners. Still, if you do speak up, you at least give the old fart a chance. Haemon did not prevent the tragedy, but he did give his father an opportunity to prevent it himself. Opportunities are valuable even when not taken.

Why do students button their lips when commanded to do so? Or even when all they receive are subtle hints to be quiet? Obviously, they are young and feel powerless in the presence of authoritarian professors. Often, students fail to speak up because speaking up is not consistent with their goals—one of which is to get an A in the course, or at least pass, with a minimum of fuss. That's a reasonable goal. But there are other goals than getting good grades, ones that belong more properly to education, and one of them is exercising leadership. Many students arrive wanting to exercise leadership, but do not find ways to do this in class. A leader among the students would speak up, or, if afraid to do so alone, would organize a group to go together to protest the tyrannical teaching, either to the professor or to the administration.

Administration

Why does the Housekeeper do no more than protest at what the Professor does? And why does she dispose of the bodies so efficiently? Why does she protect the tyrant? Ionesco does not explain.

In today's university, the answer comes down to one word—rankings. Most universities aim to raise the rankings of their departments and research programs. To do that, they must hire and retain professors with strong research profiles. And to do that, they must often turn a blind eye to small tyrannies in the classroom. Academic rankings are not sensitive to the quality of teaching.

Graduation rates are now under scrutiny, but administrations have not changed their priorities for hiring and retaining faculty. Instead, they improve student support services, admit students with greater care into challenging programs, and offer faculty members opportunities to learn better teaching methods. But much of this is merely cosmetic. An ambitious university will still promote a top research scholar with a mediocre teaching record, while terminating a brilliant teacher with a mediocre record of research.

Part of the problem is that we do a poor job of evaluating teaching. Student evaluations are the principal tool; they are useful but limited. The professor to whom students gave the worst student evaluations in a program I directed was the one whom alumni praised most often for having given them tools they used in their careers. Why? He required his students to learn to solve problems that he refused to tell them how to solve. As students, they hated that, because they did not know what to do to ensure winning an A in the course. As alumni, however, they found that the course had given them a high level of confidence in tackling real-life problems in business (or elsewhere) that no one could tell them how to solve.

I am proud that I encouraged the professor to soldier on. I knew what he did in the course, and why. And I knew how deeply he cared about putting new life into his students' minds. That is the sort of thing an administrator needs to know. But the information behind it is not quantifiable, and the housekeepers of academe want numbers. They think, wrongly, that numbers are the most objective indicators of success or failure. Leaders know otherwise.

Leaders have goals, based on values that are their own, values in which they believe, values they can explain and champion. Mere managers in academe tend to respond to other people's values. For example, they do that by letting outside scholars rank their faculty and their departments. That is fine, as far as it goes, but it does not go very far. It merely represents the values that a majority of scholars in a field currently hold for research in that field—values that are subject (in many fields) to fashion.

As for teaching, mere managers let students do the heavy lifting on evaluation. But where are they, the housekeepers, in this process? Where are the goals they would truly make their own? In the final chapter of this book, "A Campus Revolution," I will argue that if we are serious about cultivating a garden of leaders on our campus, we will need to change our goals—and we will need to have goals that we can all share, students, faculty, parents, administrations, alumni, corporations that hire the students—everyone concerned. Remember, there is no leadership without followership, and no followership without shared goals.

MIND-MURDER: THE PERPETRATORS

Even a smidge of tyranny means that leadership has failed. If we professors feel we have to intimidate our students, we have failed to lead them. Generally, when we turn away from leadership and start acting like tyrants, that is because we have been unable to draw our goals and our students' goals into alignment. We often bring into the classroom goals that differ from those of our students. What happens inside the classroom can make that difference even greater and tempt us to become tyrannical. Two traps await us in the classroom: authority and coverage. Let me explain.

The Authority Trap

We like to teach what we know, and what we know may be very narrow. We have to specialize in order to write dissertations and publish enough to earn tenure. In an ambitious department, we are encouraged to specialize in areas that will raise our ranking as a department. Many valuable kinds of work do not count for ranking: exploration of new fields, interdisciplinary work, translation, textbook-writing, to name a few.

In philosophy, the most important areas for rankings have recently been analytic metaphysics and epistemology—fairly technical fields. But most of our undergraduates who take courses in philosophy have interests other than these, unless they are among the tiny number each year who contemplate going to graduate school. Most students are interested in practical ethics, in the history of ideas, and more and more they are interested in non-European traditions, such as those of east or south Asia. Moreover, these fields attract the interest of students outside the department, inviting them to explore philosophy when they might never have done so otherwise. But these areas do not affect rankings; a top-ranked department need not have a single expert in classical Chinese philosophy, for example. Few professors dare to teach material on which they are not authorities, especially if they have no colleagues to set them straight. As a result, courses in non-ranked subfields are rare in top departments.

Authority is a trap for professors. I know myself to be a leading authority on certain subjects; all of us who teach at great universities are authorities on one thing or another. As an authority, I feel that I should be telling the students what I know, trying to bring them quickly to my level. That can lead me to teaching like a tyrant, insisting on my point of view, not listening to students when I think they are ignorant or misguided. Surely, if I must teach, I should teach a subject I know well, on which I am an authority. But perhaps I should not spend so much classroom time teaching at all.

There is so much more we can do in a classroom than teaching. Instead of teaching, we should consider leading our students in inquiries about subjects on which we are not authorities—or on which we can, at least, keep our authority in check. That would give students more independence and at the same time give professors opportunities to model leadership. Moreover, students tend to remember what they learn through their own inquiries and forget what professors tell them.

So, yes, Professor, you are an authority, and you know it. But don't let that go to your head. See how much authority your students can take, and let them at it. Socrates did not give lectures.

The Coverage Trap

You know the kind of lecture I have in mind: The speaker, an expert in the field, has prepared forty or so PowerPoint slides for a fifty-minute lecture. Each slide is rich with text. As she approaches the forty-minute mark, she sees with alarm that she still has twenty slides left. So she accelerates her delivery, and the slides fly past our eyes, as her words fly past our ears. "Will you please post the slides on the web?" a student asks as the class files out. "No," she answers. "I won't reward those who do not attend."

She has succeeded in covering the material she had planned to cover, but only if "covering" means getting through the slides. A very small percentage of the class, the speed-readers, may have learned something from this, but most have gained nothing. If challenged, the professor will say that she has to cover the material scheduled for each class or she won't be able to cover the material for the course. And if she doesn't cover the material for her course, her students will flounder at the next level.

Once she falls into the coverage trap, she cannot make time to listen to students, to back up and help those who have fallen behind, or to take any action that might enliven her students' minds. She is aiming at the wrong goal. Coverage is irrelevant to her mission as a teacher. Her mission is to invite students to reach a level of understanding at which they can think critically and creatively about her subject. The recent movement to invert the classroom is a step in the right direction. In an inverted classroom, students cover the material on their own, using online material or textbooks, and spend class time engaging with what they have learned, connecting with each other and the teacher. If the housekeepers expect her to cover more material than the students can learn in a semester, then she should make the housekeepers change their expectations. Her goal should not be to cover the subject. In fact, her goal should not be about what she does at all; it should be about what the students do. Her proper goal is that her students learn as much of the material as they can in a semester. It does not matter how much she says, or puts on slides, if her students are not able to make it their own.

Teachers do not need to be tyrants for any reason whatsoever. They do not need to play their cards as authorities, and there is rarely a subject that they must cover fully. Their only goal should be their students' goal: learning whatever is best for us all to be learning. Teachers, students, and administrators all need to bring their goals into alignment, as leaders and followers do in any successful enterprise.

NOTES

1. Ionesco 1950/2007, 92. Eugène Ionesco (1909–1994) was a Romanian playwright who lived in France and wrote in French after the time of the German occupation of France. Tina Howe, the translator of these two plays, is a distinguished American playwright.
2. Horace, *Satires*, 1.1.69–70, my translation. Horace, having made fun of a miser by comparing him to Tantalus, throws the lesson back at the reader. Horace wrote in Rome during the reign of Augustus. For a delightfully free translation, see Horace 2012.
3. See Chapter 15, "Teaching Ethical Failure."
4. Sophocles, *Antigone* 2003 (626–780), 30–36.

WORKS CITED

Horace, *Satires* (2012). Trans John Svarlien. Indianapolis: Hackett Publishing Company, Inc.

Ionesco, Eugen (1950/2007). *The Bald Soprano and The Lesson: Two Plays—A New Translation*. Trans. Tina Howe. New York: Grove Press.

Sophocles (2003). *Theban Plays*. Trans. Peter Meineck and Paul Woodruff. Indianapolis: Hackett Publishing Company, Inc.

Chapter 15

Teaching Ethical Failure

Shades of the prison house begin to close
Upon the growing boy.
           —Wordsworth, "Intimations of Immortality"

In the *Philoctetes*, a play by Sophocles, the wily Odysseus teaches his young student to lie. To Sophocles' audience, this wily teacher stands for the whole tribe of sophists, who have come to the city to teach rhetoric, and in doing so are widely suspected of corrupting the youth of Athens. The boy in Sophocles' play says it is not in his nature to lie, because his father, Achilles, was known to be the most honest of men. But that, says the teacher, is why people will believe the boy when he does lie; and he must tell a lie in order to carry out his mission for the army. The Greek army at Troy has sent this pair, Odysseus and the boy, to a lonely island to recruit an heroic old soldier for the war—the archer Philoctetes, who alone can use the ultimate weapon, the bow of Herakles. Odysseus believes that only deception will bring the archer back to war: The boy must lie to the old soldier, steal his bow, and then help Odysseus kidnap the soldier and take him back to Troy. Just one lie is all he asks from the boy; after that, says Odysseus, the boy can be as honest as he likes:

> I quite understand, my boy, that you were not born
> With a natural bent to tell such lies and contrive
> Such evil. But think how sweet it is to grab victory.
> Be daring! Afterwards, we will present ourselves
> As righteous men. But now, give me yourself

For one small slice of a shameless day, and then
You'll be acclaimed the most reverent man alive, forever.[1]

The boy does not need to learn that it is wrong to lie; he already knows that. Only under the tutelage of a teacher like Odysseus will he achieve ethical failure.[2] The audience of this play would have recognized the teacher as a familiar figure in Athens: the sophist who gives lessons in the art of persuasive speaking—the one who can teach a guilty man to talk his way out of punishment or teach a malicious man to talk a jury into convicting innocent people of dreadful crimes. The most famous of these was a teacher named Gorgias. More about him in a moment.

Do we have such teachers and such students in our universities? Like the boy in the play, who is eighteen, our students do not need to learn the difference between right and wrong. They know that already. Just about everyone does. By the time they come to college, our students know clearly that lying is wrong, stealing is wrong, killing the innocent is wrong. If they do any of these things then or later—and some will, in the course of business or war—we need to ask why.

The norm in behavior is ethical. We have an evolutionary explanation for this. Human beings cannot survive except in communities, and they cannot belong to communities unless they exhibit some level of moral goodness. As philosopher Peter Geach said, "Human beings need virtues the way bees need stings."[3] And, indeed, we have virtues most of the time, just as bees have stings.

All over the world, we can rely on people to tell the truth when we ask them for directions. When we go out on the street, we can be fairly sure that passersby will not do us violence. Most people in the world do not feel the need to carry weapons. We can safely lend valuables to our friends. So why can't we rely on a company that makes cars to be honest about exhaust fumes? On an energy company to keep honest accounts? On a shirt-making company to provide safe conditions for its workers? On our military officers to give honest reports on the readiness of aircraft? On a church to protect children from pedophiles? Readers can supply any number of stories about ethical failures, especially in organizations.

Where does ethical failure come from? That, I think, is one of the most important questions for us to ask in the university. Ethical failure may have many causes, but teaching can be one of them. Young people like the son of Achilles can be taught, influenced by example, pressured, or even shamed into doing wrong. Odysseus represented lying as an act of daring. Who could resist that challenge? Who wants to be called a wuss because he won't tell a little lie?

Sad to say, university education is part of the cause of ethical failure. We must face up to the fact that we teach ethical failure.

ETHICAL HUBRIS

We teach hubris—overconfidence in our own goodness. We Americans praise our own culture as exceptionally good. And yet in our prisons and in our conduct of war, we Americans have been exceptionally ruthless. As a nation, we set a bad example for our young people in lying to ourselves about how good we are.

People fail more easily in certain circumstances if they know how good they have been in life on the whole (in marriages, with children, toward friends, or volunteering in the community). The more you know how good you are, the worse for you as an ethical decision-maker—unless you still recognize your potential for going wrong. The worst thing about ethical hubris in the teaching profession is that it blinds us to the many ways in which we can teach ethical failure without meaning to do so. One way we teach ethical failure is by allowing for moral holidays.

MORAL HOLIDAYS

> When money was concerned, Vasco's conscience tended to fall into fits of obstinate silence.
>
> —Saki, "The Treasure-Ship"[4]

A famous false proverb says, "All's fair in love and war"—and all too often people seem to think that this holds in business too, especially when extreme conditions seem to justify breaking the rules. I blame many ethical failures on that proverb—and on the systems that operate under its umbrella. Some systems, such as the military at war, or business in its per-petual crises, like to shelter under some form of that proverb.

Ethical failure is most often due to the belief that we have crossed a boundary into territory where ethics no longer matters—for just a mo-ment, for now, while times are especially hard, until we win, until we get out of this hole, until . . . until when? . . . well, you fill it in. "You can be good at home, good in the community, as good as you want," they say. "But here, in this business [this war, this hospital, this organization], you must pay at-tention to nothing but the numbers that we use to measure success." Here we have a holiday from ethics.

In the play I quoted at the start, the wily Odysseus is asking his protégé to take an ethical holiday. But, in fact, the matter is more complicated. He and the boy have conflicting obligations: They owe something to the army at Troy, which sent them on this mission and desperately needs them to succeed; and they also owe something to the man whom they are about to deceive. This is a dilemma, but they do not see it that way. If they did, they would weigh their options more carefully.

Caving In to Dilemmas

We teach people to cave in to dilemmas without considering the full force of reasons on both sides. We do this by declining to present ethical problems as dilemmas, and by setting a high value on winning at all costs.

Odysseus and the boy have set out to bring a famous soldier back into the army. They need to bring him back as a willing, trusting member of the force. They will not be able to achieve this by dishonesty. A soldier who has been tricked into joining a campaign is unlikely to be a willing partic-ipant, and he is certain to have lost trust in his commanders. Why don't Odysseus and his student recognize that problem? They take the easy way: They do not think it through. Lying often seems the quickest way out of a tangle, but it has consequences: The loss of trust may be irreparable.[5]

The boy who is corrupted by Odysseus has not considered the ques-tion of lying in any depth. If he had, he might have considered the impor-tance of trust for any community such as the army, and the great danger that arises from damaging trust. He might have realized that an army of volunteers like the one at Troy would be dissolved by distrust.

Had the boy been better taught, he would have been able to consider the dilemma that faces him by deploying the reasons on both sides. But in his ignorance he is left the victim of his untutored feelings. Greedy for victory, he tells the lie; but later, when buffeted by compassion for the old man, he makes partial amends. He is unable to think himself through to a consistent line of action. That is not surprising, in view of his youth, but education is supposed to lift young people out of their youth, to give them, as early as possible, the maturity to negotiate moral difficulties.

Insisting on Solid Grounds When Reasons Are Enough

In philosophy courses, we often teach people that you can't make an ethical decision and defend it unless you have solid grounds to back it up. In doing this we are undermining our students' commitment to ethics. Our bad teaching in this area goes back to a misunderstanding of Socrates.

Socrates challenges a man named Euthyphro to state the principle behind an ethical decision he has made, and then Socrates refutes every principle Euthyphro offers. What then? Should the man do nothing until he can answer Socrates? No. Euthyphro suffers from ethical hubris; he thinks he knows how to teach people how to live well. The import of Socrates' inquisition of Euthyphro is that he should stop *teaching* ethics with such unreflecting confidence, not that he should stop trying to be ethical.

Suppose we can't find solid ground for ethics. We still will not have the option of doing nothing. Then why not do the easy thing, the thing that is most profitable? Out of one mouth, we teach students they must have solid ground for ethnics, and out of the other mouth we pull the ground out from under them. How can this push and pull do anything but make ethical failure come more easily? [6] We should not teach this way.

A Socrates can make any ground for honesty seem shaky; it's not hard to invent a case in which dishonesty might be a good ethical choice. But that does not entail that we have no reasons for being honest. We have many reasons to be honest; most of them come down to trust and respect for others. We can appreciate these reasons without moral hubris— without thinking we have found the holy grail of solid ground for ethics.

We don't have to stand up to a philosophy teacher's questions in order to make good decisions. But we do need to learn how to reason our way through a moral dilemma toward a result that does the least moral damage to us and those around us.

Quantitative Measures

In the American war in Vietnam (where I served) we used to count bodies killed; in education we are supposed to count scores on tests, graduation rates, and so forth; in business we measure shareholder equity. Such practices are attractive because they appear to provide objective measures for achieving our goals. But they generate two kinds of hazard.

First, an emphasis on numbers can distort our goals. Our true goal in Vietnam was to provide enough security for the people that democracy could grow. Piling up Vietnamese bodies was not our goal; worse, the body count led to a kind of combat that violated the ethics of war. Body counts do not win a war, and the way to high counts is rarely an ethical one. Test scores do not measure education, and the way to high scores may damage young children. As for shareholder equity, one day's numbers may not reflect long-term health in a business, and the quest for high numbers may lead to shady practices such as false accounting.

Second, even if managers choose numbers that truly represent their goals, they can introduce moral hazards to employees. If they charge employees with raising the numbers and apply pressure, the pressure to raise the numbers can overwhelm their employees' commitment to honesty. Managers need to look for better ways than simple numbers for assessing employees' commitment to the success of an enterprise.

We teach people that numbers represent objective values. But this is a lie: Numbers and values are rarely in alignment. In teaching people to follow the numbers, we are teaching ethical failure.

Bad Leadership from the Podium

We teach ethical failure by setting bad examples. Professors may treat students shabbily. They may lie from the podium. They may create assignments that invite ethical failure. A too-long term paper assignment invites plagiarism. A badly designed test invites cheating. A famous recent case involved a take-home exam at Harvard, on which students were forbidden to collaborate in any way. Of course, many of them did discuss the questions with friends, and they were convicted of cheating. What a stupid assignment! Students should be encouraged to collaborate on take-home assignments; that is how they learn best. The professor in this case created a serious and unnecessary moral hazard for his students. I don't deny that they did wrong, but I do insist this is partly the professor's fault.[7]

Leaders—and that includes professors—have a duty to protect their followers from moral hazards. Ethical failure is a complex phenomenon. Don't blame it simply on individual weaknesses. Look at our systems, the boundaries they create, and the way in which poor leadership—like that of Odysseus in my example—can bring young people into trouble.

TURNING OUR BACKS ON VALUES: THE GORGIAS SYNDROME

> People should use the art of persuasion like any other competitive skill, Socrates. They shouldn't use other competitive skills against everyone; they don't learn how to box or wrestle or fight in armor so they can beat up friends and enemies alike. Learning to fight is no reason to punch or stab or kill your own friends. Suppose someone spends a lot of time at the gym, builds up his body, and becomes an expert boxer. Then, if he punches his father or mother or some other relative or friend, that's no reason to hate the trainers or fight-teachers, or exile them from the city.
>
> —Gorgias, teacher of rhetoric, in Plato, *Gorgias* 456c7–e2[8]

Popular feeling ran against teachers of rhetoric in ancient Athens. Gorgias taught his students to win arguments, but he did not teach them which arguments they ought to win. A guilty man could take the course Gorgias taught, plead his case in court, and get off scot-free, while an innocent man who could not afford a course in rhetoric might be convicted of a crime he never committed. So there was a movement to drive such teachers out of town.

"Unfair," said Gorgias. It is not the fault of the teachers if their students use their lessons unethically. The boxing coach teaches boxing, not ethics; don't blame the coach if the athlete does not know whom to punch. Challenged on this, Gorgias says that, if necessary, he would teach his students about right and wrong. But he says this reluctantly, and two of his followers take the opposite tack. Right and wrong don't matter, they argue, so long as you win.

And that is precisely what his followers have learned from Gorgias. Gorgias taught them to win and declined to discuss values with them. What they learned from him, then, is just this: Winning is all that matters, since that is all that our great teacher teaches. Gorgias tried to turn his back on values, and look at the result—he did teach values in spite of himself, and they were odious, inverted values. His students (as we see in the later parts of the dialogue) emerged with their values upside down. Gorgias thought he was doing no harm, teaching people how to win arguments. But by making that the only thing he taught, he was teaching them that winning is what matters.

Do we find this in the modern university? Aren't there many professors who teach, say, marketing, but decline to teach ethics, because it is not their field, and because they believe students should have learned ethics at home or through their religion before they came to college?

Many professors try to turn their backs on values, and many departments decline to hire faculty members to teach practical ethics. That is because practical ethics teachers do not boost the rankings of departments (not even philosophy departments). Also, many departments hire only such faculty members who do quantitative research, and ethics (as we have just seen) is not to be done by the numbers. But teachers cannot really turn their backs on values. Like Gorgias, they are all teaching some values to their students, whether they know it or not. Every teacher teaches ethics.

NOT BELIEVING IN WHAT WE TEACH

A good example of a bad attitude:

> Philosophy, even the philosophy of human values—and for that matter the search after knowledge and understanding in general—needs practical justification like a fish needs a bicycle. In fact, of the various things that tell us apart from other apes, the ability and inclination to pursue non-practical interests is one of the truly priceless.[9]

The philosopher who said this, Nomy Arpaly, is admirable in many ways, but she is wrong about this. How can we honestly encourage our students to learn a subject when we do not think it has value for their lives? I believe we must be prepared to show students why we think the material we teach will be of value to them. Perhaps I disagree with Arpaly over the word "practical," and if we talked this through, we would find a point of agreement. I suspect that her "non-practical" is meant to cover the fine arts; but as these are necessary to a fully human life I would argue that they are eminently practical—and I would take the trouble to show why they are practical.[10]

Take the play by Sophocles that I have quoted in this chapter. I could shoot this play up to a high level in the ivory tower and teach it with an emphasis on the poet's later metrical style. I could use it as a window on ancient Athens' cultural history. I could ask students to study how the play fits Aristotle's criteria for a good tragic poem. These are all worthy things to teach, and they may be practical for certain purposes.

Whatever else I find to teach in this play, however, I can teach the play in a way that touches students' lives. Using Sophocles' safe example, we can discuss ethical failure without doing detailed case studies of Volkswagen or Enron or NASA's O-ring disaster. We can consider the temptations that a very young person might face and the issues that must be considered.

So it is with all the great books I have mentioned so far in my chapters. I could leave them swinging high in the ivory tower or bring them down to Earth. I can still teach Sophocles' metrical strategies because they are beautiful, and they make the play sing and come to life. But I should go beyond that and let the students into the life of the play, so that it may have some value for theirs.

Everything we teach should be brought to Earth.

NOTES

1. Sophocles 2007, 193, lines 79–85. The *Philoctetes* was written near the end of Sophocles' life, in the late fifth century BCE, as Athens was stumbling toward its famous defeat by Sparta.

2. The play's plot is complicated. The young man does tell a whopper of a lie, then tries to correct part of it, then seems to slip back. In the end, the audience may not be sure how far he has been corrupted by his teacher.
3. Geach 1977, 17.
4. Saki 1958, 293. Saki (H. H. Munro, 1870–1916) was an English writer of trenchantly satirical short stories. Enlisting in World War I, he refused a commission and served in the ranks, though he was too old to be drafted. He was killed by an enemy sniper.
5. See Chapter 8, "Facing Complexity: Leadership and Lying."
6. The way Socrates asks the question seems to imply that we can come to know a procedure for resolving ethical problems without regret, but Socrates does not believe such knowledge is possible (Woodruff 2018). Later, Plato seems to have realized some of the danger associated with Socratic teaching. Some of the young men who clustered around Socrates may have felt that he pulled the ethical ground from under them and gone wrong as a result; certainly some of them went wrong, (*Republic*, Book 7, 487a–d, 1992 161).
7. On moral hazards, see Woodruff 2014, 207–211. On the Harvard case, see Pérez-Peña 2013 and Clarida and Fandos 2013.
8. My translation. For the context, see Plato 1987, 15.
9. Nomy Arpaly, in Wolf 2010, 85.
10. As I have done for the art of theater in Woodruff 2008.

WORKS CITED

Clarida, Matthew Q., and Fandos, Nicholas P. (2013, September 18). "Matthew Platt, Instructor at Center of Cheating Scandal, Now Off the Tenure Track." *Harvard Crimson.*

Geach, Peter (1977). *The Virtues: The Stanton Lectures 1973–4.* Cambridge, UK: Cambridge University Press.

Pérez-Peña, Richard (2013, February 1). "Students Disciplined in Harvard Scandal." *New York Times.*

Plato (1987). *Gorgias.* Trans. Donald J. Zeyl. Indianapolis: Hackett Publishing Company, Inc.

Plato (1992). *Republic.* Trans. G. M. A. Grube, rev. C. D. C. Reeve. Indianapolis: Hackett Publishing Company, Inc.

Saki [H. H. Munro] (1958). *The Short Stories of Saki.* New York: The Modern Library.

Sophocles (2007). *Four Tragedies.* Trans. Peter Meineck and Paul Woodruff. Indianapolis: Hackett Publishing Company, Inc.

Wolf, Susan (2010). *Meaning in Life and Why It Matters.* Princeton, NJ: Princeton University Press.

Woodruff, Paul (2008). *The Necessity of Theater: The Art of Watching and Being Watched.* New York: Oxford University Press.

Woodruff, Paul (2014). *Reverence: Renewing a Forgotten Virtue.* 2nd ed. New York: Oxford University Press.

Woodruff, Paul (2018). "Wrong Turns in the *Euthyphro*." *Apeiron.* Forthcoming.

Chapter 16

A Campus Revolution

WHAT WE LEARN

How many students now read history with a view to leadership? How many are allowed time to ponder the moral dilemmas of leadership? The nature of courage? The challenge of human wisdom? Very few. And there will be even fewer if the self-styled reformers of higher education have their way. They want students to learn skills that have a market value, and so do too many parents. Human values—the values we prize in leaders and followers—are all too easily left behind.

In the central section of this book I touched on the questions future leaders should be thinking about while in college. I gave reasons why leaders should think about how to confront evil, how to face danger, and how to cultivate the moral beauty that makes a leader magnetic—to say nothing of their need to know how to listen well and communicate powerfully. Where in our curriculum do these elements of leadership belong? They have some place in every course, in every program, and in every student–teacher interaction. That is because every teacher models leadership and should consciously try to do that well.

Humanities courses, in particular, should focus on one or more of the elements of leadership. Part II of this book was a sustained argument that studying the humanities is essential preparation for leadership.[1] We are human, and we need to understand what it is to be human if we are to lead each other well. But how much of our current curriculum in the humanities actually helps us understand the human predicament? Not a history of facts and figures, not analysis of literature in accordance with the latest literary theory, not abstract work on the foundations of ethics. We need to put more time into studying the humanities with a view to leadership. And the same goes for the social sciences. In ethics, we need to look into a marriage of philosophy with psychology, with the aim of learning how to address the real causes of ethical failure.[2]

We need a revolution in *what* we learn and teach. We also need a revolution in *how* we teach and learn.

HOW WE LEARN

Leaders are creative and independent. Are we teaching in ways that promote those values? Much of what we do now in the classroom inhibits the growth of leaders. High school and college classes often promote the reverse of leadership—silence, craven obedience, conformism. They do this in order to teach skills and knowledge—the sort of thing that is easily measured by multiple-choice tests—as efficiently as possible. They want to generate as many students as possible with credentials—with certificates and degrees. But credentials earned that way have little to do with leadership. In fact, they may undermine it by training students to be blindly obedient to authority. Leadership requires independence and creativity. It also requires something I will call "followership." If you know how to lead, you also know how to follow. The difference between followership and obedience is crucial. How is that to be learned?

When we see that something important is missing from the curriculum, our first thought is to add a requirement. Are you worried about the ethics of our business graduates? Then make the next generation of students take an ethics course. Do you find that medical school graduates lack empathy? Throw in a required course on empathy. Do employers complain that our graduates write poorly? Then require more writing courses. Are you hoping our graduates will emerge as leaders? Make them take courses on leadership—as many courses as they need.

That approach does not work. Take writing, for example. We know that a course on writing does not make students better writers. To become a better writer, you need to change yourself fundamentally, and it takes a lot of courses, spread out over the years, to do this. One course in trigonometry may suffice to prepare you for calculus, but one course in writing will not change you in the way you need to be changed.

The same goes for leadership. Subjects like ethics, empathy, and leadership—these are not skills like trig or topics like U.S. history. These are about growing into a certain kind of person. A few courses are not enough to help you grow into a different kind of person. That is especially true if other courses are pushing you in a different direction.

Now consider empathy. Whatever we tell medical students about empathy, once they start following doctors on clinical rounds, they will learn that efficiency and time management take precedence over empathy. Medical schools in fact have a hidden curriculum—they teach things that undermine empathy without knowing that they are doing it. To make matters worse, empathy comes in several forms, some of which can be destructive to medical professionals. Maintaining healthy empathy is difficult.[3]

Or consider ethics. If 90% of courses in a given business school hammer home the message that nothing matters more than shareholder equity, those schools will eviscerate whatever good was done in their three-hour ethics courses—or in few days of ethics reserved in each course for the last blow-off week of the semester.

And now, consider leadership. At military academies, leadership is emphasized from the first day of the first-year summer program, and so is followership. The whole four-year program reinforces these, and the result is that graduates of the military academies are changed in ways that make them more promising as leaders. Of course there too we find hidden curricula in military instruction—methods of teaching that give incentives for cheating, gender attitudes that wink at sexual abuse, a "don't rock the boat" culture that silences complaints, and a commitment to success in all things that promotes dishonest reporting. But the leadership and ethics programs at the academies do provide a serious counterweight to the hidden curricula.

In civilian colleges, we do not have the options that military academies have (outside of the ROTC programs). Military academies require experience in leading and following out of the classroom during all four years. At most, civilian schools as they are now could require a semester's internship with an outside organization, but we cannot be sure that even such an internship would be a leadership experience.

So I am calling for a campus revolution both in the classroom and outside it. The inside classroom revolution would have two consequences: first, students would benefit from leadership experience in most of their courses, and, second, courses on material relevant to leadership would be conducted in practical ways. Meanwhile, the outside revolution would radically expand opportunities for students to practice leadership in sports, religious associations, and other activities.

We have many books on how to teach better, on how to use technology, and on how to help students succeed academically. This has not been one of those books. I am asking only one question: Suppose we agreed that one of our goals was to make each classroom a fertile patch in the garden of leaders. How would that change what we do, both students and teachers?

Here are six recommendations. They apply to every kind of school of higher education, whether large or small, technical or liberal arts, vocational or ivory tower.

FIRST, AGREE ON GOALS

The classroom is an opportunity for leadership. Good teachers show leadership when they induce students to learn more than they have to. Students also can show leadership in the classroom, if they have the chance, but they rarely do. In most courses, professors and students bring different goals to the classroom, and these can be incompatible. Ideally, students and teachers will be aiming for the same goals.

Whatever else we do, we must recognize the hidden curricula in our programs. If they are compatible with our goals, reinforce them. If not, confront them and try to change. The style of most high school and college teaching is inimical to leadership. We train students to sit passively in class and to accept the teaching objectives of their professors without a murmur. We habituate them to giving professors what professors want on assignments, whether students see the value in this or not. We encourage conformity of the mind.

As one recent author has pointed out, colleges seem to aim at graduating herds of excellent sheep.[4] The people involved do not want that result, so why do they unconsciously promote it? Many professors do not pay attention to independence, and so they keep on teaching in authoritarian ways that have the undesired result. And it's easy: Passivity on the part of students is easier for students and professors alike.

Keats wrote of his feeling of wonder on first reading Chapman's Homer, in a poem I quote below. To ask students to be like Keats and discover something as wonderful as Keats did on their own is to give them a challenge that is often painful. Discovery methods of teaching are not new, but they have not caught on because they are difficult. Students would rather be taught than challenged to discover on their own.

Still, the winds of change are blowing on campus these days. The inverted classroom seeks to put an end to passivity in the classroom. Research initiatives for undergraduates have already shown that they can change lives—drawing students into a new eagerness to learn. If the only goal were learning, we might stop there. But leadership is also a goal. Leaders are independent. Remember how obedient Billy Budd was, and how his obedience was a fatal flaw?

We need to set a goal of promoting followership in place of obedience. A good follower keeps an open, questioning mind and is prepared to step up into a leadership role at any time. How can we promote this best in a classroom?

SECOND, RECOGNIZE THAT EVERY TEACHER TEACHES ETHICS

Most teachers don't know it, but every teacher teaches ethics. Some of them, as we have seen, teach ethical failure. But the best teach leadership by being exemplary leaders in the classroom. Most of us with teaching jobs do not realize we are teaching ethics and leadership. "Not me," you might say. "I teach math." Or "I teach Beowulf. That's my subject. I was not trained to teach ethics. I did not take this job to teach ethics. I don't believe ethics can be taught anyway. I insist on teaching only the subject I signed on to teach: Beowulf."

If you say this, you are fooling yourself. Every time you deal with a student, you are setting an example. Remember: They are young and impressionable, not fully formed in character. Your influence is more powerful than you may know. Ask college graduates, after twenty years, what they remember from their most memorable teachers. They will not tell you they remember how to do differential equations, and they will not recall the causes of the Peloponnesian War. Instead, they will tell you how a teacher treated them: "He terrified me." "She opened my mind." "He bored me to tears." "She would not listen to my excuse." "He was kind when my mother was taken ill." Watching a teacher, students learn by example how to treat people who are under their power.

Good treatment starts with respect, all you professors. *Don't call your students kids!* Don't even think of them that way. They are adults, albeit young ones. Your job is to help them think of themselves as having all the powers of adults. After all, they are old enough to make babies or serve in the military. Joan of Arc was old enough to lead an army to victory as a teenager. Washington was a surveyor at seventeen. Leaders always treat followers like grownups, no matter how young they are.

So once we set leadership as a goal in the classroom, professors had better pay attention to the examples they set. And students should look critically at those examples. They may learn how to be leaders from a professorial example, but they may also learn how *not* to be, by observing the effect of a bad professor on their classmates.

THIRD, STOP TEACHING

To his dying day, Socrates denied he was a teacher. He told the people of Athens that he didn't know enough to teach, but who would believe him? They thought he lied. They convicted him of corrupting the youth of Athens and sent him to his death. Not believing his denial, they were right to convict him, in principle, as Socrates himself recognized: if he had been guilty of teaching he should have been punished. Teaching is harmful to students. It corrupts them by eating away at their independence. To make students objects of the verb "to teach" is to put them in a passive position. Something is being thrust upon them. But students at college are just beginning to revel in the freedom of adulthood. They know how to resist the abuse we call teaching; they will come out of the experience unscathed if they can, free from any change unless they have decided to make it themselves.

That is why Socrates did not teach. He asked questions and refused to take responsibility for answering them. Young people hung around him, but how they turned out was their affair, not his. He claimed that he was looking for a teacher himself. Maybe, just maybe (he seemed to hope), someone would turn up in Athens with godlike wisdom—someone who could teach Socrates and others how to live. If he could find such a teacher, he would gladly become a passive student. But he never found such a one. In the absence of a divine teacher, each one of us, like Socrates, must do the best we can—learning without being taught.

Lectures have never been a good way to teach. Iconic teachers such as Socrates and Confucius avoided lecturing. Lectures put students in a passive position—for a short time. Soon their active minds will be off on some other topic, social life or sex, while the professor drones on. Technology gives us alternatives to straight lecturing, but there have always been ways for students' minds to stay active and focused on the subject at hand.

When teaching does go on, the one who learns the most is usually the teacher. So, since we want students to learn, let them take over and do some teaching. Since they are the ones who need to learn, and one learns a subject best by teaching it, students should do the lion's share of teaching.[5] Then they will do the learning, in your place.

That is the revolution.

On any subject, students can be organized into teams of three to five, with missions to solve problems, help each other learn, conduct research, present results to the larger class, engage in debates with other teams, and so on. Leadership in the team can rotate, so that everyone has a chance to lead as well as to follow. Professors and teaching assistants can help, and course design can give strong incentives for full-hearted participation in teams. Technology can help but isn't necessary. Teams can have meetings that are face to face or virtual, as they prefer. In online courses, teams can still function, although I would expect them to have better meetings over pizza or lattes or beer than over the Internet.

Having students engage in research has good results, whether done by individuals or teams. But teamwork allows for the experience of following and leading. Science has the advantage here over the humanities. Most scientific research is done by teams; in contrast, the humanities have a sad record of sending individuals off to do research in lonely isolation. But the humanities need not be like that: Students and faculty can work in teams in the humanities—and more effectively than as lonely individuals.[6]

If every course set students to leading and following in teams, then every course would be an experiential course in leadership. Teaching people about leadership will never make them leaders by itself. Leaders grow on ground where they can gain experience. That ground could be a course in math or philosophy or history if it is well designed. In fact, every course we offer could be ground for growing leaders through experience.

We should aim for that.

FOURTH, HAVE STUDENTS HIRE ATHLETIC COACHES

The new track coach knows what's best for her high-school team. She is a sprinter, and she will give them all drills to increase their speed—and nothing else. The milers and half-milers complain: "Our old coach gave us workouts to increase our fitness. Can't we do that kind of workout as well?" These runners had been very successful in the past, winning high honors for the school. They know a lot about their sport. But the new coach knows how to respond when anyone challenges her authority: "No. You will do the workouts I prescribe, and you will do them precisely as I prescribe them."

The team buckles down to her regimen, grumbling. At the first meet the distance runners are smoked by the competition. They go out fast, but they soon fade. And, of course, they blame the coach for not training them as they had asked. The coach, of course, blames them, for not working hard enough. Reluctantly, the star distance runners quit, and the team's prospects are diminished.

When I ask college freshmen to write about their experiences of tyrannical behavior, such stories are all too common. Tyrant coaches abound in high schools and colleges. They leave little room for students to develop independence or leadership. Yes, they choose someone to be captain of a team, but they are afraid to give the captain any real authority.

The first thing is to fire all the coaches at the college level. They are expensive and harmful. They undermine the spirit of sport. They are hired more to win victories than to educate students through sport. Fire them all. By the time they reach college age, most student athletes know enough to coach each other effectively, and they are old enough not to be treated like children by highly paid father and mother figures.

This is not an outrageous suggestion. Many campuses today have club sports—sports that are not heavily financed by the college or university—such sports as lacrosse, wrestling, rowing, men's soccer, or rugby. In such cases, the club is organized by the student members of the team. They may, if they wish, hire a coach whom they choose. They will generally follow the coach they have hired (just as we generally follow the advice of financial experts we hire). But if coaches for a club are incompetent or tyrannical, students can fire them. And because the students are free not to follow their coaches' advice, the coaches must serve as leaders rather than tyrants.

With that done, strongly encourage students to engage in club sports. Find incentives for them to do so. In the clubs they will have great opportunities for following and leading.

FIFTH, GIVE STUDENTS TIME TO LEARN OUTSIDE THE CLASSROOM

This plea I address to the housekeepers, the administration: Please, please give students time and opportunity to grow outside class. Never forget that they can learn more about leadership outside class than in it. A healthy campus is a hothouse for leadership.

Club sports take time. So do prayer groups, theater troupes, a capella singing groups, student newspapers, and student government. All these things take time, but that time is well spent.

A former student of mine is now a successful entrepreneur. In his second year he launched a newspaper for students in his program (this was in the age of print media). He had many obstacles to overcome—funding, printing, corralling good writers. But years later he told me: "That is how I learned what I could do."

Higher education these days, though, is beset by enemies who think about nothing but the efficient generation of young people with credentials. They want to expedite student progress toward degrees in every possible way, shortening the time to complete degrees and giving college-level credit for high-school work. High-school students may be mature enough to master college-level skills and knowledge, but I do not think they are mature enough to take advantage of the leadership opportunities on a college campus.

Credentials without experience are not enough. We need to give students course loads that are relaxed enough that they can be active outside the classroom. Residential universities and colleges can provide extraordinary leadership experiences. In three years or less a young student can emerge as the leader of a powerful student organization. The value in experience for a student body president is obvious, but there is only one of those at a time; so what of all the other students? They too, on a healthy campus, may have experiences that form them as leaders.

Three students suffice to start a new organization in which they will experience independent leadership. This experience will be even better than what we can offer in a classroom, because it is unsupervised by older people, and because students may create something new and wonderful through it—something no older person might have imagined. Starting an organization may be more valuable than rising to the top of an old one. The founders of student clubs are on their way to becoming entrepreneurs.

A virtual campus may come to present the same opportunities, but I do not believe we have seen that yet. I remain agnostic about the virtual campus. For now, a brick-and-mortar campus plainly provides the best ground for leaders. Can you imagine turning West Point into a virtual campus? No uniforms? No drill? No face-to-face teamwork? I am trying to imagine it, but I have not yet succeeded.[7]

One common leadership opportunity calls for a special note. On most campuses there are fraternities and sororities—Greek-letter organizations. (Please respect our friends who are Greek by origin. There is nothing Greek about these groups aside from the letters they use in their names, and ethnic Greeks are not unreasonably offended by hearing them called "Greek.") Greek-letter organizations are touted as giving students opportunities to grow into leadership; they are often the source for officers in student government. Do they belong in the garden of leaders? The matter is controversial.

I see two problems with Greek-letter societies. First, these groups are segregated by sex and often by race. Practicing leadership in such an environment will not prepare students for the leadership they should provide in the real world, where such segregation is illegal. Administrators should consider banning all groups that segregate by sex or race.

Second, these groups have been known to develop cultures that are far distant from their stated ideals, as documented in a recent book, *True Gentlemen: The Broken Pledge of America's Fraternities.*[8] Leadership requires allegiance to values, as we have seen in earlier chapters. If a group practices hypocrisy on a massive scale, its members cannot be practicing genuine leadership. Whether these groups can be reformed is an open question. But if they remain like the ones described in *True Gentlemen,* their claims about producing leaders are bogus.

SIXTH, TRUST STUDENTS

Young people can be trusted to make good decisions, to teach each other, to work well in teams, to start new organizations, to lead old organizations, to change a campus for the better. They can even be trusted to offer the truth when they make excuses. Well-designed assignments rarely lead to cheating. Ask your students to pledge academic honesty on their papers. Explain the value of academic honesty: We have good reasons for wanting to know where words and information come from. In my experience most students are trustworthy, and they improve for being trusted. The first five recommendations can be summed up in this one: Trust students.

AND, LAST, A PLEA TO PARENTS

Students who live on campus are more engaged, both in their studies and in campus life, than students who live at home. Parents, you need to let your children go and become adults. Don't hover. Don't come to campus to do their laundry for them. Don't check up on their timeliness in doing assignments. Don't ask to know their grades on papers and tests. They need to take responsibility for managing their lives on campus. And, in order to take responsibility, they need the freedom to screw up; that experience too is part of growing into leadership. I have seen too many college students infantilized by parents.

And (if you can afford it) give them time—time to explore and find their passions, time to engage with each other outside class. Time to be leaders.

DISCOVERY

> Then felt I like some watcher of the skies
> When a new planet swims into his ken;   *10*
> Or like stout Cortez, when with eagle eyes
> He stared at the Pacific—and all his men
> Look'd at each other with a wild surmise—
> Silent, upon a peak in Darien.
>   —From Keats, "On First Looking Into Chapman's Homer"

Only a few men were among the first from Europe to stare at the Pacific. But anyone can stumble on a great poet for the first time and feel—as Keats felt—the thrill of a great discovery. When you do make a discovery—when you stare at something new with your own eyes—you become a new person, because you now have something new in your mind, and your thrill in discovering it has made it indelible. That's learning. "Stout Cortez" (the poet should have said "Balboa") will never forget the Pacific, and Keats will never forget what he found in Homer. That's learning.

Keats found his way to Chapman's Homer by himself. No one required him to read Chapman. No one made him sit quietly in class, submit assignments on time, or show due deference to elderly professors. He took himself to Chapman's Homer, and led the way for others by writing this sonnet, which is so beautiful in itself that it is hard to forget. From the first time I heard it, at age seven, I have been unable to get these last six lines out of my mind. That's learning. Can we—students, professors, parents, and all—make all learning feel like an exciting discovery? If we did, then students would have the thrill of independence in every class. And wouldn't that make our campus a more fertile garden of leaders?

NOTES

1. See Appendix A, "Humanities and the Soul of Leadership."
2. A good example of this approach is the series of videos in "Ethics Unwrapped" at the University of Texas at Austin, developed by Cara Biasucci and Robert Prentice (http://ethicsunwrapped.utexas.edu).
3. Research now distinguishes between the kind of empathy that causes distress and the kind that leads to compassionate understanding. Medical professionals and others who face human suffering are vulnerable to empathic distress, which they must learn to prevent. But they may still be open to compassionate understanding. See Singer and Klimecki 2014.
4. Deresiewicz 2015.
5. See Appendix C for details of a course that follows this model.
6. Every team needs clear goals, and these may be given in humanities courses. See Appendix C for an example of such a course, along with a rubric for students' self-evaluation on leadership.
7. On the virtual campus issue, see Chapter 1, note 11.
8. Hechinger 2017.

WORKS CITED

Deresiewicz, William (2015). *Excellent Sheep: The Miseducation of the American Elite and the Way to a Meaningful Life*. New York: Free Press.

Hechinger, John (2017). *True Gentlemen: The Broken Promise of America's Fraternities*. New York: Hachette Book Group.

Keats, John (1951). *The Complete Poetry and Selected Prose of John Keats*. Ed. Harold Edgar Biggs. New York: The Modern Library.

Singer, Tania and Klimecki, Olga M. (2014). "Empathy and Compassion." *Current Biology* 24.

Summary of Recommendations for Change

We have choices. There is no one best way to work toward any of the goals on which we agree. Future leaders don't even need formal education, as the example of self-educated giants such as Abraham Lincoln makes clear. That is why I have centered the book on goals, and the few recommendations I make are general. I assume that readers from institutions of higher learning will know of particular ways to implement these goals in their particular schools. The arguments to support these recommendations are in the body of the book.

I make three kinds of recommendations for change in higher education—for curriculum, for teaching methods, and for co-curricular activities. I propose these for every kind of college or university—two-year colleges, four-year colleges, universities, and technical institutes. The recommendations apply to students in every major, whether it be nursing, business, violin, classics, engineering, or molecular biology. They apply to brick-and-mortar schools as well as to ones that offer online education.

First, curriculum. This takes up the bulk of the book, Chapters 5 through 13, because of its importance and its complexity. All students, regardless of major, need a general education that includes subjects and skills that are valuable for leaders. Communication skills are essential. Ideally, all students should have at least one course that requires good writing, good listening, and good speaking in each year of their studies. Such courses can be taught across the curriculum. In addition, all students should be exposed to history, literature, social science, and ethics. This material must be taught in such a way that students can see how it applies to their lives. A purely academic approach is wasted on most of them.

To make room for such a curriculum, some disciplines may have to reduce their requirements for majors. Most disciplines find it easier to add requirements than to delete them. In the fine arts, for example, conservatory-trained oboe teachers may be reluctant to make room for a course in Asian studies, but they need to recognize that they produce more graduates in oboe than there are positions, and many of their students will need to make their way outside music. In technical fields, as knowledge grows, departments make their requirements so heavy that they may leave no time for electives. That is a mistake. Technical faculty need to recognize two important truths: First, their graduates will learn most of what they need for their careers in the labs they join or the jobs they take after graduation, and, second, many of their graduates will grow into leadership positions in science or technology, and some will find work outside of that sphere altogether. An undergraduate major should prepare students for lifelong learning in the field; it does not need to teach students everything they will need to know later on. Once faculty members realize that, they should be willing to make more space for the skills and knowledge that will help their students grow into leaders.

To offer such a curriculum, we in the liberal arts need to make sure that we hire into the faculty people who can teach such material and make it relevant to our students. That may change hiring priorities for departments that put research first.

Second, teaching methods. I assume that my readers who are on the faculty in various disciplines will know more than I about how to teach their subjects. This is not a book on teaching technique, as that would have to be discipline-specific. What I most want to do here is to urge all teachers to keep the goals I discuss in mind as they enter the classroom. Above all, that means that teachers should realize that they are teaching leadership by the examples they give through their behavior as teachers. This is as true of an engineering whiz as of a virtuoso violinist or a groundbreaking scholar in classics. Being an ace in your field is not enough: You need to be a leader as well. Professors, keep asking yourselves whether you want your students to lead others in the way you are leading them.

I discuss teaching generally in Chapters 14 through 16. I have one specific recommendation: More and more courses in all fields are now emphasizing teamwork. This is especially true in business and engineering, but the use of teams is growing even in the humanities. It should grow. If you assign teamwork in your courses, keep in mind that wherever there is a team there are leadership issues, which you should address. The military has gotten many things wrong in the area of leadership, in my view, because it is so authoritarian. But it got one thing right: Leadership and followership are learned in the same way and at the same time, through working on teams that have rotating leaders who are made conscious of their roles as leaders.

I use teams in many of my courses in philosophy and literature. I assign leaders in each team, on a rotating basis, so that everyone does some leading—running meetings, face to face or virtually, and completing meaningful projects in competition with other teams. I give detailed examples in Appendix C.

I urge faculty members to use teams for learning the material of their courses and, at the same time, to give practice in leadership—for any subject whatever. Student teams may seem most appropriate for engineering or business courses, but I have found that they work for philosophy as well.

Third, co-curricular activities. We all need to recognize the value of what students do outside the classroom and to encourage them to try their wings in starting new organizations or leading old ones. The scope for this is larger on four-year residential campuses, but there is scope for such activity as well on a two-year campus and even on a virtual campus. Education should never be limited to the classroom or the online course.

This principle requires more than lip service. We need to make sure students are not so heavily loaded with requirements that they have no time outside the classroom. And we should not try to force students to slash the time it takes them to complete a degree. Varsity teams with professional coaches should be replaced, wherever possible, by club teams led by students who hire their own coaches. Student organizations that discriminate by race or sex (such as many Greek-letter groups, fraternities and sororities) should be phased out; students need opportunities to practice leadership in inclusive communities.

APPENDICES

APPENDICES

Humanities and the Soul of Leadership

This book began as a thought experiment about Billy Budd: What were his most serious gaps in education? It did not begin as a defense of the humanities, but I should not have been surprised by the large role they play here. Billy's main weakness is his inability to understand the human world in which he has been dropped. Leaders understand human beings and the human situation with heartfelt feeling (not just in an abstract way). And leaders communicate well. All of that belongs to the humanities.

Nevertheless, this is not a book about the humanities or the liberal arts. Much has already been written about the value of these studies for leadership. This appendix is a gesture toward the existing literature, which is too wide for me to summarize here. Interested readers should read all the articles in Wren et al. (2009) and explore the other works cited at the end of this appendix.

To start them off, here is a set of recent quotations:

The most important set of understandings that I bring to [my] position of citizen, the most important stuff I've learned I think I've learned from novels. It has to do with empathy. It has to do with the notion that the world is complicated and full of grays, but there's still truth to be found, and you have to strive for that and work for that. And the notion that it is possible to connect with some[one] else even though they are very different from you. (President Barack Obama[1])

The central virtue of a liberal education is that it teaches you how to write, and writing makes you think. (Zakaria 2015, 72)

The second great advantage of a liberal education is that it teaches you how to speak. (Zakaria 2015, 75)

The third great strength of a liberal education: It teaches you how to learn. (Zakaria 2015, 78)

Liberal arts colleges, graduate schools in the arts and sciences, and other professional schools could, in principle, perform the same functions as the business schools. Indeed, many increasingly do. (Stewart 2009, 301)

Management theory, in fact, is already a branch of the humanities—it just may not know it yet. (Stewart 2009, 302)

A good manager is someone . . . in short, who understands oneself and the world around us well enough to know how to make it better. By this definition, of course, a good manager is nothing more or less than a good and well-educated person. (Stewart 2009, 303)[2]

It is in Apple's DNA that technology alone is not enough. It's technology married with liberal arts, married with humanities, that yields us the result that makes our hearts sing. (Steve Jobs,[3] quoted in Zakaria 2015, 82)

Facebook is "as much psychology and sociology as it is technology." (Mark Zuckerberg, quoted in Zakaria 2015, 181, note to p. 83)

Get a liberal arts degree. In my experience, a liberal arts degree is the most important factor in forming individuals into interesting and interested people who can determine their own paths through the future. (Edgar Bronfman, quoted in Zakaria 2015, 90)

Poetry isn't, after all, a bully pulpit, a place to preach. It's not even a forum for sharing information. It operates in a different way, as a location where the emotions of being human can be put out, can be received. Poetry allows readers to exercise their own emotional possibilities through the words of others. (Poet Donald P. Hall)[4]

Poetry teaches the ethical nature of choice. (Hoagland 2014, 203)

These ideas have roots in antiquity. I quote here, in my translations, famous passages from ancient Rome:

Even if it were only pleasure that led you to read poetry, still I think you'd judge this turn of mind to be highly humane and genteel. Other pursuits are fit only for specific times or ages or places. But reading poetry sharpens our youth, lightens old age, adds grace to success, provides escape or solace in failure, gives delight at home, and doesn't trouble us in business. It is with us through the night, on our travels, and in the country (*pernoctant nobiscum, peregrinantur, rusticantur*). (Cicero, *Pro Archia Poeta*; 16)[5]

Only one line of study is truly liberal—the one that makes you free. And that is the pursuit of wisdom, which is sublime, powerful, generous. Other subjects are puerile and petty. (Seneca, Epistle 88 to Lucilius, *De liberalibus studiis*, 2)[6]

You ask, "Where did Ulysses go on his wandering?" You'd do better to ask how to keep ourselves on track. . . . Teach me this instead: how to love my native land, my wife, and my father [as Ulysses did], and how to keep sailing, after shipwreck, towards those noble goals. (Seneca, Epistle 88 to Lucilius, *De liberalibus studiis*, 7)

What good is it for me to know how to divide land into [mathematical] parts if I don't know I should share these with my brother? (Seneca, Epistle 88 to Lucilius, *De liberalibus studiis*, 11)

I finish with quotations from the great Karl Jaspers, who was meditating on German guilt immediately after the close of World War II (1945):

No one can morally judge another. It is only where the other seems to me like myself that the closeness reigns which in free communication can make a common cause of what finally each does in solitude. (33)

Blindness for the misfortune of others, lack of imagination of the heart, inner indifference toward the witnessed evil—that is moral guilt. (64)

Whoever has not yet found himself guilty in spontaneous self-analysis will tend to accuse his accusers. (84)

The first thing each of us needs in disaster is clarity about himself. (84)

In tracing our own guilt back to its source we come upon the human essence—which in its German form has fallen into a peculiar, terrible incurring of guilt but exists as a possibility in man as such. (94)

In inner action before the transcendent we become aware of being humanly finite and incapable of perfection. Humility comes to be our nature. (113)

Purification is the premise of our political liberty, too; for only consciousness of guilt leads to consciousness of solidarity and co-responsibility without which there can be no liberty. (114–115)

For further texts from the humanities bearing on leadership, see Samet 2015.[7]

WORKS BEARING ON THE VALUE OF LIBERAL ARTS TO LEADERSHIP

Braham, Jeannne (2007). *The Light Within the Light: Portraits of Donald Hall, Richard Wilbur, Maxine Kumin, & Stanley Kunitz*. Boston: David R. Godine.

Cicero (1923). *Pro Archia Poeta*. In Cicero in Twenty-Eight Volumes, Vol. 11. Trans. N. H. Watts. Cambridge, Massachusetts: Harvard University Press.

Grafton, Anthony, and Grossman, James (2015, Winter). "Habits of Mind: Why College Students Who Do Serious Historical Research Become Independent Analytical Thinkers." *American Scholar* 84.1, 31–47.

Gregory, Marshall (2009). *Shaped by Stories: The Ethical Power of Narratives*. Notre Dame, IN: Notre Dame University Press.

Hipps, J. Bradford (2016, May 21). "To Write Better Code, Read Virginia Woolf." *New York Times*. http://www.nytimes.com/2016/05/22/opinion/sunday/to-write-software-read-novels.html?smprod=nytcore-iphone&smid=nytcore-iphone-share.

Hoagland, Tony (2014). *Twenty Poems that Could Save America and Other Essays*. Minneapolis: Graywolf Press, 201–219.

Jaspers, Karl (1945/2001). *The Question of German Guilt*. Trans. E. B. Ashton. New York: Fordham University Press.

Landy, Joshua (2012). *How to Do Things with Fictions*. New York: Oxford University Press.

Nussbaum, Martha C. (1997). *Cultivating Humanity: A Classical Defense of Reform in Liberal Education*. Cambridge, MA: Harvard University Press.

Robinson, Marilynne. (2015, November 19). "President Obama & Marilynne Robinson: A Conversation in Iowa." *New York Review of Books*.

Samet, Elizabeth D. (2015). *Leadership: Essential Writings by Our Greatest Thinkers*. New York: W. W. Norton & Company.

Seneca (1920). *Ad Lucilium Epistulae Morales*. Vol. 2. Trans. Richard M. Gummere. New York: G. P. Putnam.

Stewart, Matthew (2009). *The Management Myth: Why the Experts Keep Getting It Wrong*. New York: W. W. Norton & Company.

Wren, J. Thomas, Riggio, Ronald E., and Genovese, Michael A. (2009). *Leadership and the Liberal Arts: Achieving the Promise of a Liberal Education*. New York: Palgrave Macmillan.

Zakaria, Fareed (2015). *In Defense of a Liberal Education*. New York: W. W. Norton & Company.

NOTES

1. Robinson 2015, 6.
2. Stewart's complete definition of a good manager includes abilities for analysis and synthesis, an eye for details and big picture, knowledge of the world and the way people work, and the capacity for respecting others.
3. See Zakaria 2015, 181n82 for source. See also Hipps 2016; coding and creative writing are judged by many of the same standards: elegance, concision, even beauty.
4. Quoted in Braham 2007, 19.
5. Cicero (106—46 BCE) was a brilliant lawyer and philosopher writing in the last days of the Roman republic. He wrote this speech in defense of the Greek poet Archias, whose claim to Roman citizenship was challenged as a result of an anti-immigrant movement in Rome. The speech, a seminal defense of the liberal arts, was delivered in 62 BC.

6. Seneca (4 BCE—65 CE) was a Stoic philosopher and a tragic poet. He served the emperor Nero, who eventually caused him to take his own life. The letters to Lucilius were written toward the end of his life, 62–63 CE.

7. Authors quoted include Shakespeare, Lincoln, Montaigne, Virgil, Machiavelli, Thucydides, Herodotus, Melville, Homer, Marcus Aurelius, Mencius, Babur, and many more.

APPENDIX B

Study Guides and Further Reading

This section is designed to help people who wish to develop courses on the material mentioned in Parts I and II. Refer to the "Works Cited" list at the end of each chapter for bibliographic information.

CHAPTER 1. ALEXANDER THE GREAT HAD ARISTOTLE

Recommendation

Choose someone you think has shown leadership and do a little research. What was this person's education? Did it help the person grow into leadership? If so, how? Famous leaders such as Washington and Lincoln are worth study, but you may learn more from reading up on leaders who are not well known or are known only to you. You may also wish to interview leaders in your own community whom you consider to be effective in the context of freedom—including student leaders. What do they think prepared them for leadership?

For Washington, the best recent work overall is Chernow. Fischer is especially good at describing Washington's way of chairing meetings, Brookhiser on Washington's reading and education. For Lincoln, I recommend Wilson and Kaplan.

Further Thinking About Leadership

The bibliography on the concept of leadership is enormous, and the definitions of "leadership" are legion. I do not recommend dipping into this literature in a first course about leadership; readers will find too many conflicting concepts labeled "leadership." Instead, I would invite students to ask themselves and each other what they look for in leaders and followers both. What sorts of behavior help them wish to follow a coach, a band director, or a student body president? What actions turn them off?

CHAPTER 2. LEADING FROM FREEDOM

Recommendation

Read Sophocles' *Antigone*, one of the most famous plays ever written. Antigone is opposed by her uncle Creon, who is the king. Like most authority figures in the real world, Creon shows leadership in some of his actions and tyrannical tendencies in others. Can you sort these out in the action of the play?

Go beyond silent reading of the play. Choose some scenes to act out with friends or in class. The debate between Creon and his son Haemon is especially valuable to act out. For a change, I have rewritten the scene as between mother and daughter. You will find the altered text of this debate at the end of this appendix.

Further Reading

History and fiction are full of vivid accounts of tyranny. The best way to start thinking about how to lead from freedom is to look at the opposite. Read up on tyrants and ask whether they would have been more effective in the long run if they had shown more leadership and allowed more freedom than they did. And if not, why not?

Whether you read up on Stalin or Lincoln, you should be asking about specific actions they took, whether those actions are tyrannical or "leaderly." If you ask whether they are, simply tyrants or leaders, you will not have understood this chapter.

You will not find many women in history who have had a chance to be tyrants or leaders, but women who have shown leadership in history are especially interesting because they have rarely had authority to fall back on. In your further reading you would do well to focus on examples of women. On women leaders, see Betty Sue Flowers.

CHAPTER 3. MESSIANIC LEADERSHIP: JOAN THE MAID

Recommendation

Read Shaw's play, *Saint Joan*. What do you think is the source of her strength? Of her weakness? Is she a good example of messianic leadership? If so, how does she illustrate the power and limitations of that kind of leader? Notice that even the king whom she crowned does not want her bought back to life. Why? Why is there such a bad fit between her and the people she tries to support? Would formal education have helped her or hindered her?

Act out all or part of the trial scene. Try it with genders reversed and see how you feel about it that way.

Further Reading

The literature on Joan is copious. The documentary evidence from the trials is fascinating, more captivating than any play. For this, see Taylor. Also helpful is Wilson-Smith. Recently we have Harrison, who brings out the messianic character of her story by telling it in parallel to the story of Jesus' capture, trial, and execution. She also makes interesting use of the plays and films that have made Joan their subject. For the historical context, read Castor—an excellent book by a professional historian.

On reverence and religious warfare, look at Chapter 1 of Woodruff (2014), and reread the famous speech by Lincoln on his second inauguration:

> Neither party expected for the war the magnitude or the duration which it has already attained. Neither anticipated that the *cause* of the conflict might cease with or even before the conflict itself should cease. Each looked for an easier triumph, and a result less fundamental and astounding. Both read the same Bible and pray to the same God, and each invokes His aid against the other. It may seem strange that any men should dare to ask a just God's assistance in wringing their bread from the sweat of other men's faces, but let us judge not, that we be not judged. The prayers of both could not be answered. That of neither has been answered fully. The Almighty has His own purposes.

CHAPTER 4. NATURAL LEADERSHIP: BILLY BUDD

Recommendation

Read *Billy Budd*. Why does Billy bless the captain who has ordered his execution? Is Billy a believable character, or do we have to think of him as a figure in a fable? Could anyone, brought up as he has been brought up, be so good in so many ways? In what ways does Billy use his influence over the crew of the ship of war?

Captain Vere and Claggart exercise authority in different ways. Does Claggart show leadership at any point? Does Vere? In what actions?

Stage a debate over clemency for Billy Budd.

Further Study

See Truffaut's 1970 film *L'Enfant sauvage* (*The Wild Child*) for a dramatic adaptation of the life of one wild child, Victor of Aveyron. Marin Kitchen tells the story of Kaspar Hauser, one wild child that Melville mentions in *Billy Budd*.

CHAPTER 5. EDUCATING BILLY

Recommendation

Read the narrative of the life of Frederick Douglass in any of its versions and ask at least these questions: How did he learn what he needed to know in order to grow into the leader he was? What can we learn about suffering from his story? What can we learn about evil from reflecting on the various people who thought they owned him?

Further Reading

On education for leadership, Ciulla et al. and Wren et al. are places to begin. On the idea that virtue grows from seedlings that are planted in us by nature, read Ivanhoe.

CHAPTER 6. FACING EVIL, LEARNING GUILE

Recommendation

Read the Melian dialogue from Thucydides, along with the debate over Mytilene. Stage debates along these lines using these stories or current events. What are the best strategies for leading people who are facing evil in others?

Further Reading

Sophocles' *Philoctetes* and the list of readings for Chapter 8. On Machiavelli, revisionist views are presented in Bobbitt and Viroli. A more conventional view is found in Skinner. On the Socratic approach to people who claim to hold immoral views, read Plato's *Gorgias*. The opening argument between Socrates and Gorgias is enough to show that Gorgias' practice is not consistent with the views that he states under questioning. Is he really committed to the value of justice, or only pretending? Let the reader decide. Our point is that although you may not be able to change Gorgias, he may be able to change himself once he becomes aware of the conflict within him.

From Rupert Brooke, "Tiare Tahiti"

> All are one in Paradise,
> You and Pupure are one,
> And Taü, and the ungainly wise.
> There the Eternals are, and there
> The Good, the Lovely, and the True,
> And Types, whose earthly copies were
> The foolish broken things we knew;
> . . .
> Snare in flowers, and kiss, and call,
> With lips that fade, and human laughter
> And faces individual,
> Well this side of Paradise! . . .
> There's little comfort in the wise.

CHAPTER 7. FACING EVIL IN OURSELVES: COMPASSION AND JUSTICE

Recommendations

Measure for Measure is a fine challenge for students to discuss. The ending poses a problem: How can anyone forgive Angelo? "Bartleby" is also good for discussion. On self-knowledge, Plato's *Apology* is essential reading. After that, almost any tragic play, ancient or modern, shows characters that do not know themselves. *A View from the Bridge* is a fine modern take by Arthur Miller on a tragic theme; so is his *Death of a Salesman. Oedipus Tyrannus* of course shows the classic failure of self-knowledge.

Further Reading

Justice and compassion are enormous subjects. On justice, the first book of Plato's *Republic* should be required reading for everyone, and today's students should know something about John Rawls' theory of justice as fairness. On compassion, Woodruff's *Ajax Dilemma* is a place to start.

CHAPTER 8. FACING COMPLEXITY: LEADERSHIP AND LYING

Here there are many options. Read and discuss a few chapters of *The Prince,* along with large sections of Bok, which is very student-friendly. Is Machiavelli right that good results excuse bad actions ("When the act accuses the result excuses"—*Discorsi* 1.9)?

Literary works that bear on this are the plays by Sartre and Camus, but I do not think these have worn well in the twenty-first century. Better, I think, is their ancestor: Molière's *Misanthrope*, about a man who tries always to tell the truth and is therefore banished from polite society. Read this in the Wilbur translation (see the "Works Cited" list in Chapter 8).

If time permits, wrestle with the philosophical problem of moral dilemmas.

Evil is perplexing to philosophers and theologians who believe that the world is governed by a beneficent power. You can explore the theological issue in the literature of your own religious tradition. As for the philosophical issue, read the *Meditations* of Marcus Aurelius in any translation. For many generations, and still today, his work has been comforting to leaders in trying situations.

CHAPTER 9. FACING FEAR, SHOWING COURAGE

Recommendation

Look for examples of quiet courage from history outside warfare. Do scientists need courage? Engineers? In what circumstances? Also consider where courage fits into the business world. What fears must corporate leaders face? Leaders in small businesses? Entrepreneurs? According to a recent article (see Jones in "Works Cited" in Chapter 9), the top five fears of CEOs are:

1. Being seen as incompetent (the "imposter syndrome")
2. Underachieving
3. Appearing too vulnerable
4. Being politically attacked by colleagues
5. Appearing foolish.

What dangers do these CEO fears pose for us? How should we prepare ourselves to face such fears?

Closer to home, ask this: Does our classroom today promote cowardice or courage? Are teachers influenced by fear? What do teachers fear? What do students fear? You would do well to ask these questions about the course you are now teaching.

Further Reading

Plato's *Laches*; Washington's Farewell Address can be found in Spalding and Gentry.

CHAPTER 10. FINDING COURAGE

Recommendations

Research: What thinkers have done the best in explaining what courage is? Could courage be a fixed trait? What does empirical science say about this?

Discussion: What does courage require of people in politics? Is there cowardice or courage in your representatives in Congress? If you think there is courage, where do you think it came from? If cowardice, is this due to lack of respect within Congress? Or is it a symptom of a wider failure of respect, or of courage, in our society?

Can you show true courage only by acting totally outside of the norms of your culture? Is it courage or a miracle to be good in an evil society? Must you feel fear in order to act with courage? My friend William Gibson, a Marine veteran with experience of extreme combat, writes me this:

> On courage, I have often taught it as you present it here. However, I have begun to wonder if the presence of fear is a necessary component. It seems to me that fear is an emotion that over time can be "burned out." What of courage then? Is it something that can also be extinguished? Combat numbness and the "two thousand yard" stare are not uncommon, yet these soldiers continue to fight resolutely. During my second tour [of combat in Vietnam], I stopped fearing death. I felt euphoric during action and a numbness thereafter but I was indifferent to death in either case (of course, I would not take foolish risks just for the hell of it). I have never regained a fear of death. As I age, the main feeling I have is exasperation at my diminished capacities. I suppose one can find other things to fear, but it seems to me that to continue with what remains as does Sisyphus is to be resolute which may or not be courage because of the absence of fear.

Suggested Readings

Aristotle, Books 2 and 3 of *Nicomachean Ethics*; Conrad's *Lord Jim* (only if there is time to read the whole book); Grant's memoir; Miller, pp. 1–46 and 281–284; O'Brien; Plato's *Laches*.

CHAPTER 11. PERFORMING LEADERSHIP

Recommendations

Find out if fellow students have opinions about the following questions. When Harry Potter learns the truth about Dumbledore, has he at last grown up (see Rowling 2007,

686–691)? Has Harry outgrown hero worship and started growing into an understanding of the real world? Did Dumbledore's mask set a good example for Harry? Would Harry have been better off as a child had he known the full truth about his headmaster? Was Dumbledore a hypocrite, or a successful performer of leadership?

Shakespeare wrote, "Love's best habit is in seeming trust," and Clancy Martin, in his book, *Love and Lies*, urges lovers to conceal some truths about themselves. How much truth must there be in a loving relationship?

Read further about Washington and other leaders. How important was performance to their success? For Washington, see the authors recommended in Chapter 1. Notes on valuable passages in Chernow:

> The loss of Fort Washington. GW weeps at the loss, 262: Washington Irving said he heard from eyewitnesses: the defeat "was said so completely to overcome him that he wept with the tenderness of a child." In that defeat, GW had advised Greene (who commanded the fort) to evacuate. Greene screwed up. GW forgives Nathaniel Green for the defeat. "He seemed to know that no loyalty surpassed that of a man forgiven for his faults who vowed never to make them again," 263.

> Greene to Congress: "There never was a man that might be more safely trusted," 277.

> Crossing a bridge near Trenton, with Hessian bayonets threatening, Private John Howland reported: "the firm, composed, and majestic countenance of the general inspired confidence and assurance in a moment so important and critical," 279.

> On not alienating civilians (as British did), GW wrote: "the spirit and willingness of the people must in a great measure take [the] place of coercion," 286.

> "He never insulated himself from contrary opinions, having told Joseph Reed early in the war to keep him posted on even unfriendly scuttlebutt. 'I can bear to hear of imputed or real errors,' he wrote. 'The man who wishes to stand well in the opinion of others must do this, because he is thereby enabled to correct his faults or remove the prejudices which are imbid[e]d against him.' Washington made excellent use of war councils to weigh all sides of an issue," 292.

> Washington characteristically hid his grief and tears. A maid often saw him in tears, 294.

CHAPTER 12. GOOD EARS, STRONG VOICES

Recommendations

Always couple a speaking assignment with a writing assignment. Writing assignments should be set up as articulated processes, from topic selection through research to a draft and from the draft through revision to a final version. Never simply ask for a paper at semester's end.

Listening, speaking, and writing all need practice throughout a college career. Listening assignments are unusual. How would you develop them?

Make use of each other. Scholars read each other's drafts and make helpful suggestions. Students should have the same privilege, but they need help learning how to help each other.

Further Reading

Great speeches, of course. I also recommend Reynolds for speaking and Trimble for writing. There is a scholarly literature on the use of peer evaluations for writing (including peer review that is calibrated to the professor's review method).

CHAPTER 13. BECOMING MAGNETIC

Recommendations

Read and discuss Plato's *Symposium* and the ladder of love. What sort of thing is beauty of soul? Discuss the attributes you would want in a follower. Are they the same as those you look for in a leader?

Further Reading

On virtues, classic readings in Confucius, Mencius, Plato, and Aristotle. Modern readings on virtue ethics tend to be too technical for our purposes. A good beginning for the Chinese tradition is Ivanhoe's book on Confucian self-cultivation. For Plato, start with the *Apology of Socrates* and the *Crito*. For Aristotle (who is harder), start with the first two books of the *Nicomachean Ethics*.

THE GENERATIONAL DEBATE FROM PSEUDO-SOPHOCLES' *ANTIGONUS* (WOMEN'S VERSION)

Altered from the translation by Paul Woodruff, copyright Hackett Publishing Company, 2001. Find the original version (for two men) in that translation.

Chorus
Now, here is Haimosa, the last of your children.
Is she goaded here by anguish for Antigonus,

Who should have been her groom?
Does she feel injured beyond measure?
Cheated out of marriage?   630

Creusa
We'll know the answer right away, better than prophets:
Tell me, girl, did you hear the final verdict?
Against your fiancé? Did you come in anger at your mother?
Or are we still friends, no matter what I do?

Haemosa
I am yours, Mother. You set me straight,   635
Give me good advice and I will follow it.
No marriage will weigh more with me,
Than your good opinion.

Creusa
Splendid, my girl! Keep that always in your heart,
And stand behind motherly advice on all counts.   640
Why does a woman pray that she'll conceive a child,
Keep her at home, and have her listen to what she's told?
It's so the girl will punish her mother's enemies
And reward her friends—as her mother would.
But some women beget utterly useless offspring: 645
They have planted nothing but trouble for themselves,
And they're nothing but a joke to their enemies.

Now then, my girl, don't let pleasure cloud your mind,
Not because of a man. You know very well:
You'll have a frigid squeeze between the sheets   650
If you shack up with a hostile man. I'd rather have
A bleeding wound than a criminal in the family.
So spit him out. And because the boy's against us,
Send him down to marry somebody in Hades.
You know I caught him in the sight of all,   655
Alone of all our people, in open revolt.
And I will make my word good in Thebes—
By killing him. Who cares if he sings "Zeus!"
And calls him his protector. I must keep my kin in line.
Otherwise, folks outside the family will run wild.   660
The public knows that a woman is just
Only if she is straight with her relatives.

So, if someone goes too far and breaks the law,
Or tries to tell her rulers what to do,
She will have nothing but contempt from me. 665
But when the city takes a leader, you must obey,
Whether her commands are trivial, or right, or wrong.
And I have no doubt that such a woman will rule well,
And, later, she will cheerfully be ruled by someone else.
In hard times she will stand firm with her spear 670
Waiting for orders, a good, law-abiding soldier.

But reject one person ruling another, and that's the worst.
Anarchy tears up a city, divides a home,
Defeats an alliance of spears.
But when people stay in line and obey, 675
Their lives and everything else are safe.
For this reason, order must be maintained,
And there must be no surrender to a man.
No! If we fall, better a woman should take us down.
Never say that a man bested us! 680

Chorus
Unless old age has stolen my wits away,
Your speech was very wise. That's my belief.

Haemosa
Mother, the gods give good sense to every human being,
And that is absolutely the best thing we have.
But if what you said is not correct, 685
I have no idea how I could make the point.
Still, maybe someone else could work it out.

My natural duty's to look out for you, spot any risk
In speech or action that someone might find fault.
The common woman, you see, lives in terror of your frown; 690
She'll never dare to speak up in broad daylight
And say anything you would hate to learn.
But I'm the one who hears what's said at night—
How the entire city is grieving over this boy.
No man has ever had a fate that's so unfair
(They say), when what he did deserves honor and fame. 695
He saved his very own sister after she died,
Murderously, from being devoured by flesh-eating dogs
And pecked apart by vultures as she lay unburied.

For this, hasn't he earned glory bright as gold?
This sort of talk moves against you, quietly, at night.   700

And for me, Mother, your continued good fortune
Is the best reward that I could ever have.
No child could win a greater prize than her mother's fame,
No mother could want more than abundant success—
From her daughter.

And now, don't always cling to the same anger,   705
Don't keep saying that this, and nothing else, is right.
If a woman believes that she alone has a sound mind,
And no one else can speak or think as well as she does,
Then, when people study her, they'll find an empty book.
But a wise woman can learn a lot and never be ashamed;   710
She knows she does not have to be rigid and close-hauled.
You've seen trees tossed by a torrent in a flash flood:
If they bend, they're saved, and every twig survives,
But if they stiffen up, they're washed out from the roots.
It's the same in a boat: if a sailor keeps the foot line taut,   715
If she doesn't give an inch, she'll capsize, and then—
She'll be sailing home with her benches down and her hull to the sky.
So ease off, relax, stop being angry, make a change.
I know I'm younger, but I may still have good ideas;
And I say that the oldest idea, and the best,   720
Is for one woman to be born complete, knowing everything.
Otherwise—and it usually does turn out otherwise—
It's good to learn from anyone who speaks well.

Chorus
Ma'am, you should learn from her, if she is on the mark. And you,
Haemosa, learn from your mother. Both sides spoke well.   725

Creusa (to the Chorus)
Do you really think, at our age,
We should be taught by a girl like her?

Haemosa
No. Not if I am in the wrong. I admit I'm young;
That's why you should look at what I do, not my age.

Creusa
So "what you do" is reverence for breaking ranks?   730

Haemosa

I'd never urge reverence for a criminal.

Creusa

So you don't think this boy has been infected with crime?

Haemosa

No. The people of Thebes deny it, all of them.

Creusa

So you think the people should tell me what orders to give?

Haemosa

Now who's talking like she's wet behind the ears?   735

Creusa

So I should rule this country for someone other than myself?

Haemosa

A place for one woman alone is not a city.

Creusa

A city belongs to its mistress. Isn't that the rule?

Haemosa

Then go be ruler of a desert, all alone. You'd do it well.

Creusa (to the Chorus)

It turns out this girl is fighting for the man's cause.   740

Haemosa

Only if *you* are a man. All I care about is you!

Creusa

This is intolerable! You are accusing your own mother.

Haemosa

Because I see you going wrong. Because justice matters!

Creusa

Is that wrong, showing respect for my job as leader?

Haemosa

You have no respect at all, if you trample on the rights of gods!   745

Creusa

What a sick mind you have: You submit to a man!

Haemosa

No. You'll never catch me giving in to what's shameful.

Creusa

But everything you say, at least, is on his side.

Haemosa

And on your side! And mine! And the gods' below!

Creusa

There is no way you'll marry him, not while he's still alive.   750

Haemosa

Then he'll die, and his death will destroy Someone Else.

Creusa

Is that a threat? Are you brash enough to attack me?

Haemosa

What threat? All I'm saying is, you haven't thought this through.

Creusa

I'll make you wish you'd never had a thought in your empty head!

Haemosa

I'd say you were out of your mind, but you are my mother.   755

Creusa

Don't beat around the bush. You're a man's toy, a slave.

Haemosa

Talk, talk, talk. Why don't you ever want to listen?

Creusa

Really? Listen, you are not going on like this. By all the gods,
One more insult from you and the fun is over.

(To attendants)
Bring out that hated thing. I want him to die right here,   760
Right now, so his bride can watch the whole thing.

Haemosa
Not me. Never. No matter what you think.
He is not going to die while I am near him.
And you will never, ever, see my face again. Go on,
Be crazy! Perhaps some of your friends will stay by you.   765

(Exit Haemosa through stage right wing.)

Chorus
Sir, the woman has gone. She is swift to anger;
Pain lies heavily on a youthful mind.

Creusa
Let her go, her and her lofty ambitions! Good riddance!

APPENDIX C

Using Teams for Leadership Experience

INTRODUCTION

I learned in the military that the best way to sharpen leadership ability is to work in a team, taking turns leading and following. That model works well in military training, of course, but it also works in the classroom. I have used this method in courses on philanthropy, democracy, and the arts. I think it can be used for any subject in which students can be given tasks to carry out in teams. I also believe that this approach is more effective than the courses in which I teach directly. I would like to start a movement to introduce elements of leadership into our pedagogical methods in most courses. We can reach many more students this way than through courses with "leadership" in their titles. I propose a rubric for team leaders' self-evaluation at the end of this section.

FIRST EXAMPLE: PHILANTHROPY

I have experimented over the years with various ways of engaging students with each other, and I am currently having some success with setting teams of students in competition with each other. A few years ago, I had good experiences with classes that I divided into competitive teams. For example, a Philanthropy Lab course I taught some years ago went very well. The class was given $100,000 to give away to reputable causes (other than the university) at the end of the semester. These were real dollars provided by a foundation called Once Upon a Time . . . The foundation's goal was to make every dollar work twice—once in the education of the students, and once again in the good causes to which the students gave the money.

My class—all first-year students—divided itself into teams representing such causes as the arts, education, poverty, health research, and human rights. They were required to do extensive research as individuals in the causes that interested them and present their results to their teams. Each team then chose one student's cause to support and prepared to debate the other teams. All this left me little time for lecturing or conducting the usual class discussions, but the students were learning like wildfire—how to use library databases, how to evaluate charitable causes, how to write up strong papers about them, how to make the case orally for their causes. Along the way they were also learning to work better in groups. There were no laggards, because the dollars were real, and they all cared where those dollars would go.

SECOND EXAMPLE: PHILOSOPHY OF THE ARTS

In this example, the tasks for each team were two: to teach the class for a week and then to compete for grants in the arts. Having students teach classes is not appropriate for every subject, and it did not succeed when the topic was literature. But the method worked well in this course on the arts because I gave a very clear template for the teaching to be done by each team.

At the end of the semester the students were to constitute a foundation and award a grant to support a project in the arts. The money was imaginary, but the proposals had to be real enough to be carried out. Teams of students developed these projects over the semester, under rotating leadership. I gave no lectures on leadership, but when the dust settled, all students agreed they had learned something about leadership in the process. Although I had not advertised the course at the start as having anything to do with leadership, toward the end I did admit that leadership was among my goals.

Before turning the teaching over to the students, I introduced them to Aristotle's *Poetics* and a few classic works on the arts, while developing a list of questions that a poetics for any given art form should answer. By a "poetics" I meant answers to a series of questions about an art form. I gave an example by introducing them to the art of chamber music and developing a short poetics for that: a definition, an enumeration of elements, a theory about what makes it good when it is good, and an account of its value for performers and audience.

Meanwhile, students expressed interest in art forms that interested them, forming six teams of five members each. My main interests in the arts—painting, poetry, and theater—did not appeal to them; the six art forms they chose were rap music, film, modern dance, architecture, popular music in general, and fiction.

In the middle six weeks of the course we learned from the students about each art form and came to some understanding of what a poetics for that form would look like. The oral presentations (for which I had given them guidance as to content, delivery, and timing) went well, and we all felt we had learned something about the arts. Modern dance was new to all but its team members, architecture was little better known, and film was quite unknown as an art form. Rap was familiar to the whole class, but its aesthetics were not.

Meanwhile, students were writing papers presenting the material they would bring before the class, each student taking one part of the poetics of the team's choice. They were also beginning to develop—and do research for—their grant proposals. As with the Philanthropy Lab, each team would choose a student's project and work together to promote it in the debate section that would end the course.

The teams chose readings for the class, in consultation with me, and also proposed questions for the final exam—knowing that they would have to answer the questions posed by other teams than their own. So I gave my students the full experience of teaching—choosing material, thinking it through, and devising ways to assess student learning. They seemed to relish this and learn from it.

At the end of the course, each team made a pitch for a grant to support a project in its art form. A committee with representation from each team devised the ballot, choosing an approval form of voting. The class awarded its imaginary grant to the team I (silently) thought had made by far the best pitch. All members of the team that won the grant got bonus points on their grades. Students whose participation in the teams was weak were docked penalty points (I had only one case of this).

Each member of the team participated in each of the team's many assigned activities. Each member had a turn as leader for two weeks and submitted a report on what the team had done under his or her leadership. I graded students individually on their presentations and on the formal papers that grew out of them. This is essential for an academic team-based course; students rightly insist on being graded on the merits of their own work, which shows what they have individually learned. Nonacademic teamwork, such as for military operations, is rightly evaluated on a team basis; if one member fails, the whole team might die, and so the members need to learn by experience that individual achievement, by itself, is irrelevant in certain situations. But in academic work, individual recognition is indispensable. Nevertheless, the teams wanted to do well as teams and to win bonus points.

What did the students learn? That is hard to assess. At the end of the semester I asked students to write up what they had learned about leadership from the experience. It turned out that most of them learned a lot by observing each other's successes and failures, and writing that up seemed to cement what they had learned. The final exams showed that they had learned enough to write good essays on the art forms they had presented, while giving accurate answers to test questions on the readings chosen by other teams. Besides learning some new things, the students had good practice writing, doing research, and speaking about topics they cared about.

The skills involved are useful in any line of work, I believe, since they are easy to transfer from the arts to other subjects.

In my career as a teacher I know I have learned more by teaching than I could have learned as a student. I infer that my students could learn more from taking the role of teachers in this class than they would have if I had made them listen patiently to my lectures on art forms that meant little to them. I believe they did. I am sure they made progress toward leadership during the course.

What would I do differently another time? First, I would give students better guidance in selecting the readings. Second, I would devise a better way to evaluate the performance of each student as a leader. The military model, a 360-degree peer evaluation, is unpopular with students. It can be devastating, when you are very young, to find that your peers all dislike you. It's far better, I think, to ask students to evaluate their own learning about leadership. A self-evaluation should be graded on a pass/fail basis, and could be built around questions like these: What have you learned about how to chair a meeting effectively? What would you do differently as a leader next time? I have devised a rubric for leadership self-evaluation, which appears at the end of this appendix.

I will share student comments only because they bear on the design of the class.

Complaints

"I did not like the student taught class model . . . Many of the presentations were a bit too shallow for me." "Didn't meet my expectations in terms of directly teaching philosophy." Other students also complained that the student-given lectures were not as informative or as philosophical as they would have liked.

They are quite right: The course did not cover as much as is expected of a philosophy course. Students were exposed to less material, but I expect that they will retain more of what they were exposed to than they would have from a traditional lecture course.

Some students wanted more guidance than I gave them on selecting readings to assign to the class, as well as on writing their papers. This is important and I have resolved to do better; letting students run a class actually requires more work from the teacher than conventional teaching.

Positive Reactions

All the students were positive about the course.

> "Most valuable experience of my academic career thus far." (There were several similar remarks, two of which came from graduating seniors.)
> "An effective way of 'teaching' leadership skills."

"If we had more than one leadership-based class like this, far more developed leadership behaviors would arise. Our team had some difficulty, but we all learned how to prevent it in the future. Hopefully we will have this in future."

"Typically, group assignments are not fun, but Woodruff made it thoughtful and simple by breaking it down."

RUBRIC FOR SELF-EVALUATION IN LEADERSHIP

To readers: This rubric is designed for use by students in teams with rotating leadership and clear goals. I have used this successfully. Most students easily diagnosed problems in their leadership that they would try to correct in future.

To the student: This is for your own satisfaction; the score you give yourself will not figure into your grade for the course. It is a pass/fail assignment. Give yourself up to ten points for each item you can check off for the period during which you were the team leader.

If you do not give yourself a full ten points for any items on the list, write down what you would do differently another time. Add any other comments you see fit. Don't be too easy on yourself. To receive credit for the assignment, you should identify at least three areas for improvement. If you find this hard, ask your teammates.

A. Meetings
1. Started on time, ended on time.
2. Had a clear agenda: usually a decision to make.
3. Everyone on the team participated in the meeting and was heard.
4. Everyone was willing to buy into the decision, whether or not they totally agreed with it.

B. Project
5. The project goals during your term of office were clearly defined.
6. Everyone contributed to the project.
7. You did NOT do all the work yourself or take over other people's tasks.
8. The team met its goals during your term of office.

C. Communication
9. Every member of the team had the same understanding of the team's goals and of the decisions the team made during your term.
10. You understood the point of view of each team member.

INDEX

Printed in the USA/Agawam, MA
February 7, 2020

749792.001